BESTSELLING
BOOK SERIES

Mexican Cooking For Dummies®

Cheat Sheet

P9-CME-260

Great Tips for Mexican Cooking

Follow these tips to get the most out of cooking Mexican:

- **Garnish freely.** We don't mean a sprig or two of wilted parsley strewn across a plate. In the Mexican kitchen, the garnishes — fresh diced onion, sliced radish, chopped cilantro, lime wedges, diced chiles — are integral to the dish. They add the crunch, the freshness, and the bright acidity that completes a dish.

- **Recycle.** Yesterday's salsa and chips are today's tortilla soup is tomorrow's chilaquiles. It's good for the planet, and it tastes good, too!

- **Start good taste at home.** Try making our homemade corn and flour tortillas and our salsas rather than purchasing the store-bought variety. Then you'll recognize the difference between a so-so tortilla and something great.

- **Try unusual cuts of meat.** Mexican cooking provides an excellent opportunity to explore inexpensive cuts of meat. Slowly cooked butts, shoulders, and shanks will reward you with silky tenderness and intense flavor at half the cost of prime cuts. To take the plunge, turn to Chapter 11 for Menudo and Chile Braised Lamb Shanks and Chapter 14 for two great uses for pork butt: Carnitas Norteñas and Cochinita Pibil.

- **Aspire to be an acid queen or king.** Acid accents, particularly from lime juice, are necessary in Mexican cooking to balance the richness and spice, especially in posoles, ceviches, and tacos. Just about every savory Mexican dish in this book will benefit from an additional squirt of lime.

- **Roast and toast freely.** Roasted tomatoes, onions, and chiles add a unique layer of complexity to salsas and sauces that is characteristic of real Mexican cooking. Don't skip this step. The same advice applies to toasting pastas or grains.

- **Make homemade beverages.** Mexican cuisine offers an array of wonderfully vibrant beverages, alcoholic and not. Get in the spirit and abandon predictable soft drinks and wines for a refreshing change. (See Chapter 4 for all kinds of beverage recipes and recommendations.)

- **Embrace chiles.** Don't be intimidated by chiles. With a little know-how, you will find that they are easy to work with and extremely healthy and add a wallop of lowfat flavor that will grow on you if you give them a chance. (See Chapter 2 for a chile primer.)

- **First say yes.** Before you automatically say no to a new food or taste experience, think again and take a bite. Remember that it took Europeans about 400 years to figure out what to do with a tomato. Just think of all that great tomato sauce they were missing.

Temperature Conversions

° Fahrenheit	° Celsius	° Fahrenheit	° Celsius	° Fahrenheit	° Celsius
250	120	350	175	450	230
275	135	375	190	475	245
300	150	400	205	500	260
325	160	425	220		

Mexican Cooking For Dummies®

Cheat Sheet

It's Chile Time!

Take this list with you to the store to help you keep the various types of chiles straight. (Chapter 2 tells you more about these chiles.)

- **Serrano:** A small, fresh, green hot chile. Used for spice and flavor in cooking and as a garnish.

- **Jalapeño:** Larger than a serrano, though still small. This fresh green or red chile is probably the easiest to find in America. The ripe red version is sweeter; the green version can be spicy.

- **Poblano:** A dark green, medium-sized fresh green chile often roasted and stuffed.

- **Habañero:** A tiny, lantern-shaped fresh chile of extraordinary heat. Interchangeable with the incendiary Scotch Bonnet.

- **Chile de arbol:** A small, red dried chile. It's the chile used for the dried red chile flakes in the spice section of the market.

- **Chipotle:** A medium-small, wrinkled, dried brown chile with a unique smoky flavor reminiscent of bacon. It's the dried, smoked version of jalapeño.

- **Chile negro,** or **pasilla:** A long, narrow, dark brown dried chile used for grinding into moles.

- **Ancho:** A medium-sized, wrinkled, brown dried chile with a mellow, earthy, sweet flavor. It's the dried version of the poblano.

Liquid Measurements

This Measurement . . .	. . . Equals This Measurement
3 teaspoons	1 tablespoon
2 tablespoons	1 fluid ounce
4 tablespoons	¼ cup
1 cup	8 fluid ounces
2 cups	1 pint
4 cups	1 quart
4 quarts	1 gallon

Dry Measurements

This Measurement . . .	. . . Equals This Measurement
3 teaspoons	1 tablespoon
4 tablespoons	¼ cup
5 tablespoons plus 1 teaspoon	⅓ cup
16 tablespoons	1 cup
16 ounces	1 pound

Metric Conversions

This Measurement . . .	. . . Equals This Measurement
1 tablespoon	15 milliliters
1 cup	250 milliliters
1 quart	1 liter
1 ounce	28 grams
1 pound	454 grams

For Dummies: Bestselling Book Series for Beginners

Praise for Mary Sue Milliken and Susan Feniger

"Mom was never as amusing as Susan Feniger and Mary Sue Milliken . . . the two banter and bicker as they cook Latin American food and dispense cooking tips . . . " — Forbes

"They exhibit a patience, a palpable love for their work." — Los Angeles Times Magazine

"Milliken and Feniger . . . [are] friendly, familiar, and unabashedly enthusiastic about all sorts of food." — Los Angeles Times Magazine

" . . . Their philosophy is avante garde: They want to bridge the gap between their formal French training and the world's ethnic cuisines with their bold flavors and rustic textures . . . multiculturalism at its best. As superb teachers, hip personae, and (in their own words) 'serious sensory junkies,' Mary Sue Milliken and Susan Feniger are doing much more . . . " — Camille Paglia, The Advocate

Praise for Border Grill

"So-Cal's most innovative Mexican cuisine . . . " — Esquire

Feniger and Milliken's knowledge of and reverence for Mexican food runs as deep and rich as its flavors . . . They are (among) its pre-eminent American translators." — New York Newsday

"The fiesta-bright Border Grill is a stylishly funky, pleasantly raucous place, serving wildly authentic Mexican and Central American food." — Travel and Leisure

Praise for Ciudad

"This is lighthearted yet gutsy cooking. The kitchen revels in bold flavors and exotic ingredients." — Los Angeles Times Magazine

"Ciudad's menu is a fantasy, a giddy, Bacardi-fueled Latin American journey . . ." — Los Angeles Magazine

" . . . an exciting world on the plate . . . Feniger and Milliken are true visionaries — and Ciudad shows us the rich diversity of Los Angeles at the turn of the twentieth century." — Gourmet

"The Too Hot Tamales have done it again. At Ciudad, Mary Sue Milliken and Susan Feniger have renewed their passports as intrepid intercultural trendsetters with a wildly inventive menu that showcases the tastes of Central and South America . . . " — "The Top Ten" new restaurants, Los Angeles Magazine

" . . . And if there ever was a Roy Rogers and Dale Evans of the kitchen range, it's the Too Hot Tamales, Mary Sue Milliken and Susan Feniger . . . With influences from Havana to Rio and Buenos Aires, and across the Atlantic to Lisbon and Barcelona, Ciudad pays tribute to the bold flavors of the Latin world . . . From Ecaudorian salmon tartare and quinoa fritters to plantain gnocchi and grilled Argentine gaucho steak, these Too Hot Tamales deliver." — Flaunt

" . . . For a parade of Pan-American dishes in a sleek, humming setting, head for Ciudad . . . the latest venture of the Too Hot Tamales team of Mary Sue Milliken and Susan Feniger. The ingredients, not to mention the exotic house cocktails, may be unfamiliar, but plunge in the mixed Spanish antipasto plates . . . and you'll never look back." — The New York Times

TM

References for the Rest of Us!®

Mexican Cooking

FOR

DUMMIES®

**by Mary Sue Milliken
and Susan Feniger
with Helene Siegel**

WILEY

Wiley Publishing, Inc.

Mexican Cooking For Dummies®

Published by
Wiley Publishing, Inc.
909 Third Avenue
New York, NY 10022
www.wiley.com

Copyright © 1999 by Wiley Publishing, Inc., Indianapolis, Indiana

Published by Wiley Publishing, Inc., Indianapolis, Indiana

Published simultaneously in Canada

For general information on our other products and services or to obtain technical support, please contact our Customer Care Department within the U.S. at 800-762-2974, outside the U.S. at 317-572-3993, or fax 317-572-4002.

Wiley also publishes its books in a variety of electronic formats. Some content that appears in print may not be available in electronic books.

Library of Congress Cataloging-in-Publication Data:

Library of Congress Control Number: 99-65875

ISBN: 0-7645-5169-8

Manufactured in the United States of America

10 9 8 7 6 5 4 3

1O/SV/QS/QT/IN

About the Authors

Mary Sue Milliken and **Susan Feniger** may be "two gringas from the Midwest," but they fell deeply in love with Mexican food when first introduced to it more than 20 years ago. The two chefs became friends in the late 70's while working in the otherwise all-male kitchen of a prestigious French restaurant in Chicago called Le Perroquet. After honing their skills in fine restaurants in France and America, they opened their first restaurant, the highly celebrated City Cafe, in Los Angeles in 1981. These days, they divide their time between their three restaurants, Border Grills in Santa Monica and Las Vegas, and the upscale Ciudad in downtown Los Angeles. They also have authored four previous cookbooks, host the popular Television Food Network series, *Too Hot Tamales,* and are heard regularly on Southern California radio.

Helene Siegel is the co-author with Mary Sue and Susan of *City Cuisine, Mesa Mexicana,* and *Cooking with the Too Hot Tamales.* She also is the author of *The Ethnic Kitchen* series and 32 single-subject cookbooks in the best-selling *Totally Cookbook* series. Her articles have appeared in the *Los Angeles Times,* the *Times Syndicate, Fine Cooking,* and on the Web at cuisinenet.com.

Mary Sue and Susan value your feedback and would love to hear from you! Visit their Web site at www.bordergrill.com.

Authors' Acknowledgments

Thanks to Martha Wright, for her enthusiasm and constant good cheer in keeping such an unwieldy project on track.

Thanks to Kim Romero, for her Spanish translations, pronunciations, and help with the recipe writing.

Thanks to friend and photographer Ann Johanssen, who made her wonderful photographs taken in Mexico available for this book. And for their work in the photo studio, we'd like to thank prop stylist Linda Johnson and food stylist Polly Talbott.

Thanks to the hard-working team at Hungry Minds: our ever-patient project editor, Mary Goodwin, Acquisitions Editor Holly McGuire, Copy Editor Tina Sims, and Laura Penseiro, who enthusiastically tested each and every recipe — twice.

And, finally, thanks to our agents, Mari Florence and Skye Herzog, who made the match.

Publisher's Acknowledgments

We're proud of this book; please send us your comments through our Online Registration Form located at www.dummies.com/register.

Some of the people who helped bring this book to market include the following:

Acquisitions, Editorial, and Media Development

Project Editor: Mary Goodwin

Acquisitions Editor: Holly McGuire

Copy Editors: Tina Sims, Billie Williams, Janet Withers

Technical Editor: Diana Conover

Recipe Tester: Laura Penseiro

Photographer: Lou Manna

Illustrator: Liz Kurtzman

Editorial Coordinator: Maureen F. Kelly

Acquisitions Assistant: Heather Prince

Acquisitions Coordinator: Jonathan Malysiak

Editorial Manager: Kristin Cocks

Editorial Assistant: Alison Walthal

Production

Project Coordinators: Tom Missler, Regina Snyder

Layout and Graphics: Brian Drumm, Kelly Hardesty, Angela F. Hunckler, Barry Offringa, Brent Savage, Janet Seib, Michael A. Sullivan, Brian Torwelle, Maggie Ubertini, Mary Jo Weis, Dan Whetstine

Proofreaders: Melissa D. Buddendeck, Nancy Price, Marianne Santy, Rebecca Senninger

Indexer: Cynthia D. Bertelsen

Publishing and Editorial for Consumer Dummies

Diane Graves Steele, Vice President and Publisher, Consumer Dummies
Joyce Pepple, Acquisitions Director, Consumer Dummies
Kristin A. Cocks, Product Development Director, Consumer Dummies
Michael Spring, Vice President and Publisher, Travel
Brice Gosnell, Publishing Director, Travel
Suzanne Jannetta, Editorial Director, Travel

Publishing for Technology Dummies

Richard Swadley, Vice President and Executive Group Publisher
Andy Cummings, Vice President and Publisher

Composition Services

Gerry Fahey, Vice President of Production Services
Debbie Stailey, Director of Composition Services

Contents at a Glance

Cartoons at a Glance

By Rich Tennant

page 5

page 49

page 265

page 107

page 235

page 283

Cartoon Information:
Fax: 978-546-7747
E-Mail: richtennant@the5thwave.com
World Wide Web: www.the5thwave.com

Recipes at a Glance

Side Dishes

Braises, stews, and moles

Fish and seafood

Chicken and turkey

Meat dishes

Desserts

Breakfast Foods

Table of Contents

Introduction

. . . .

*I*f you like to eat Mexican food, you're going to love cooking it. This casual style of cooking relies on the same few easy-to-find ingredients — tomatoes, limes, onions, cilantro, and chile peppers — simple home-based techniques like roasting and frying, and nothing more complicated than a blender in terms of equipment.

Mexican food is also great for serving to large groups. We love to serve Mexican food family-style, in great heaping platters or tureens placed in the middle of the table, for sharing.

When Mexican food is on the menu, fun and high spirits are bound to follow.

How to Use This Book

You can use this book as your one and only, all-inclusive Mexican cookbook, or you can use it as your jumping-off point to go deeper into Mexican cooking and culture. We've been exploring the world of Mexican cooking both in our travels and our kitchens for the last 20 years, and it's a world rich with thousands of years of culinary culture.

Our goal has been to boil our cooking experience down to its essence so that you can open the book at any point, roll up your sleeves, and start producing real Mexican food with ease and confidence. After cooking a few dishes, you should be as comfortable around Mexican cooking as you would be making a peanut butter and jelly sandwich.

How This Book Is Organized

This book is organized according to the traditional cookbook, or menu, format. There's a soup chapter, a salad chapter, and so on, straight on through to dessert. The other chapters, at the front and the back of the book, introduce the beginner to new ingredients, techniques, and equipment and give you ideas for how to put the food together for parties and special occasions. Like most cookbooks, it is not meant to be read from cover to cover. But if you feel like doing so, we hope it's a page-turner.

Part I: Getting the Juices Flowing

Everything you need to know to set up your kitchen for maximum Mexican cooking enjoyment is here: how to shop for ingredients, tame a wild chile pepper, and cook perfect beans. Refer to this part if you're following a recipe and you suddenly draw a blank on how to toast seeds or forget the difference between a chipotle and a poblano.

Part II: Taking a Quick Trip

The foods in this part represent some of the best and easiest party foods. If you're more interested in wowing your guests with the best margaritas in town and a selection of homemade salsas than creating a complex mole, this is the part for you. Start with great guacamole, a fresh fish ceviche, one or two of our excellent tacos, or any of the street snacks in this part and work your way up to the moles when you're ready for a commitment.

Part III: Enjoying an Extended Tour

When you're feeling comfortable in your huaraches (Mexican woven sandals) and you're ready to delve more deeply into the heart and soul of Mexican cuisine, turn to this part. Here you can find the great traditional stews, soups, tamales, roasted and grilled meats, fish, and poultry. These more complex foods pay back many times for the time you spend in the kitchen with complex, soul-satisfying flavors and aromas. We finish your tour with a chapter on desserts.

Part IV: Menus for Every Occasion

Here's where we put it all together for you. Mexican food is meant to be shared, so this part gives you ideas on how to do that. We offer suggestions on how to throw several great Mexican theme parties and include some new recipes, music and lighting tips, instructions for building a beach barbecue, do-ahead game plans, and a whole chapter of brunch recipes.

Part V: The Part of Tens

This part of the book includes those little lagniappes (a fancy word that simply means gifts with purchase) that round out a meal (or a cookbook). We give you more party tips for making the scene sizzle, suggest what to do with a pantry overflowing with yesterday's tortillas, provide a few Spanish food phrases for your first trip to Mexico, and recommend the best places to visit on the Internet for food and Mexican cooking information.

Part VI: Appendixes

For reference we include an alphabetical list of the Spanish words that appear in the text, including pronunciations. In this part, you also find a helpful appendix of common substitutions, abbreviations, and equivalents.

Conventions Used in This Book

Okay, you've heard this advice a million times in cookbooks, and frankly you're bored. But trust us. Read the recipes all the way through and pay attention to the stuff in the notes at the beginning and end of the recipes before cooking. You'll be glad you did. You'll know whether you need any special equipment, how much time to allow, and whether you need another recipe from a different part of the book to complete the dish. We also include tips and hints that can make your cooking easier — wouldn't want to miss those!

To keep the ingredient lists in this book concise, we follow certain conventions:

- All milk is whole unless noted.
- All butter is unsalted.
- All salt is coarse kosher salt.
- All pepper is freshly ground black pepper.
- All cream is heavy unless noted.
- All eggs are large.
- All flour is all-purpose.
- All sugar is granulated unless noted.
- All herbs are fresh unless noted.
- All citrus juices are freshly squeezed.
- Tomatillos are husked and rinsed unless noted.

In the recipes, we tell you when you need special equipment or gadgets to complete the recipe. Here's what we assume you have in your kitchen:

- A few frying pans or skillets, preferably cast iron, 10 or 12 inches wide and a small 8-inch skillet for spices and small quantities.
- A medium or large heavy saucepan.
- A large, heavy Dutch oven or soup pot with cover that can be used for stewing and braising.
- A large glass, ceramic, or metal roasting pan and rack.

✔ A large pot with cover that can be used for soups, pasta, stews, and improvising a tamale steamer. (See Chapter 8 for more information on soup pots.)

✔ A steamer basket.

✔ One or two baking sheets or cookie trays with edges.

✔ Small everyday tools like wooden spoons, ladles, a slotted metal spoon, spatula, tongs, strainer, whisk, measuring spoons, and dry and liquid measuring cups.

✔ A cutting board, kitchen towels, and mixing bowls.

✔ Paper towels, aluminum foil, and plastic wrap.

✔ A blender.

Icons Used in This Book

Look for these icons next to tidbits of useful information.

Even business partners can disagree sometimes. This icon flags Mary Sue's personal pet peeves, ideas, and suggestions.

When you see this icon, expect some words from Susan — she's the short one who can't stop cooking and talking, in her own words.

These are technique tips or shortcuts for reducing kitchen stress. They usually show an easy, fast way to do something.

This icon indicates ways to avoid common pitfalls and problems. Remember, you've been warned!

A variation following a recipe gives instructions for different ways to tweak and turn the preceding recipe to give it another twist or flavor. Variations can help you make a dish even though you are missing an ingredient, and they can also help you develop a more flexible way of viewing recipes in general.

And for you vegetarians out there, we put a little tomato icon next to the vegetarian recipes in the "Recipes in This Chapter" list that begins each chapter. That way, if you're looking just for veggie dishes, you can simply scan for the tomato icon and then flip right to the recipes that you want.

Part I
Getting the Juices Flowing

The 5th Wave   By Rich Tennant

"A molcajete, huh? How many attachments does it come with?"

In this part . . .

You don't have to read this book from beginning to end (but, of course, we'd be thrilled if you did). However, if you've never cooked Mexican food before, we suggest that you stroll through this part of the book before moving on to the recipes. Doing so will give you a basic introduction to Mexican cooking, the ingredients and tools used in the Mexican kitchen, and a few basic techniques that you'll need along the way.

Chapter 1

Understanding Mexican Cooking

• •

In This Chapter

▶ Debunking common Mexican food myths

▶ Getting a taste for Mexican cooking

• •

*E*xperiencing pasta overload? Burnt out on grilled chicken breasts and left cold by one more turkey burger? Ready to take a culinary adventure full of sizzle and spunk, exciting seasonings, terrific party foods, and world-class cocktails? Open your heart, mind, and kitchen to Mexican food, and your guests and family will thank you a thousand times.

Forget about those cheesy restaurant combination platters of yesterday, with their heaping portions of rice, beans, and fried foods. Our style of Mexican cooking is much lighter than that, and it can be as hot and spicy as you like. Big flavors, inexpensive ingredients, ease of preparation, and casual presentation are what our kind of Mexican cooking is all about.

The recipes in this book include a range of dishes — a whole fish marinated in citrus juices and spice and tossed on the grill, succulent pork and chile tamales, bracing raw and cooked fish cocktails, big soups and stews brimming with chunks of fresh vegetables and lime juice, and enough interesting new salads to please the vegetarians and light eaters in the house. And don't worry about our choices for dessert — they're luscious.

Before you begin your journey into Mexican cooking, we want to tell you a couple of things to get you started out right, including blasting a few myths about Mexican cooking and giving you a few hints about how to approach this great cuisine.

Dispelling Mexican Cooking Myths

Although it's one of the world's most beloved cuisines, Mexican food has been severely misunderstood and sloppily translated north of the border. Here are a few myths you can toss aside once you start cooking with us.

Myth #1: Mexican food is too spicy

To think of Mexican food as merely hot and spicy is to oversimplify a much more complicated set of sensations. The great traditional foods of Mexico, like moles and posoles, are a complex blend of savory and earthy flavors, with chopped condiments and spicy salsas generally served on the side to use as a seasoning and for textural contrast.

For some reason, perhaps because it was a hot concept that could be easily communicated, spiciness became the defining characteristic of all things Mexican in the United States. It just ain't so.

Seeking out great tastes in Mexico

You may be lucky enough to travel to Mexico and experience the great flavors of the country firsthand. If so, then we have a few tips to help you find wonderful, authentic foods.

Tourism plays such a large part in the Mexican economy that certain places have been developed specifically to make tourists feel at home, or not quite in Mexico. Destinations like Acapulco, Puerto Vallarta, Baja, Cancun, and Cozumel may be great for kicking back and sipping margaritas by the pool, but if it's a culinary adventure you're after, you're unlikely to find it in those sanitized, prepackaged locales. Twenty minutes outside of town, however, it's another story.

The best way to sniff out real regional foods is to visit the main marketplace, usually located near the center of town, or *zocalo* (ZOH-ka-low). Inside the market, and along the streets surrounding it, you can find vendors at stands, pushing carts, or stationed on blankets on the street, who sell the very best, homemade regional specialties. The cart may be tattered and worn, but as long as it looks clean, we don't hesitate to order up whatever may be offered. Chances are it's delicious.

For scrumptious street snacking, you can't go wrong with roasted corn slathered with mayonnaise, lime juice, and cayenne; cold mango on a stick; any fruit juice or liquado (see Chapter 4); salted tamarind seeds; garbanzos roasted in the shell; and beautifully sliced and seasoned fruit.

We recommend *A Cook's Tour of Mexico,* by Nancy Zaslavsky, published by St. Martin's Press, to the seriously food-possessed. This Angeleno has traveled extensively over a 20-year period to complete her research. She can tell you where to go in each region for the best marketplaces, vendors, snack stands, and informal restaurants for a truly authentic dining experience when travelling in Mexico.

Our favorite regions for authentic food are the southern state of Oaxaca, with its ancient mole recipes and active Zapotec culture, and the Yucatán, along the Caribbean coast, with its super citrus-marinated seafood and lightly grilled foods.

Mexico City is a great, sophisticated city for eating. We like to avoid the big-deal, upscale restaurants that lean toward the quasi-Continental in favor of authentic street stands that cater to the locals. Here's a trio of favorites:

- **For breakfast:** El Jarocho, Tapachula #94, Esq. Manzanillo, Col. Roma

- **For tortas:** La Castellana, Revolucion #1309

- **For quesadillas:** Los Panchos, Tolstoi #9, Col. Anzures

Myth #2: Mexican food is too heavy

Old-fashioned Mexican-American restaurant food is heavy. Real Mexican food and the modern updates we favor feature lots of fresh fruits and vegetables, herb garnishes, fresh chopped salsas, rice, beans, tortillas, and a small serving of meat or chicken. Modern Mexican cuisine is light and healthful, with a large dose of flavor.

All that sour cream and melted cheese associated with Mexican food is actually an American restaurant innovation. Typical corn and tortilla snacks, such as enchiladas, tacos, and quesadillas, are meant to be delicate, nutrient-dense morsels, not the leaden doorstops they can be in the United States. Think back to the big, heavy platters of meatballs and spaghetti of the 1950s that have become the refined vegetable pastas of today and you can see the direction Mexican food is taking.

Myth #3: Mexican food is hard to cook

It's ironic that such a rustic, family style of cooking is intimidating to American home cooks. For many, it remains a food to go out to restaurants for, rather than something to cook themselves. One reason may be the exacting authenticity demanded by stern cookbook authors who shall remain nameless.

After you gain experience handling a few unfamiliar ingredients, and you start keeping them on hand, Mexican cooking should fit right into your already overflowing schedule. The Mexican food we love has its roots in the home kitchen and the market, with no fancy last-minute techniques or special equipment necessary to create great soul-satisfying dishes.

Getting Started with Mexican Cooking

Cooking a new cuisine, like speaking a new language, can be intimidating. Here are some pointers for taking those first few tentative steps.

Keeping things manageable

Start small, with familiar, accessible foods like tacos or marinated and grilled meats with salsas. (Look in Chapter 5 for salsas, Chapter 6 for tacos, and Chapter 14 for meaty recipes.) Save the 28-ingredient mole and the more technique-intensive tamales for some time down the road when you have a weekend to tool around the kitchen and linger over a pot of stew.

Experimenting with chiles

Get to know one or two chiles well — serranos and poblanos are a good place to start. After you feel comfortable with your "starter chiles," then branch out to other, more exotic chiles. The techniques for roasting, peeling, and seeding are the same no matter what kind of chile you cook with.

Chapter 3 gives you all kinds of helpful hints on working with chiles. You can check the Web sites listed in Chapter 21 if you'd like to order chiles over the Internet that you can't find in your local markets.

Entertaining, Mexican style

If you're a weekend cook, increase your popularity by entertaining Mexican-style. (See Chapters 16 and 17 for specific tips on planning menus for parties and other special events.) You can't go wrong with chips, salsas, guacamole, two or three kinds of tacos, and a pitcher full of margaritas in the house.

Keeping your mind (and mouth) open to new experiences

Be daring: Taste that baby goat taco at the ethnic food stand, mix up a drink with dried hibiscus flowers, and surprise your friends with homemade tamales or salsas during the holidays. Mexican food is all about expanding your horizons and breaking out of familiar, dull food habits. Just for the fun of it!

Remember that before you started cooking pasta every night of the week, Italian food was new and foreign.

Montezuma's revenge: Fact or fantasy?

Confession time. Even macho tamales with iron-clad stomachs have been known to waste precious time in the ladies room when visiting Mexico. The main reason for traveler's diarrhea, or Montezuma's revenge, is that the water contains a bacteria that can be foreign to your intestinal tract. There's nothing wrong with the water per se; many people are just sensitive to this bacteria.

To avoid embarrassing downtime, you need to be mindful of anything containing water, including iced drinks, unpeeled fruits or vegetables that may have been rinsed in the water, or raw salads.

Some travelers use purified water for everything, including brushing their teeth — though we've never been that careful. There's really no need to go overboard cross-examining food servers. As long as you take these few precautions, you needn't ruin your vacation by worrying about every bite you take. It's not good for the digestion.

The best way to counteract a rambunctious gastrointestinal tract and return to eating with a vengeance is eating a diet of plain white rice, horchata (a rice beverage), and ginger ale until the storm passes.

Chapter 2

Ingredients for Mexican Cooking

· ·

· ·

Mexican cooking doesn't call for a wide array of esoteric ingredients. In Mexican cooking, you use common fruits and vegetables like chiles and tomatoes, easy-to-find cuts of meat, inexpensive cooking oils and vinegars, and a few seeds and spices. The secret to successful Mexican cooking lies in the care and time you take transforming these simple ingredients into exotic dishes. To us, the end result of working with the ingredients of the Mexican kitchen is always magic.

Fruits and Vegetables

Fresh fruits and vegetables are an integral part of everyday eating in Mexico. Tropical fruits like mango, pineapple, guava, and watermelon — beautifully sliced and seasoned — are sold on the street as snacks and pureed into mouthwatering drinks at juice stands all over Mexico.

And vegetables are not some sad little afterthoughts that appear alongside a big serving of meat. They're sliced, diced, and pureed into sauces, stews, and garnishes that make any vegetarian smile. Along with fruits, vegetables such as cucumbers and jícama are also eaten as snacks throughout the day.

Avocado

Pebbly-skinned greenish brown Hass (rhymes with pass) avocados are our first choice for Mexican cooking (see Figure 2-1). Their rich, nutty flesh strikes the perfect balance with fiery Mexican foods, and this avocado is irreplaceable for guacamole, salads, sandwiches, tacos, and soups.

Avocados

Figure 2-1:
The best
avocados
for Mexican
cooking.

Hass   Fuerte

Our second favorite type, if you can't find high-quality Hass avocados, is the leaner, smooth-skinned Fuerte. Its flesh is more watery and the seed bigger than the Hass.

When shopping for avocados, remember that this is one fruit that shouldn't be judged by its cover. The condition of the skin is not necessarily an indication of what lies within. Sometimes scaly, blemished skin can cover the most luxurious flesh.

For judging ripeness, we rely on the squeeze test. If the flesh has a little give when you press it with a finger, you should plan on using the avocado within a day. However, if it puts up no resistance and squishes beneath your thumb, you should put it back. The flesh inside is probably already turning brown and losing its flavor.

Rock hard fruit takes about a week to ripen. To ripen avocados, store them in a sealed brown bag on the counter for about a week. An apple placed in the bag speeds up the process.

Let's hear it for avocados!

According to the California Avocado Commission, this fabulous fruit has been unfairly maligned by the fat police. Avocados contain neither cholesterol nor sodium. They are nutrient-dense, containing Vitamins C, E, and B6, as well as high ratios of potassium and mono-unsaturated fat — that's the good kind of fat that protects your heart. One avocado contains about 275 calories (high for a fruit) — that could be where its bad reputation got started.

To remove the pit from an avocado and extract the meat, just follow these steps (see Figure 2-2):

1. **Cut the avocado in half lengthwise and pull the halves apart.**
2. **Place the half with the pit in it on a counter and hit the pit with the sharp edge of a heavy knife until it plunges in.**
3. **Twist the blade to remove the pit.**
4. **Scoop out the meat with a spoon.**

How to Pit and Peel an Avocado

Figure 2-2:
Pitting and extracting the meat from an avocado.

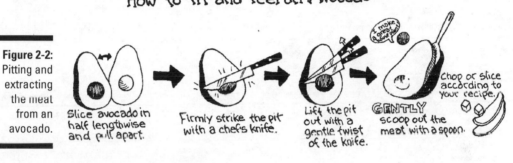

After you cut an avocado, the flesh spoils quickly. To slow down the aging process, you can sprinkle the flesh with lemon or lime juice or cover the avocado skin-tight with plastic wrap and store the fruit in the fridge.

Banana leaves

Large, green banana leaves are available all year-round in the freezer section of Latin American markets. They're popular in the southern and Gulf coast states for wrapping fish, tamales (see Chapter 7), pork, and chicken. In addition to keeping foods moist, these fragrant green leaves impart a delicious fruity flavor of their own. They can also be used to line and cover pans for roasting meats.

To soften banana leaves for folding, use a knife to trim out and discard the tough stalk in the center. Then pass the leaf over a low gas or electric burner less than a minute until it becomes pliable. Because the leaves are huge, trim them into 9-inch squares for wrapping. Unused leaves can be tightly wrapped and stored in the freezer for several months.

If you can't find banana leaves, a good substitute is briefly blanched collard greens. As with banana leaves, trim and discard any tough stems so that the leaves are pliable.

Cactus paddles

The type of cactus most often eaten in Mexico is the prickly pear, the one traditionally pictured in movies about the Old West. Cooks in Mexico simply go into their front or backyards and cut off the tender, young paddles, no larger than about 6 by 8 inches, of the cactus as needed, just as you might harvest an herb or vegetable.

Look for cactus paddles, or *nopales* (noh-PAHl-es), also from the prickly pear, at farmers markets or ethnic grocers. They're usually sold already cleaned (with their needles removed), in plastic bags (see Figure 2-3). The best, freshest paddles are bright green and firm and reverberate when flicked with a finger.

Figure 2-3:
Cleaned cactus paddles.

cactus paddles

You may have to buy your cactus paddles au naturel and clean them yourself. The best way to remove the needles is to shave across the paddle with a sharp paring knife. Store the cleaned paddles in plastic bags in the vegetable bin of the refrigerator.

Our favorite way to cook 'em is grilled, as we describe in the recipe for Cactus Tacos in Chapter 6. Boiling, which some cookbooks recommend, enhances their okra-like quality, but we don't recommend it. If you wish to try it anyway, simply bring a large pot of salted water to a boil and blanch the paddles as you would any green vegetable to soften slightly, about 3 minutes.

Chayote

This pale green, pear-shaped squash was one of the principal foods of the Aztec and Mayan people of Central America. We admire the bland little vegetable for its versatility, ease of preparation, and low cost. Also known as the *mirliton* in Louisiana, the chayote mixes the mild taste of zucchini with the firmer texture of a kohlrabi. Chayote is low in calories and an excellent source of potassium.

You can use chayote in any recipe calling for a summer squash such as zucchini, and everything, including the large seed in the center, is edible. You can also eat it raw in salads.

Look for chayote in Latin and Asian markets year-round. Choose small, unblemished squashes and store them in the vegetable bin of the refrigerator as long as a month.

Corn husks

Dried corn husks (see Figure 2-4) are sold in packages at the supermarket year-round. They are the traditional wrapper for tamales (see Chapter 7), but you can use them to wrap other foods for steaming or grilling: Achiote-marinated fish strips for the steamer or slices of lime-marinated pork loin for the grill are two mouthwatering examples. Corn husks protect tender foods as they cook, while infusing them with corn essence.

corn husks

Figure 2-4:
Corn husks
infuse food
with corn
flavor.

One package of husks is usually enough to wrap about 1 dozen tamales. Store dry husks in an airtight package in the pantry as long as a year.

Dried husks should always be soaked in hot water before using — you'll need to soak them for at least 2 hours. Choose the largest pieces for wrapping and shred thin strings from the edges for tying tamale packages closed. (See Chapter 7 for more information on how to wrap tamales using corn husks.)

Jícama

Jícama (see Figure 2-5) is one root vegetable it pays to know. This plain, round, brown-skinned root yields crisp, white flesh that's terrific for adding sparkle to salads and raw vegetable platters.

Mexico's gifts to world cuisine

When Columbus and Cortez returned to Europe after their travels in the 15th century, they brought from Mexico several ingredients that changed the way the world eats. Chocolate, corn, tomatoes, and chiles were all being raised for agricultural purposes when the explorers arrived. In turn, the Spanish brought beef, pork, lamb, and dairy products to Mexico. Typical pre-Hispanic sources of protein were turkey, duck, dog, bee, and the cochineal insect, used today as a source of red dye.

Figure 2-5:
Jícama is one versatile vegetable.

Like water chestnuts in Chinese cooking, jícama is primarily a texture food. In Mexico, jícama is cut into sticks, sprinkled with salt, cayenne, and lime juice, and sold on the street as a snack. Because its flavor is rather bland (it's mildly sweet like a water chestnut), it always needs at least some salt and lemon or lime to perk it up.

Look for jícama in the produce section of the supermarket. Always remove the fibrous brown skin with a knife and, once cut, cover the flesh with plastic wrap to avoid drying. You can store jícama in the vegetable bin of the refrigerator for a few days.

As a mom, I rate jícama as one of my all-time favorite summer snacks. During the summer, I cut it into sticks (like carrots), sprinkle the sticks with salt and lime juice, and just leave them out on the counter for healthful nibbles. The kids don't even know they're eating vegetables.

Lime

Mexican cooks use the yellow-skinned key lime, or limón as it is called there, and the taste is sweeter than the limes typically eaten elsewhere. The lime is used in Mexico for marinating fish and chicken, perking up salsas, garnishing soups, and balancing margaritas, among other uses.

If you can't find key limes in your local supermarket, you can create a similar taste at home. Just mix half lemon juice and half lime juice any time a recipe calls for lime juice to get closer to the true Mexican flavor.

In the United States, the green Persian lime is the most widely available lime. Persian limes can be disappointingly hard, juiceless, *and* expensive to boot. Choose them wisely: Look for small, soft, thin-skinned fruit, with a yellowish tint in the supermarket or farmers market.

Store limes in a bowl or basket on the countertop. Don't put them in the refrigerator — they go bad faster in there!

We prefer to juice limes by hand (see Figure 2-6). Roll them on the counter first, bearing down to break up the juice sacs. Then cut the lime in half across its width and, holding a half in one hand, plunge the tines of a fork into the pulp. Twist the fork to loosen the juice and pour into a bowl.

How to Juice a Lime

Figure 2-6:
Juicing a
lime.

Cut a lime in half, across the middle.

Hold a half in one hand at an angle. Use a fork to apply pressure and squeeze out the juice!

If juicing a quantity of limes in advance, you can store the juice in a sealed jar in the refrigerator up to 2 days. Or, if your quantity is really large, transfer the juice to freezer bags and freeze it. For smaller portions, freeze the juice in ice cube trays. You never want to be caught without lime juice.

For an extra-concentrated pop of lime flavor in rich stews and soups, try using diced pulp rather than the juice and zest. Using a serrated blade, first remove all of the zest and the white pith beneath it. Then dice the pulp and add it toward the end of your recipe's cooking time.

I know it can be tempting in the rush to get the meal on the table to substitute bottled lime or lemon juice for fresh citrus juice, but don't! There is such a difference in taste between that chemical cocktail sold in bottles and the real thing. I suggest making something else, or substituting another acid (like vinegar) rather than using the bottled product.

For neat little lime wedges, as they are cut in Mexico, first trim off the ends of the lime with a sharp paring knife. Then cut the lime in half crosswise. Laying each half on the counter, cut side down, cut in half and half again.

Plantains

These large, thick, cooking bananas (see Figure 2-7) are a staple food in the Caribbean, where they're fried, mashed, boiled, simmered, pureed, and baked into soups, stews, breads, and side dishes. Though classified as a fruit, like the banana, plantains are used more as a starchy root vegetable like a yam by Caribbean cooks, including those of Mexico's Yucatán peninsula.

Figure 2-7:
The many
faces of the
plantain.

The trick to handling plantains is knowing their stages of ripeness. Their color ranges from green when picked to black when thoroughly ripe, and though you can cook them at every stage, they only turn sweet when their skin has entirely blackened, and their starch has turned to sugar. A cooked green plantain more closely resembles a potato than a banana.

If you plan to enjoy them sweet, purchase plantains that are yellow to black rather than entirely green because green fruit may be difficult to ripen. To speed up the ripening process, store fruit wrapped in newspapers or a brown paper bag out of sunlight, and add an apple if you wish to speed up the ripening process.

Look for plantains in the supermarket or Latin markets. Turn to Chapter 10 for terrific Fried Plantains.

Tomatillos

These small, pale green fruits (see Figure 2-8) are the key to most green salsas. Though they resemble green tomatoes when out of the husk, tomatillos are acidic, pale-green members of the Cape Gooseberry family, and bear no relation to tomatoes.

Figure 2-8:
The tomatillo, no real relation to the tomato.

Look for tomatillos that are small, not rock hard, and still in the husk in the supermarket produce section. Store tomatillos, in the husk, in the vegetable bin of the refrigerator. When you are ready to use them, just pull off the papery husks with your fingers and rinse off the fruit's naturally sticky coating with cold water.

Our favorite way to eat tomatillos is raw or very briefly cooked in order to retain their crunch and spunky bright flavor. Try them chopped in place of the tomatoes in a Fresh Salsa (Chapter 5) or diced and marinated in some lime juice and olive oil and spooned over raw oysters.

Chiles 101

Though chile peppers are enjoyed all over the world (China, Thailand, India, and Korea are big chile-growing and -eating countries), no other country matches Mexico's passion for peppers. Mexican farmers grow over 140 varieties, and Mexican cooks are legendary for their skilled appreciation of every facet (not just the heat) of this complex vegetable that's technically a fruit.

Chiles have been misunderstood as an ingredient, perhaps because of their striking heat. If you stop to appreciate chiles, you'll start to notice a wide range of exotic flavors. From snappy, sparkly jalapeños to smoky chipotles and earthy poblanos, chiles are a light, healthful way to bring a wide range of strong, new flavors to your cooking. Just start with a little at a time, find out what you like, and don't let all the macho hype about the heat deter you.

If you're totally new to chiles and you're the type who likes to dip a toe in the water before diving in, start out gently. Try adding a dried pepper or two to a pot of your favorite soup or stew and let it steep until it plumps up. Then remove the chile before serving. The flavor of the chile will infuse the broth, but no one will be scorched by a mouthful of heat.

Don't let the heat drive you out of the kitchen

We know this seems a little scary, but we always recommend tasting a small slice of a fresh chile before you begin cooking with one. Just as the sweetness and texture of an apple can vary enormously from batch to batch, the same type of chile can run the gamut from mild to incendiary depending on growing and storage conditions. Make the bite teensy-weensy, don't eat the seeds, and keep a tortilla nearby for any cough attacks.

The main idea to keep in mind when you let chiles into your life is that the heat is carried mostly in the seeds and veins inside the fruit. To pump up the heat, use more chiles and include the seeds. To maximize the heat of those fiery little seeds, chop them to release their oils. For great chile flavor without so much heat, simply remove and discard the seeds and veins and use only the flesh.

Shopping for chiles

The names of chiles aren't consistent all over the United States, so study the chart in this section and judge chiles by their appearance and taste, not only their name.

A general rule for predicting the flavor and heat of a chile is the smaller the chile, the hotter the heat. Red indicates a ripe, and probably sweeter, chile than green. Cutting off and tasting a tiny piece of a slice of fresh chile is really the best way to predict its heat and flavor when cooked.

When purchasing fresh chiles, look for bright, smooth, shiny skin and buy about a week's supply. Store the chiles in the vegetable bin of the refrigerator and rinse them before using.

Dried chiles should be fragrant and flexible enough to bend without breaking. Look for unbroken chiles that are not too dusty. (Because chiles are dried outdoors, they can become dirty and dusty and need to be wiped off before cooking.) Store dried chiles in airtight bags in the freezer and let them soften a minute or two at room temperature before using. (See "Plumping up dried chiles" later in this section for more information.)

Handling fresh chiles

After chopping or otherwise handling chiles, you want to be mindful of the other surfaces that have come in contact with cut chiles. The hot oils from the cut chiles will spread like, you guessed it, wildfire.

Immediately after handling chiles, wash off your cutting boards, knives, and hands with hot, soapy water. Be careful not to touch your face or eyes before hand washing because chile oil in the eye is not fun.

Some cooks like to wear gloves when handling chiles, and some cooks coat their hands with a layer of cooking oil to protect them. Just wash with soap and water to remove the oil.

Plumping up dried chiles

Dried chiles are often rehydrated by taking a long soak in hot water or stock before joining the dish. Softening a not-too-hard chile takes about 20 minutes.

Read the recipe all the way through before tossing out the soaking liquid because this chile-infused liquid is often called for later in the recipe.

Dried chiles have a whole other texture and taste, and should not be used as a substitute for fresh chiles. Just like fresh chiles, they can be toasted to improve flavor (see Chapter 3) and seeds can be removed to reduce heat.

Types of chiles

In our cooking, we rely on the nine types of chiles described in this section and shown in Figure 2-9.

Taming the heat

The immediate antidote to a mouth on fire is a milk product like ice cream or yogurt that coats and soothes. Cold drinks like water or beer only spread the sensation down your throat and actually increase the uncomfortable feeling.

The best solution is to taste while you're cooking and try to correct foods that are too spicy before you serve them. Frequently, a dish tastes overwhelmingly spicy because the spice hasn't been brought into balance with other flavors.

You can counteract the heat by adding more salt or acid. Or, if it's still too spicy, serve the spicy dish with plenty of bland rice, beans, tortillas, or potatoes as accompaniments.

The best plan, however, is to make a dish moderately spicy and serve it with an extra spicy salsa so that guests can add spiciness to taste at the table. That way you can please all the palates at the table while gently introducing them to the joys of chile.

Ancho

Anchos are the dried version of our favorite green pepper, the poblano. This wrinkled red-brown, wide-shouldered chile has a mellow, sweet flavor, similar to a bell pepper, with just a touch of heat. We like to add it, julienned, to sauces for its chewy texture or pureed at the beginning of a sauce to add body and pure pepper flavor.

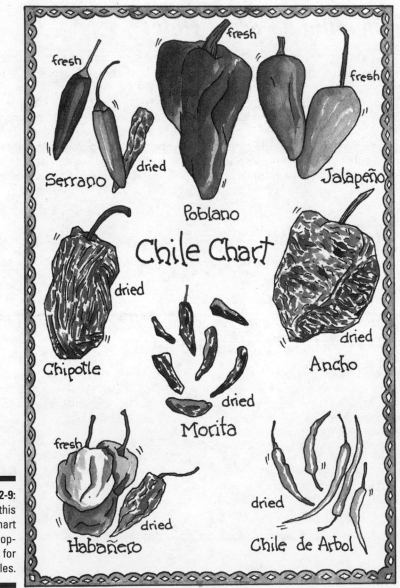

Figure 2-9: Consult this chile chart when shopping for chiles.

The healthy chile

In 1937 the Nobel prize was awarded to Albert Szent-Gyorgyi for isolating vitamin C, which he happened to discover while experimenting with his Hungarian wife's chile pepper plant. Since then, we've come to recognize how great the pepper's health-giving properties are. It's the plant highest in vitamin A; it is a good source of potassium, folic acid, and vitamins E and C; and it is incomparable for clearing sinuses. Chemical capsaicin, the element that gives chiles their heat, is the ingredient in commercial cold medications that makes people cough to break up congestion.

Chile de arbol

Arbols, also known as dried red chiles, are the papery thin, long, dried chiles sold by the bag in the supermarket. Used extensively in Chinese and Mexican cooking (they put the pow in Kung Pau chicken), these inexpensive little peppers pack a powerful punch of heat, especially after they're chopped and cooked. To tame their heat, you can add them whole to stews and soups and remove them before serving.

Chile negro or dried pasilla

This long, narrow, dark brown chile is a dried chilaca chile. Similar in flavor to the more popular ancho, pasillas are often used in combination with other dried chiles in traditional moles. Look for them via mail order or in ethnic markets.

Chipotle

Chipotles, or dried, smoked, red jalapeños, are one of those life-changing ingredients. Once we tasted chipotle salsa, on our first tasting expedition to Mexico back in 1984, we never looked back. We've been using these wrinkled, reddish-brown chiles to add a mysterious, smoky, sweet flavor to everything from salad dressings to grilled chicken and salsas ever since.

If you can't find dried chipotles at the market, try ordering them mail order from one of the specialty suppliers mentioned in Chapter 21.

Though usable as a substitute, canned chipotles en adobo (dried chiles packed in a sweet, sour, spicy sauce) are quite different. They're actually hotter and their texture is softer. If you use chipotles en adobo, wipe them off to remove excess sauce and reduce by half the quantity called for in the recipe.

Roots of the chile plant

The chile plant originated in what is now Bolivia or Peru about 7000 B.C. The tiny, pungent red fruit was widely cultivated by native people all over Central, South, and southwestern North America who used it for cooking, healing, and trading. It was considered a valuable enough commodity to be included at burial sites.

When Columbus "discovered" the chile pepper in 1492 he didn't realize what he had found. He thought he had found the prized black pepper plant and so named the plant "pepper." But when the seeds were planted, back in Europe, brand new fleshy green and red chiles emerged. Europeans were impressed by how easily the plants grew and their pungent flavor. Even if they didn't know exactly what to do with them, chiles fascinated cooks from the start.

As the Spanish and Portuguese explorers continued to chart the new world's trade routes, they sprinkled chile seeds in their wake. Africa, India, China, Southeast Asia, and the East Indies continue to be major chile producers and users. Today 25 percent of the world's population eats chiles on a daily basis.

Habañero

This is one little pepper that lives up to its reputation. It's pure heat. Along with the Scotch Bonnet, the habañero is considered the world's hottest chile.

These small, lantern-shaped (usually) peppers are most often used in the Yucatán. You can shop for them at Latin and farmers markets where their color can range from dark green to orange and even red. We prefer the taste of fresh rather than dried habañeros and recommend substituting a larger quantity of serranos (seeds and all) in a pinch.

Cooking with our favorite chile

We hate to pick favorites, especially among chile peppers, but if we had to choose one chile that we could not live without it would have to be the little brown chipotle. Its meaty, smoky flavor is so distinctive that we always recommend it to our vegetarian friends who still crave bacon. Chipotles are that luscious.

Susan's favorite quick salsa features chipotles. First she soaks them in simmering red wine vinegar for 15 minutes to plump them up. Then she chops the chiles and combines them with olive oil and chopped green onions. Tossed with strips of beef, this combination is fantastic!

Another diehard chipotle-lover's trick is to reconstitute them first in vinegar. Then carefully split the chiles open, remove the seeds, and stuff them with cheese. Batter and fry the chiles like Chiles Rellenos (see Chapter 7) for a real treat.

If you're still not convinced, try the variation on Fiesta Bean Salad in Chapter 9. If that dish doesn't sell you, you may be immune to this smoky little chile's charms.

It's hot no matter how you spell it

We're not sure who makes these rules, but as far as we can tell, the word *chile* refers to the pepper plant, *chili* refers to the traditional meat and bean dish from Texas, and *chilli* is the Nahuatl, or Mexican Indian spelling. The plant Columbus brought back from his journeys was called *aji* by the native people and got renamed Calcutta Pepper by a German botanist because folks still thought Columbus may have found India.

Jalapeño, red and green

The jalapeño, America's favorite chile pepper, is a thick-fleshed, small (about 3-inch long), bright green or red pepper. With its sweet, fresh, garden flavor and medium heat, this versatile pepper is great for garnishing just about anything.

In Mexico, we've even seen jalapeños eaten as an accompaniment to rich stews and tacos. In fact, at the Border Grill staff meals, a bowl of fresh jalapeños is always nearby. They're easy to find at the market, but you can substitute serranos if you prefer.

Canned jalapeños are not a good substitute for fresh peppers because their taste and texture are quite different.

Morita

These small, brown, dried chiles look like thin chipotles but are less smoky with a spicier taste. They are a variety of dried, smoked jalapeño. Use fewer moritas to replace chipotles in a recipe.

Poblano

These dark green, medium-sized, thick-fleshed chiles are our favorite fresh green peppers for cooking. We feature them in soups, sauces, and chilis, and they are always our first choice for stuffing because of their wide shoulders, thick skin, and smoldering flesh. They are superb as *rajas* (roasted pepper strips) because of their meatiness.

Sometimes mislabeled pasilla in the West, look for smooth-skinned poblano chiles with nice wide shoulders for stuffing. Less spicy, skinnier Anaheims can be substituted for stuffing, but poblanos should be easy to find in a well-stocked supermarket.

Serrano

Small, thin serranos are similar to jalapeños but pack a little more punch. We mostly use the green variety (the reds are a bit sweeter) in salsas and as a raw garnish in salads and soups. They're easy to find at the supermarket, and you can use them interchangeably with jalapeños.

Herbs

If the variety of herbs on the market makes you feel insecure, you can relax. The Mexican kitchen uses the same three herbs over and over again: cilantro, oregano (fresh and dried), and epazote. If you start cooking Mexican often, you may want to buy a few of these easy-to-grow plants for the garden and save last-minute shopping trips.

Cilantro

Cilantro (see Figure 2-10) is one of those ingredients that arouses emotions. People either love it or hate it, and it's not easy to change a hater's taste. Still, we do recommend that you give this unique flavor a few chances if you don't immediately care for it. It just might grow on you.

cilantro

Figure 2-10:
Give cilantro
a try.

On the other hand, if the thought of a cilantro leaf passing your lips still makes you quiver after a few tastes, please don't give up on Mexican (or Thai or Chinese) food. Simply replace it with flat leaf parsley or an herb that you love and, if anybody asks, tell them two highly trained chefs gave you permission.

Cilantro, also known as Chinese parsley or fresh coriander, was brought to Mexico by the Spanish. It is primarily used fresh in salsas and as a garnish, but is also cooked into green moles, sauces, and stews. Look for it in the supermarket produce section and store the bunch, loosely covered with a plastic bag, stems down, in a glass of water in the refrigerator.

If the roots are still attached, leave them on. In Thai cuisine, even the roots are eaten, and even if you don't eat them, they help the plant stay fresh longer.

Because cilantro is so delicate, it's best not to chop it in advance. Likewise, don't stress about removing the thin stems; they're entirely edible. Dried cilantro should never be used to replace fresh. This is one herb that doesn't dry well.

Epazote

Stronger-tasting than most herbs, epazote (see Figure 2-11) grows like the weed that it is all over North America. It's difficult to find in the supermarket (though you're liable to find it in the weeds growing alongside the highway in Los Angeles), but you can easily grow it from seed in the garden or a pot. We've tried the dried variety and do not recommend it because it's virtually flavorless.

Figure 2-11:
Epazote, a
very flavor-
ful weed.

The flavor of fresh epazote is so dominant that it should be used alone, not in combination with other herbs, when flavoring a dish. In Mexico, it's often used to complement mushrooms, black beans, squash, and even quesadillas.

When cooking with epazote, always trim off the tough stem.

Oregano

Oregano, familiar from Italian-American cooking, is the most popular herb in the Mexican kitchen. Thirteen varieties of this small, soft, green-leafed plant grow in Mexico. Look for it in the supermarket produce section and always remove the leaves from the tough stems.

Mexican cooks also use dried oregano. You can purchase cellophane bags of Mexican dried oregano, containing larger pieces of leaves and stems, and crumble the large pieces by hand before adding or just use common dried oregano. We sometimes add a smoky edge by toasting the dried herb first in a dry skillet over low heat.

The Spice Shelf

The Mexican spice shelf is reassuringly short: cumin for savor and cinnamon for sweetness. The magic lies in how these spices are combined with chiles, salt, pepper, assorted seeds, and other flavorings to make this simple soul-satisfying cuisine.

Cumin

If we had to pick the one fragrance that instantly identifies Mexican food, it would be cumin. We recommend using it liberally in your Mexican cooking, combined with cinnamon, nutmeg, cayenne, and arbol chiles for a sweet spicy kick, or combined with onion, garlic, ground ancho, paprika, and cayenne for a full, earthy, chile flavor.

Use it ground, if you want its flavor to pervade the dish, and always develop the flavor by cooking it first in fat. Use about 1 teaspoon of whatever fat is in the dish to each teaspoon of spice. If it's just dropped into a bubbling soup or stew, the flavor never goes as deep. Use cumin seeds whole when you're looking for an assertive pop of flavor when you take a bite.

As with all dried spices, you can purchase cumin in small enough quantities to last on your shelf no longer than six months. Store out of sunlight and check expiration dates in the store before purchasing. You're likely to find fresher cumin in an Indian or Mexican market where cooks purchase it a lot.

Cinnamon

Cinnamon (see Figure 2-12), known as *canela* in Spanish, is used in the Mexican kitchen to flavor both savories and sweets. The thin, papery, brown bark known as Mexican cinnamon has a rougher edge and is less expensive than the tightly wound variety commonly found in the supermarket. Look for the Mexican variety (actually from Sri Lanka), packed in hanging cellophane bags, in the ethnic section of the market. Use the bark to infuse drinks, stews, moles, and sauces and then discard it. Ground cinnamon can always be used in its place.

Figure 2-12:
Sweet
cinnamon
sticks.

cinnamon

Store cinnamon in airtight containers away from the sun and replenish after about six months because the bark dries out.

Nuts, Seeds, and Seasoning Pastes

Nuts and seeds are much more than a snack food or dessert ingredient in the Mexican kitchen. Since pre-Columbian times, peanuts, pecans, and pumpkin seeds have been used to thicken sauces and moles. And the Spanish influence can be seen in the use of almonds and walnuts in rich ground-nut sauces and stuffings. Nut- and seed-based sauces come under the general heading of pipians, of which Green Pumpkin Seeds Mole in Chapter 11 is one.

Annatto seed and achiote paste

These tiny, rock hard, brick red seeds from the South American annatto tree give Mexican food its characteristic orange tint (see Figure 2-13).

Figure 2-13:
Annatto
seeds in
their simple
splendor.

The seeds alone have a slightly musky flavor but when ground and combined with garlic, oregano, cumin, cinnamon, pepper, and cloves they make fragrant achiote paste, a seasoning mixture popular in the Yucatán for marinades and sauces. To sample the flavor firsthand, try Cochinita Pibil from Chapter 14 and Grilled Red Snapper Tikin-Chik from Chapter 16.

Annatto seed, available in ethnic markets and by mail order, is used by American food producers to add an orange tint to butter and cheddar cheese. You can use the seeds to flavor an oil by simply heating them in the oil and then straining out the seeds, or you can grind them in a coffee or spice grinder and use them to color masa for tamales. Annatto or achiote should always be cooked in fat to remove any chalkiness.

Achiote paste, sold in bricks in Mexican markets, is an easy-to-use spice rub for fish and meats. When the paste is thinned with vinegar or citrus juices, the spices develop a wonderful tropical fruitiness. Achiote paste can be kept, well wrapped, in the refrigerator for a long time.

Be sure to wash off any utensils or cutting boards that come into contact with annatto or achiote right away. There's a reason this is an industrial-strength dye. A little goes a long way.

Tamarind seeds and paste

Tamarind is a leathery, dried brown seed pod that produces a deliciously sticky, sweet-sour paste when cooked (see Figure 2-14). One of the key ingredients in Worcestershire sauce, it is popular in Indian, Mexican, Indonesian, and Thai cuisines as a tart balance to fatty foods. It is available in brick as well as pod form in ethnic markets.

Figure 2-14:
Tamarind
pods in their
natural
state.

To reconstitute dried tamarind pods, first remove the hard outer pods by hand and discard the pods. Place the fruit in a pan, generously cover with water, and cook at a boil about 15 minutes, until soft. Strain before using. The finished paste should be the consistency of ketchup.

Bricks of tamarind pulp should be soaked in hot water to soften about 30 minutes and then pressed through a strainer to separate any solids from the thick puree.

A good substitute for tamarind paste is pureed, dried apricots, enhanced with some lemon juice.

Coconut

Coconuts are available year-round in the supermarket. The best ones feel heavy in your hand and sound full of liquid when shaken. If the eyes are soft and the coconut smells spoiled when you sniff it, chances are that it's rotten inside.

In some Latin markets, coconuts are sold already husked and wrapped to go in plastic. But if you can't get to a Latin market, here's how to get to that sweet, white meat: Poke a hole in two or three eyes with a screwdriver or ice pick and drain the liquid. Place the coconut on a baking tray in a 350° oven for about 10 minutes, and then remove it and crack it open with a hammer on the floor (to avoid damage to your expensive kitchen counters).

For delicious, large shards of coconut meat ready-to-go, shop for unsweetened, shaved (not shredded) coconut in health food markets. Store the coconut in plastic bags in the freezer.

Pepitas

Pumpkin seeds, or pepitas (see Figure 2-15), are native to Mexico and show up in sauces, salads, moles, and, of course, snack foods. The seeds sold in Mexico, often with the thin, white husks still on, have much more flavor than those sold in the United States. The thin husks are edible.

Figure 2-15:
Give your dishes some pep with pepitas.

Call us nuts

We like to buy our nuts, seeds, spices, and beans from health markets that sell in bulk. After spending so many years in the restaurant business, we can never get used to the idea of buying tiny quantities and paying for excess packaging. Still, for our home needs, we need to be careful not to overstock. Even dried foods like spices and beans age and turn stale.

Our general rule is to buy about a six-month supply (about 1 pound) of any nut, seed, or bean. Store all nuts and seeds in your refrigerator or freezer in well-sealed containers. For the best flavors, always toast nuts and seeds first in a 350° oven or in a dry pan, shaking constantly, for about 10 minutes.

We like to purchase the long, thin green seeds raw from bulk markets and season them with Chili Mix Powder (Chapter 11) and salt, spread them on a baking sheet, and roast them in the oven until crisp.

Like all seeds and nuts, pepitas should be stored in airtight containers in the freezer. They need not be defrosted before using.

Beans and Starches

These beans and starches are the simple and substantial backbones of every Mexican meal. No good Mexican cook is ever without them.

Beans

The two beans Americans most often associate with Mexican cooking are black beans and larger mottled pink pintos, but in Mexico, people enjoy a wider variety. Beans and rice are served at virtually every meal to ensure a daily dose of protein in diets that don't depend upon a large portion of meat.

Most important when shopping for beans is to purchase from a store that does a brisk business. There is such a thing as a bean that's gotten too old to ever cook up soft — and it's impossible to spot these little scoundrels before they're cooked.

 TOQUE TIP

If you don't have time for all the boiling dried beans require, you can always substitute a good canned bean. A good way to enhance the flavor of canned beans is to sauté a clove or two of garlic with a chopped onion in some oil until they are soft and nearly brown. Add this to the beans with their cooking liquid and warm through.

Tortillas

You can't eat Mexican food without tortillas. Would you ask a Frenchman to sit down to a meal without his baguette? Not only are tortillas the sustaining bread of the Mexican people, but they also make a darn good fork in a pinch. Just hold the tortilla in your hand and pinch the food in between for instant taco transport.

If you do much cooking, you should stock up on large packs of 6-inch taco-sized corn tortillas (which are widely available in stores) because they are so versatile. Deep yellow corn tortillas are our favorite, but white can be good too, depending on your preference. You can use corn tortillas for making chips, enchiladas, chilaquiles, and tostadas, to name a few dishes, and they'll keep a long time in their sealed package in the fridge. (Chapter 10 tells you how to make your own corn tortillas at home.)

Flour tortillas, with or without lard, are also available in various sizes and packs in the supermarket. You may want to stock these tortillas if you like making burritos and quesadillas. Also, search for uncooked tortilla dough in the supermarket freezer next to the cookie dough. (Chapter 6 tells you how to make flour tortillas.)

Masa harina

Masa harina is flour made from corn dough that has been dried and then ground into a powder. Quaker Oats sells it in the supermarket baking section. Ordinary yellow cornmeal for making cornbread is not a good substitute.

The Mexican Dairy

Authentic Mexican cheeses can be found in most supermarkets. With the three basic cooking cheeses — panela, añejo, and manchego — or their substitutes, you have all the cheeses you ever need to cook authentic quesadillas or queso fundido, or just add a bite of richness to salads, soups, and enchiladas. Remember, as a general culinary principle, just say no to orange cheese.

Añejo

Also known as Cotija (koh-TEE-jah), for the town where it was first made, añejo (ah-NYEH-hoh) is a dry, aged cow's milk cheese prized for its salty bite. Because it's not a good melter, it should always be combined with another cheese in cooked dishes, but for sprinkling over beans, soups, and salads it is perfect alone. Use it as you would grated Parmesan in your Italian cooking. Either Parmesan or Romano makes a good substitute.

Panela

Panela, a semi-soft white cow's milk cheese, has a delightfully fresh milky flavor. In the freshest panela, the curds are still visible, as well as the circular pattern imprinted from the basket in which the curds were set to drain. We like it diced, as a garnish for soup or posole, and in cubes in a salad because it holds its shape so well.

Contrary to its mozzarella-like appearance, panela is not a good melter and always needs to be teamed with a Jack-like cheese for quesadillas. We recommend dry curd farmer's cheese, dry cottage, or dry ricotta as substitutes.

Mexican manchego

This inexpensive semi-soft cheese should not be confused with Spanish manchego, a stronger aged eating cheese. Soft, mild Mexican manchego is the melter in the group. You can substitute Monterey Jack cheese for manchego.

Crema

Mexican crema, sold in jars in the refrigerator case of the supermarket, is a soured milk product similar to buttermilk and sour cream. This salty, white drizzling cream is thinner and less sour than sour cream and used most often as a garnish or dressing.

We're not big fans of commercial produced crema because of the additives. The best substitute is crème fraiche, but sour cream thinned with a bit of lime juice or buttermilk to the consistency of a creamy salad dressing will do in a pinch. Chapter 15 contains a recipe so that you can make your own crema at home.

The cheese mix

We like to use a grated mixture of one part manchego, one part panela, and one part añejo rather than one cheese in our cooked dishes. The mix results in a more complex texture and flavor. Manchego lends its texture, añejo its salt, and panela its milkiness.

Weird things we've eaten in Mexico

Before we tantalize you with descriptions of some of the strange things we've tasted on our travels in Mexico, you need to understand that we eat weird things wherever we go. Our job is to travel the world and taste it, so we can bring back new ideas to keep our palates and restaurant kitchens alive and growing.

Because so much of eating is mental, we try to enter each new eating experience with an open mind or blank slate. By erasing any negative, preconceived notions based on cultural taboos before we dive in, we're prepared to embrace the new experience. Unless we're being served eyeballs, that is. Then we just close our eyes and keep a big bottle of tequila nearby for instant taste memory loss.

On our Mexican tasting trips, we've eaten (and enjoyed) the following: an appetizer of roasted crickets with chiles and guacamole, roasted worms, pig's feet, tail, snout and ears, goat brains, and blood sausage — a memorable dish of sheep's lung stuffed with blood and diced vegetables and roasted underground. Let us know if you can top that!

Of course, if you can't get your hands on all three, feel free to improvise with substitutes or use two rather than three types of cheese. The basic idea is that a variety of cheeses is always preferable to one in any melted cheese dish.

Olives

The most authentic olives for Mexican cooking are little green Manzanillas from Spain, with pits, not pimentos. They're sold in ethnic markets and the ethnic section of the supermarket.

Oil and vinegar for the pantry

The olive oil we use for most of our cooking is a strong, fruity one from Spain that we discovered while visiting a restaurant kitchen in the Yucatán. Extra-virgin olive oil can be lovely for dressing salads, but we don't find it necessary for Mexican cooking. As for vinegar, cheap red or white wine vinegar in big jugs from the supermarket is just fine. We use it all the time.

The kind of ingredients it does pay to spend the time and money seeking out are those that can really dominate a dish and make a difference. The best, freshest fish from a specialty market for Tikin-Chik (see Chapter 16), a great steak for a chile-stuffed rib eye, or an expensive aged tequila for sipping after dinner is well worth the money. Those ingredients can raise the whole meal to another level of enjoyment.

Chapter 3

Mastering a Few Simple Tools and Techniques

If you've never cooked before, the few tools and techniques you need for Mexican cooking are a good way to get started in the kitchen.

Equipping Your Kitchen

We hate to disappoint any closet yuppies in the crowd, but you can forget about some big shopping spree before you start cooking Mexican food. If you have the basic cooking utensils, you probably don't need any new equipment at all. (See the Introduction for the basic equipment list.) And anything you may decide to buy (like a blender or a bean masher) won't cost much. After all, terrific Mexican food has been coming out of shacks and street stands since before stainless steel restaurant-style kitchens were invented.

On the other hand, if you're not only new to Mexican cooking but your previous forays into the world of cuisine consisted mainly of dialing for takeout, you may want to treat yourself to some good pots and pans to make your time in the kitchen more fun. Here's what we recommend for working on all four burners:

✔ Invest in a starter set of cookware that includes 14- and 10-inch skillets, a 3-quart saucepan, and a 10-quart stockpot. Purchasing pieces that may be too large for your present needs is better than buying small pans. Empty space in a skillet is less of a problem than overcrowding. A brisk sauté can become a slow steam in moments in a pan that's too small.

✔ Our favorite materials are heat conductors like copper, aluminum, and cast iron. Heavier pots and pans not only cook better but also last longer.

✔ Avoid fancy cookware with bottoms made of a different material from the body of the pan. Those sandwiched bottoms can separate and warp over time. Also avoid plastic handles because they'll melt and warp in the oven.

✔ If you can afford only one good knife, make it a large, 10-inch heavy chef's knife (see Figure 3-1). Hold the knife in your hand and make sure that the grip is comfortable. The blade should be well-balanced with a full *tang* — the metal running the length of the knife from tip to handle.

The best metals are high-carbon stainless and plain carbon steel. We do not recommend stainless steel knives, because they don't hold an edge. Some brands we can recommend are Takayuki, Forchner, Friedr, Dick, Henckels, and Wüsthof. They're not all expensive (a good chef's knife can range in price from $35 to $150), and a good knife should last a life-time. Invest in a sharpening steel at the same time, and you'll be chopping with the best of them before you know it.

Figure 3-1:
Invest in a
chef's knife.

chef's knife

To sharpen knives with a steel, hold the knife at a 30-degree angle and swipe the entire edge of the blade against the steel. Repeat about 10 times on each side for an even edge (see Figure 3-2). After a knife has totally lost its edge, take it to a professional cutlery store to put the edge back on with a device known as a stone.

How to Use a Sharpening Steel

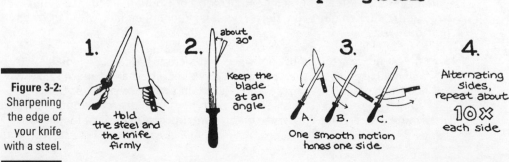

Figure 3-2:
Sharpening
the edge of
your knife
with a steel.

1. Hold the steel and the knife firmly

2. about 30° — Keep the blade at an angle

3. A. B. C. One smooth motion hones one side

4. Alternating sides, repeat about 10X each side

Why we love cast iron

Cast iron is the best! It is inexpensive and heavy, heats up quickly and evenly, and never warps. The only downside, aside from the weight of really large pots, is the time and care to properly season cast iron.

Cast iron, the classic American cooking material, needs to be coddled in its youth with several coatings of grease and time on the burner in order to properly coat the surface. Then, once

it's in use, you need to wipe it clean with sudsy water rather than scrub it to leave the seasoning intact. The payoff for such special treatment is a first-rate pan for life.

If you're on the lazy side, look for old, lovingly seasoned, and cared-for cast-iron pans at flea markets or try to inherit one from a generous grandma.

Blenders

We're always shocked to see blenders in remote villages in Mexico, but there is really nothing like them for all the grinding and pureeing involved in making Mexican beverages, sauces, moles, and stuffings. It's the only piece of electric equipment you'll ever need, and we would choose a blender any day over a food processor.

Although a processor has a bigger work bowl and more powerful motor, it whirs everything around so quickly that some pieces of food get pushed to the edges, never getting properly ground. But a blender, because of the tall shape of the container and blade design, processes foods up and down, resulting in an even grind every time.

Any inexpensive blender will do, but a blender with a heavier case and more powerful motor is always a better investment over the long haul because it will last longer.

Read "Ready, set, puree" in this chapter for some tips on working with a blender.

Stovetop grills and griddles

Those circular cross-hatched grates that fit over a burner are great for heating tortillas on the stovetop, although a hot, dry skillet works just fine.

We also like heavy stovetop grill pans for getting a grilled effect indoors (see Figure 3-3). And a low-edged pancake griddle is great for reaching right in and flipping freshly made tortillas.

Figure 3-3:
Use a stove-
top grill pan
to get the
grilled effect
indoors.

Tortilla presses

Metal and wooden tortilla presses (see Figure 3-4) for pressing out dough are sold at Mexican markets and by mail order from cookware catalogs.

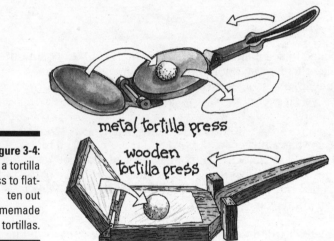

Figure 3-4:
Use a tortilla
press to flat-
ten out
homemade
tortillas.

The cheaper the better — you shouldn't pay more than about $8 for one. Just look for a press that presses the dough evenly at all points. They pretty much explain themselves once you get one in your hands. (Press down with the lever to squash the dough.) In a pinch, we've pressed tortillas between sheets of plastic, with a good heavy dictionary — Spanish or English.

You can put your tortilla press to work by making flour tortillas (Chapter 6) or corn tortillas (Chapter 10).

Bean mashers

We like the inexpensive, wiggly, wire, handheld variety — good for mashing refried beans (see Chapter 10) and potatoes but leaving a few lumps of authenticity.

Steamers

The little perforated baskets that fit in a saucepan for steaming vegetables are great for Mexican cooking. You can improvise a larger steamer for tamales by fitting a colander, with an inch or two of water beneath, on top of a deep soup pot. Cover the top of the pot with aluminum foil to trap the steam. Or treat yourself and purchase a big pot with a steamer attachment.

Tackling a Few Techniques

The techniques of the Mexican kitchen do not call for split-second timing or finicky, precise movements. Just roll up your sleeves and get ready to chop, dice, slice, and occasionally whir the blender or sizzle foods in hot oil. Mexican cooking methods, based on techniques honed by home cooks over the years, depend only on your willingness to dive in and do the work.

Toasting and seeding vegetables and seeds

If, in your previous attempts at cooking, you've taken heat for burning the food, you're in luck now. Good Mexican cooking calls for lots of roasting, toasting, and charring to give the food that mysterious deep, smoky, rustic edge. This may be the only time in your cooking career where to blacken is not only okay but preferred. Here's how to roast and toast some ingredients typically found in Mexican foods.

Fresh chiles and bell peppers

Fresh chiles and bell peppers can be roasted directly over a gas flame or on a tray under the broiler. Keep turning until the skin is evenly charred, without burning the flesh. Transfer charred peppers to a plastic bag, tie the top closed, and let the peppers sit until they're cool to the touch, about 15 minutes. (To speed things up, you can place the bag in a bowl of iced water.) Remove the blackened skin by pulling it off by hand and then dip your fingers in a bowl of water to remove any blackened bits. Once peeled, cut away stems, seeds, and veins with a paring knife.

Do not peel roasted peppers under running tap water or tasty, precious juices will be washed away.

Figure 3-5 shows how to roast, peel, seed, and julienne a chile.

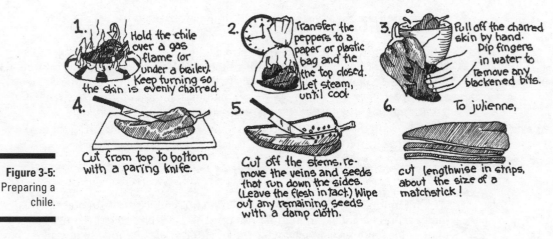

Figure 3-5: Preparing a chile.

How to Roast, Peel, Seed, and Julienne a Chile

1. Hold the chile over a gas flame (or under a broiler). Keep turning so the skin is evenly charred.

2. Transfer the peppers to a paper or plastic bag and tie the top closed. Let steam, until cool.

3. Pull off the charred skin by hand. Dip fingers in water to remove any blackened bits.

4. Cut from top to bottom with a paring knife.

5. Cut off the stems, remove the veins and seeds that run down the sides. (Leave the flesh intact.) Wipe out any remaining seeds with a damp cloth.

6. To julienne, cut lengthwise in strips, about the size of a matchstick!

Dried chiles

Dried chiles, like anchos, develop more flavor if lightly toasted. Just place them directly over a low gas flame or in a dry skillet over low flame and warm a few seconds on each side, until the flesh is bubbly and lightly toasted.

Vegetables

Tomatoes, tomatillos, onions, and garlic are often roasted on a tray under the broiler when making salsas, soups, and stews. Simply arrange all the vegetables to be roasted on a large baking sheet, protecting small garlic cloves by tucking them under larger vegetables. Stay nearby and keep turning the vegetables with tongs until everything is evenly blackened. Be careful to transfer the juices that collect on the baking sheet to the blender because they carry lots of delicious flavor.

You can also roast vegetables in a heavy, dry cast-iron skillet over a medium flame. Cook, turning frequently, until blackened.

Seeds

Whole coriander, cumin, and fennel seeds can be toasted on the stovetop. Place the seeds in a dry skillet over medium heat and keep shaking and tossing the pan until their aroma is released, less than a minute.

Ready, set, puree

We are huge fans of the humble blender that can be purchased for about $40 at the local hardware store. Nothing beats it for a uniform puree. If we had to live without it, our next best choices for grinding would be a hand-cranked food mill or sieve.

When using the blender to puree hot liquids for soups or stews, follow these tips:

- ✔ Never fill a blender more than halfway. Always leave a crack open at the top for steam to escape.

- ✔ Control the proportion of liquids to solids in the container by lifting solids from the pot with a spoon and then pouring a small amount of liquid from the pot to the blender. A combination of about half liquid and half solids is good.

- ✔ Always cover the top of the blender with a towel to protect yourself from escaping liquids.

- ✔ Begin the action by briefly pulsing a few times to start liquefying. When the blades are moving freely, you can let it rip.

To puree garlic in quantity, first break the bulbs apart. Peel them by first flattening the cloves with the flat side of a heavy knife or cleaver and then removing the skin. Puree with a small amount of olive oil in a blender or food processor fitted with a metal blade. Store in the refrigerator for as long as a week. Pureed garlic can always be used in place of minced garlic. One tablespoon pureed equals about 3 cloves, minced.

Welcome to the beanery

Here are some suggestions to help assure perfectly cooked beans every time:

- ✔ Never salt the water. It will toughen the bean's skin. Add salt to flavor after the beans are done.

- ✔ For maximum creaminess, always cook over low heat, with the cover on, to prevent drying.

- ✔ To prevent scorching, stir with a wooden spoon several times during cooking, always reaching down to the bottom of the pot. Burnt beans on the bottom of the pot will infuse the whole pot with their unlovely aroma.

- ✔ To test for doneness, taste a few of the smallest beans because they take the longest to cook through. If their centers are smooth and creamy, the batch is done.

✔ Use cool water in your sink to cool beans in a hurry, as shown in Figure 3-6.

✔ Pressure cookers are great for cooking beans. Just follow the machine's instructions.

Figure 3-6:
Cooling beans down quickly.

Fill the sink with COLD water... submerge the pot of beans into the water. Don't get the beans wet! stir up from the bottom! Repeat, until cool.

Poppin' peppercorns for flavor

TOQUE TIP

To crack peppercorns, place the whole peppercorns in the middle of a cutting board. To keep the peppercorns from flying away when you crack them, roll up a towel and use it to surround the corns. Place the heel of a skillet or saucepan on top and push down and away from you several times (see Figure 3-7).

How to Crush Peppercorns

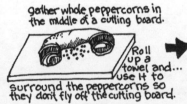

Figure 3-7:
Cracking pepper-corns down to size.

gather whole peppercorns in the middle of a cutting board.

Roll up a towel and... use it to surround the peppercorns so they don't fly off the cutting board.

Use the heel of your hand to press down the edge of a small pot on to the peppercorns.

Repeat steps one and two until the peppercorns are crushed to a desired size...

Mexican cooking light

Authentic Mexican cooking is light and healthful, with an emphasis on fresh fruits and vegetables and sauces thickened with seeds, nuts, chiles, and tor-tillas rather than fattening butter and cream. Mexican food's bad rap can be traced to the old Mexican-American restaurant combination platter, which was based on the concept of lots of inexpensive rice, beans, and melted cheese to accompany the margaritas.

Here are some pointers for lightening Mexican food, both at home and in restaurants:

- ✔ Order soft tortillas rather than crisp, fried shells.

- ✔ Order more _ceviches_ (raw fish salads) and vegetable dishes than richer stews and cornmeal dishes.

- ✔ Start the meal with chips and salsa, but, once the meal is under way, hide the chips.

- ✔ In your own cooking, do more grilling and use strongly flavored marinades matched with salsas rather than a cooked sauce to jazz up meats and poultry. See Chapter 13 for marinating and chicken-grilling tips.

- ✔ Serve a selection of vegetables, starches, grains, and protein. Divide that 16-ounce sirloin into four portions and serve it with flavorful accompaniments. It makes for much more interesting and healthful eating.

- ✔ If you crave crisp tortillas, try baking flour tortillas until crisp rather than frying corn tortillas. See Chapter 19 for directions.

- ✔ Replace that devilish sour cream or Crema (see Chapter 15) in your garnishes with full-fat yogurt — equally delicious and satisfying, with hardly any calories. But don't go overboard and use nonfat yogurt. It tastes so bad that you'll end up eating more in search of some satisfaction.

Part II
Taking a Quick Trip

The 5th Wave   By Rich Tennant

"Why don't you start with some guacamole and I'll finish charring the peppers."

In this part . . .

The chapters in this part of the book give you a short tour through the Mexican kitchen. None of the recipes you find in these chapters is very complicated or time consuming — in short, they make a great place to start with Mexican cooking.

With the help of the Mendoza sisters, who are local Oaxaca restaurateurs, Mary Sue and Susan get a lesson in the art of the *metate*. The sisters use the three-legged stone *metate* to grind corn and other grains for cooking.

A farmer shows Susan and Mary Sue how to harvest the heart of an agave plant in Oaxaca. The heart, which looks like a pineapple, will be roasted and distilled into mezcal, which is a form of tequila.

Susan and Mary Sue cook quail with rose petal sauce with Emilia Arroyo, a retired nurse turned herbalist in Oaxaca.

Mary Sue and Susan check out the fresh ingredients and food stands at a local market in Oaxaca City, which offers a wide variety of culinary attractions — not surprising for a city whose name comes from the Nahuatl word *Huaxacac*, which means "in the eye of the squash."

(Top to bottom) Mexican Chopped Salad, which features green apples, corn, and pine nuts, provides a great alternative to the standard side salad. Bread Salad will make you think of a sandwich in a bowl (both in Chapter 9).

Serve Gazpacho (Chapter 8) with Aztecan Quinoa Salad (Chapter 9) as a first course to cool off your guests in the heat of summer.

(Clockwise from bottom left) Smoky Chicken Quesadillas combine the richness of cheese and the spice of chiles to create an authentic treat your family and guests will enjoy. Serving Cactus Tacos will please the choosy vegetarians in your life. For a twist on the traditional taco, try making Fish Tacos with Cucumber Salsa (all in Chapter 6).

(Top to bottom) You combine roasted pork, Adobo Sauce, and a bolillo to create this delicious Barbecued Pork Torta. Chicken Poblano Enchiladas showcase the wonderful flavor of the poblano chile (both in Chapter 6).

(Top to bottom) Either Chile Braised Lamb Shanks (Chapter 11) with White Rice (Chapter 10) or Caldo de Pescado (Chapter 11) can be served as a filling and hearty main course.

(Top to bottom) Mushroom Empanadas offer the rich flavors of mushrooms, cheese, and tart green salsa. Throw a tamale party and have your guests help you create traditional tamales with Green Chile Cheese Filling (all in Chapter 7).

(Top to bottom) Seared Chard adds color and vitamins to your plate. Red Rice is a basic tomato-tinged rice that accompanies many Mexican dishes, along with Refried Black Beans and the rough texture of home-made Corn Tortillas (all in Chapter 10).

(Top to bottom) Start your dinner party out right by having tortilla chips, Guacamole, Roasted Ancho Salsa, and Silky Crab and Cheese Nachos out and ready for guests when they arrive. Then watch the mingling begin (all in Chapter 5)!

(Top to bottom) Many people who don't usually like fish enjoy the fresh taste of Garlicky Squid Sauté and Grilled Swordfish with Fresh Tomato and Herb Salsa (both in Chapter 12).

(Top to bottom) Fried Plantains and White Rice make a nice alternative to warm oatmeal in the morning (Chapter 17). For a real eye opener, serve warm Red Roasted Tomato Salsa (Chapter 5) and Huevos Rancheros (Chapter 17).

(Clockwise from top) Whip up a batch of Quick and Easy Buñuelo Sticks, powdered-sugar covered Mocha Crackles, or sweet and chewy Hahas and have a perfect end to any meal (all in Chapter 15).

Chapter 4

Bright Lights, Big Beverages

. . . .

. . . .

The Mexican beverage repertoire is as varied and colorful as the country itself. We're not talking red and white wine, espresso, and diet soft drinks here. We're talking brilliantly colored fresh fruit juices, full-flavored sangrias, eggnog with a twist, and a tart red juice made with hibiscus blossoms — not to mention world-class beers, delicious spiced coffee, and tequila that will knock your socks off.

More than in most cuisines, homemade beverages play an important role in the Mexican culture. Fruit juice stands dot the Mexican landscape with the frequency of cafes or ice cream stands in Italy, and the juice stand is a place to meet a friend and gossip as well as to quench a thirst. Any of these drinks served in your home will telegraph your guests that they are in for an unusual dining experience. And if those beverages don't relax and entertain them, Mexico's legendary beers and tequilas can almost always get the party going. Salud!

Eye-Openers

Unlike Italy or France where you gradually work your way up to a large meal in the middle of the day, in Mexico you start out eating spicy, full-flavored foods and, as the day progresses, you just keep going in that direction.

The traditional Mexican hot drinks, coffee and chocolate, are rich enough to support a hearty Mexican breakfast or to stand alone any time of the day or night. Interestingly, both ingredients are native to the Americas.

The following tips will help you avoid scorching the milk in the coffee and chocolate drinks described in this section:

- ✔ If you have a nonreactive saucepan, by all means use it for heating the milk in these warm beverages.

- ✔ Rinse your pan with cold water and shake out the excess water before adding the milk to the pan.

- ✔ Heat the milk over medium heat, stirring occasionally.

Mexican Spiced Coffee

The first time we tasted *café de olla,* as it's called in Mexico, we were relaxing in the Puebla town square in the evening. When everyone started clinking their glasses with their spoons, we thought that some sort of small insurrection was starting up. Instead, people were signaling the waiter that they were ready for their coffee. He filled their glasses from two pitchers — one pitcher contained spiced coffee, the other was filled with steamed milk. Delicious!

You can make this spiced coffee up to a day in advance by boiling the spicy syrup and then keeping it in the refrigerator. Bring the mixture to a boil and then add the coffee grounds right before serving.

Special tool: *Fine strainer or coffee filter*

Cooking time: *10 minutes*

Yield: *6 servings*

4 cups water	*2 whole cloves*
¼ cup packed dark brown sugar	*1 cup dark roast coffee beans, medium grind, or ¾ cup preground beans*
2 cinnamon sticks	*2 cups milk*
2 allspice berries	

1 In a saucepan, combine the water, sugar, cinnamon, allspice, and cloves. Bring to a boil over medium heat, stirring to melt the sugar. Stir in the coffee grounds, remove from heat, cover, and steep for 5 minutes.

2 In a small saucepan, warm the milk over medium-high heat and carefully whisk until frothy. Strain the coffee through a fine sieve or a coffee filter into a pitcher. Serve the coffee in tall glasses with the frothed milk in a pitcher alongside, for adding the milk to the coffee to taste. We prefer about half coffee and half milk.

For another spice combination, replace the cinnamon, allspice, and cloves with 2 slices fresh ginger, ¼ teaspoon anise seed, and ½ teaspoon grated nutmeg. Substitute ¼ teaspoon dried ground ginger and a pinch of ground nutmeg if fresh is not available.

When I entertain at home, I love foods and drinks that can be served out of a big communal pot. Somehow it seems to pull the group together. A special beverage like this one, served in a beautiful pot at the end of a meal, can even replace dessert.

Mexican Hot Chocolate

If your hot chocolate experience is limited to the thin, instant cocoa we Americans foist on our kids, you'll be amazed at this rich, frothy drink. In Mexico, where cocoa drinking began, people of all ages enjoy their morning chocolate, especially when accompanied by *pan de yema,* the sweet egg bread. (For instructions for making *pan de yema,* turn to Chapter 16.) Adults often dilute their chocolate with water, not milk, in Mexico.

Traditional Mexican chocolate is not for nibbling. These tablets (see Figure 4-1) of chocolate, sugar, cinnamon, and ground almonds are for making hot chocolate and blending into moles. In Mexico, people bring locally grown cacao beans to their local grinder, who grinds and mixes their chocolate with almonds, sugar, and cinnamon according to their family's tastes. If you aren't fortunate enough to have a local grinder, look for the Ibarra brand of chocolate in Latin American markets and in the ethnic section of the supermarket.

Cooking time: *10 minutes*

Yield: *2 servings*

3 cups milk

1 3-ounce tablet Mexican-style chocolate, coarsely chopped

Pinch of ground cinnamon

Bring the milk to a low boil in a small saucepan. Add the chocolate and reduce to a simmer. Cook, whisking constantly (see Figure 4-2), until the chocolate is melted and the milk is frothy. Sprinkle with cinnamon. Serve hot.

Figure 4-1: Mexican chocolate is packaged in tablets.

Mexican chocolate

Figure 4-2: Making your Mexican Hot Chocolate hot and frothy.

Frothing Hot Chocolate

Put your hands together and hold the whisk between them.

'Roll' the whisk between your hands until the chocolate is good and frothy!

Afternoon Refreshers

These homemade drinks are a great place to start expanding your nonalcoholic beverage horizons. The three most popular aguas frescas, Jamaica, Tamarind, and Horchata, are sold on the street in Mexico by vendors called *vitriollas* (bee-tree-OH-yahs), who display their brilliantly colored wares in glass barrels. Take a tip from the *vitriollas* and serve these tempting drinks in clear pitchers at your next fiesta. Then watch the party take off!

Strawberry Banana Liquados

Colorful *liquados* are sold all over Mexico at juice stands where you can point — unless you speak Spanish — to the fruit of your choice and get an instant, made-to-order fruit milk shake to hold you over until the next meal. If you're not a milk drinker, water will work just fine.

Special tools: *Blender or food processor*

Preparation time: *10 minutes*

Yield: *3 servings*

(continued)

Like chocolate for drinking

Mexicans were the first to process cacao beans, or chocolate, for drinking. The cacao tree, on which the beans grow, originated in the rain forests of the Amazon and Orinoco Rivers in South America. But the first people to cultivate the cacao bean were the Mayans of the Yucatán peninsula, who in turn traded the beans with the Aztecs of central Mexico. The Aztecs are credited with figuring out how to process and drink cacao — a drink they considered the elixir of the gods, even without sugar added.

The Spanish explorer Cortez was either lucky or exceptionally charming. When the Aztec leader Montezuma mistook him for the returning Quetzalcoatl, the plumed serpent or god of light, he taught Cortez the secrets of cocoa making and brewing. Cortez brought those methods back to Spain, where a small, elite group started sipping unsweetened cocoa. The drink really caught on, though, 70 years later, when the Italians figured out how to sweeten cocoa and sell it to the masses.

Chocolate continues to have a strong presence on the streets of Mexico, especially in the southern state of Oaxaca. There, people bring their own cacao beans along with sugar, almonds, and cinnamon or other spices to the town's grinder, or *molino* (moh-LEE-noh), who makes them their own personal blend. At home, the mixture is heated with water or milk and then whipped with the traditional round wooden whisk called a *molinillo* (moh-LEE-nee-yoh), which you can see in the following figure. According to legend, the wooden whisk is a conduit, transferring a woman's energy into the comforting drink. We're not sure what happens when a man does the whisking.

Mexican Whisk for Chocolate

2½ cups chopped fruit (about 1 banana plus 10 large strawberries)	2 cups ice cubes
	3 tablespoons honey
1½ cups milk	

Combine the fruit with the milk, ice, and honey in a blender or food processor. Puree until smooth. Pour into tall glasses and serve immediately.

VARIATION

You can also enjoy the following fruits as a liquado:

- ✔ Ripe cantaloupe (2½ cups cut in cubes) makes a great, unusual liquado.
- ✔ Any berry is terrific in a liquado. In the winter when you're longing for those summer flavors, 2½ cups frozen berries are a good choice.

Horchata

Horchata (or-CHAH-tah), the chalky white drink made from ground rice, is the most traditional of Mexico's nonalcoholic drinks. Its soothing white milkiness is the perfect antidote to rich, spicy foods, and although it takes some getting used to, you'll probably learn to love it as we have.

Special tools: *Blender*

Cooking time: *20 minutes, plus 4 hours chilling*

Yield: *9 servings (3 quarts)*

1 quart milk	¾ cup sugar
4 cinnamon sticks	1 tablespoon vanilla extract
⅓ cup uncooked white rice, ground to a powder in a blender	2 quarts water

1 Place the milk and cinnamon sticks in a pot and bring to a low boil. Reduce to a simmer and cook, stirring occasionally, for 5 minutes. Remove from heat and let sit for 15 minutes. Lift out the cinnamon sticks and set them aside for later use.

2 Combine the ground rice, sugar, and vanilla in a medium bowl. Pour in the cooled milk mixture and the water and whisk to incorporate well. Refrigerate for at least 4 hours. Then pour the liquid into a pitcher, discarding the sediment that has settled on the bottom of the bowl. Serve cold over ice, using the reserved cinnamon sticks as stirrers.

Watermelon Juice

What could be cooler than a nice, tall glass of iced watermelon juice for your next summer barbecue? Serve *sandia* (Spanish for watermelon) in a clear pitcher to highlight its brilliant color. A garnish of thin lime slices looks nice against the pink of the juice.

Special tools: *Blender*

Preparation time: *5 minutes*

Yield: *3 servings*

2 cups watermelon chunks, seeded

2 tablespoons sugar

½ cup cold water

5 ice cubes

(Optional) Juice of 1 lime

Combine all the ingredients in a blender and puree until smooth. Serve over additional ice.

TOQUE TIP If you can find seedless watermelon, by all means go for it. Why waste precious moments searching for seeds when making watermelon juice?

Jamaica

This brilliant red tea brewed from dried hibiscus blossoms is a great surprise for jaded palates. It's sweet, tart, and mysteriously fruity, and as an added bonus, it packs a high dose of vitamin C.

The dried hibiscus blossoms you need for this drink are available at Mexican and Armenian markets, where they are sold by weight or in pre-packed plastic bags. Do not substitute flowers from the garden!

Preparation time: *15 minutes, plus 4 hours chilling*

Yield: *4 to 5 servings (1½ quarts)*

2 quarts water

¾ cup dried Jamaica or hibiscus flowers

½ cup sugar

Lime wedges for garnish

(continued)

Bring the water to a boil. Add the flowers and return to a boil. Reduce to a simmer and cook for about 10 minutes. Stir in the sugar, strain into a pitcher, and refrigerate for 4 hours. Serve cold over ice, with lime wedges for garnish.

Four or five slices of fresh ginger mixed in with the flowers make a delicious addition. Or try adding Jamaica to your next mimosa for a Mexican twist. Mix one-third orange juice, one-third champagne, and one-third Jamaica.

Party Boosters

The only thing that sounds like more fun than eating Mexican food is drinking Mexican drinks. Mexican beers, margaritas, and tequilas are so popular that they are the gateway for many people to tasting Mexican food for the first time. After you've munched on chips and salsa at a couple of parties, why not take the leap to tamales and empanadas, or to cactus salad, the next time you're looking for an accompaniment to that ice chest of Mexican beers?

We have been serving and drinking these popular beverages long enough to have formed a few opinions and picked up a few tidbits along the way. Here are our findings on the best Mexican beer and tequila, the difference between mezcal and tequila, a short lesson in tequila-making lingo, the riddle of the worm resolved, and our almost-secret formula for mixing the perfect margarita. Upon completion of this brief section, consider yourself a graduate of the Mary Sue and Susan course in advanced tequila drinking. Because we can't pass out diplomas, pour yourself a drink!

Choosing a Mexican drink vendor

Travelers are always a little scared to try the fantastic homemade drinks served in Mexico, but they are really missing out. I first experienced some of the more unusual flavors and textures of the Mexican kitchen in drinks — like the slightly sweet, milky drink from the mamey fruit called Texate and the tart, fruity water made from hibiscus flowers, called Jamaica.

Here is my method for choosing a drink vendor (and I've never gotten sick!):

✔ Scope out the stand and look for purified water bottles — they are big and hard to hide.

✔ If the vendor has lots of water bottles, it means that he is not only using safe water but also selling his drinks fast. The locals must be drinking them, so they must be good. Yummm.

Sparkling Fruit Punch

A light, bright fruit punch such as this one is perfect for afternoon parties. It's festive and pretty, yet it's low enough in alcohol that guests won't fall asleep in the punch bowl. Have spoons handy for nibbling on the fruit.

Preparation time: *7 minutes, plus 20 minutes cooling time and chilling time*

Yield: *12 to 16 servings*

1 cup sugar	*6 cups chopped and seeded watermelon*
1 cup water	*1 cup chopped mango or papaya*
1 bottle sparkling wine, such as Cava (Spanish champagne)	*1 cup chopped pineapple*

1 Combine the sugar and water in a saucepan. Bring to a boil and simmer, stirring occasionally, until the syrup is clear, about 4 minutes. Set aside to cool.

2 Stir together the syrup and sparkling wine in a punch bowl. Add the watermelon, mango or papaya, and pineapple and chill the punch before serving.

TOQUE TIP This punch is the perfect place to pour that inexpensive champagne that may be lurking in the cupboard. After you mix it with the fruits and sugar, no one will be the wiser.

Sangria

We love a light fruit and wine drink like sangria for casual afternoon gatherings. Sangria looks especially nice when served in sangria pitchers, which you can see in Figure 4-3.

Preparation time: *10 minutes, plus 2 hours steeping*

Yield: *4 servings*

1 orange	*1 bottle fruity red wine, such as Pinot Noir*
1 lemon	*1 cup freshly squeezed orange juice*
1 lime	*2 cups ice cubes*

(continued)

Scrub the orange, lemon, and lime under running water and cut them into ¼-inch slices. Cut each slice into quarters to form wedges. Place the fruit wedges in a pitcher, pour in the wine, and let the sangria sit for about 2 hours at room temperature so that the flavors can combine. Or it can steep as long as a day in the refrigerator. Just before serving, stir in the orange juice and ice cubes. Serve immediately.

For a sangria that stays cold longer, try making one large ice cube. Wash out a half-gallon cardboard milk carton and fill it with water and some thin slices of oranges, lemons, and limes for color. Stand the carton upright in the freezer and freeze. Empty the ice into a punch bowl by ripping off the carton just before adding the sangria.

Figure 4-3:
Serving sangria in sangria pitchers allows you to showcase the beauty of the beverages.

sangria pitchers!

Primo Margaritas

Almost as many legends surround Mexico's most popular mixed drink, the margarita, as there are needles on a cactus paddle. Our favorite story credits Mexican hotelier and restaurateur Danny Herrara with mixing up the first margarita in the 1940s when a visiting American actress named Marjorie (or Margaret as he heard it) was allergic to straight tequila.

If you love Mexican food as we do, you owe it to yourself to improve your entertaining skills by mastering basic margarita making. Now you can toss out that margarita mix and dazzle friends and relatives with your suave style behind the bar.

We prefer to make our margaritas with añejo tequila, which you can read more about in the sidebar "Tequila 101." We like ours shaken, not blended. If you're drinking them straight, use your best tequila. The traditional orange liqueur in a margarita is Triple Sec. Cointreau and Grand Marnier, if that's what you have in the house, are fine substitutes.

Special tool: *Cocktail shaker*

Preparation time: *5 minutes*

Yield: *1 serving*

1 lime, cut into 5 slices

Margarita or coarse kosher salt

2 ounces añejo tequila

1 ounce orange liqueur, such as Triple Sec

1 tablespoon freshly squeezed lime or lemon juice

½ cup ice cubes

1 Arrange 3 lime slices to cover a small plate, and cover another plate with salt to a depth of ¼ inch. Place a martini glass upside down on the limes; press and turn to dampen. Then dip the glass in the salt to coat the rim (see Figure 4-4).

2 Combine the tequila, orange liqueur, lime or lemon juice, and ice in a cocktail shaker and shake. Pour into the prepared glass, garnish with the 2 remaining lime slices, and serve.

On a hot day, even margarita purists such as ourselves, who don't often use the blender, are known to blend up a batch of margaritas for the backyard barbecue. Here's the formula for making 8 margaritas: Mix 2 cups tequila, 1 cup Triple Sec, and ½ cup freshly squeezed lemon or lime juice. Blend in 3 batches, by dividing each ingredient in thirds, adding about 1 cup ice for each batch, and processing until smooth.

Salting a Margarita Glass

Arrange 3 slices of lime on a small plate.

Turn a martini-type glass over and press into the limes to moisten the edge.

Next, press the moistened edge into a shallow dish of coarse salt.

All salted, and ready for the Margarita to be poured!

Figure 4-4: Salting the edge of the glass.

Tequili

Here is a recipe for a tequila martini, for when you're ready to start tasting your tequila, but you're not quite ready for straight shots.

Special tools: *Cocktail shaker and strainer*

Preparation time: *5 minutes*

Yield: *1 serving*

2 ounces tequila, preferably añejo

½ teaspoon orange liqueur, such as Triple Sec

4 ice cubes

Twist of lime

In a pitcher or cocktail shaker, combine the tequila, orange liqueur, and ice. Stir or shake 20 times. Strain into a martini glass. Top with the lime twist and serve.

TOQUE TIP

To make a lime or lemon twist for jazzing up martinis, first cut off a ¼-inch deep strip of the rind. It's okay for some of the white part to still be on. Squeeze or twist it to release its oils into the drink and then drop the twist into the drink. You can get an added kick of citrus flavor by rubbing the rim with the colored part of the rind.

Top tequilas

We enjoy sipping our tequila slowly, in the same way that people traditionally enjoy brandy. Although the complexity of a brandy can sometimes be overwhelming, tequilas are relatively simple and straightforward. They have a distinctive alcoholic flavor — with a slight sour edge.

Mary Sue recommends that you order a tequila, on ice with a wedge of lime, at banquets where the wine selection is not inspiring. That way, instead of sipping bad wine all night while keeping up your end of the conversation, you can enjoy a more interesting drink (without the side effects of cheap wine) and probably make some darned good conversation as well.

Here are our personal picks for the tequila hall of fame:

✔ Patrón Añejo, with a smooth rich flavor, is Susan's favorite.

✔ El Tesoro Añejo, with its strong flavor of alcohol, is Mary Sue's favorite.

✔ Chinaco Añejo is named after the "Fighting Chinacos." With a name like that, how could we resist?

✔ Porfidio Silver, an elegant, crystal-clear plata, is distilled three times making it smooth as silk going down.

✔ Del Dueño is a slightly sweet añejo.

Tequila 101

We don't know why more hype seems to surround tequila than the northern spirits like vodka or gin, but ours is not to question why. Ours is to taste, digest, and demystify.

Tequila is the distilled spirit of the heart of the agave (ah-GAH-vay) plant — a spiky succulent of the lily family, not a cactus. (You can see a picture of an agave plant on the second page of the color insert of this book.) To make tequila, the heart, or *pina,* of the agave is steamed in huge ovens, and the resulting sweet juice is fermented and distilled.

Tequila production is regulated by the Mexican government so that all tequila meets the following conditions:

- It must come from one of five north central Mexican states: Jalisco, Guanjuato, Michoacan, Nayarit, or Tamaulipas.

- It must be at least 60 percent derived from the Blue agave or Tequilana Weber plant.

- It must be distilled twice.

There are five distinct types of tequila:

- Plata, Blanco, and Silver are the youngest tequilas. They are clear like vodka, not aged, and they are frequently used for mixed drinks.

- Mixtos are the cheapest tequilas, made from 60 percent agave.

- Joven Abogado, or Gold, are unaged tequilas that are colored and slightly softened or sweetened with caramel or food coloring. Use this variety when you don't want to spend the bucks for añejo.

- Reposado is aged, but not as long as añejo. It is stored for 2 months to a year in small wood barrels, where it acquires a light gold color. Reposados combine the spiciness of a clear tequila with the smoothness of añejo.

- Añejo, the most costly tequila, must be aged in wood, preferably small oak barrels, at least a year but sometimes as long as 3 years. We prefer this type for sipping.

Sangrita

After you graduate to straight shots of tequila, sangrita is the proper accompaniment. Serve it alongside tequila and match, sip for sip. Grenadine, a sweet, red, pomegranate-flavored syrup, adds color and sweetness to this potent chaser.

Special tool: *Blender*

Preparation time: *3 minutes, plus chilling*

Yield: *10 shots*

(continued)

1 cup freshly squeezed orange juice	*½ teaspoon salt*
¼ cup freshly squeezed lime juice	*3 tablespoons Tabasco*
2 tablespoons grenadine syrup	

Combine all the ingredients in a blender and process until blended. (You can whisk this together by hand as well.) Refrigerate. Serve cold in shot glasses with corresponding shots of tequila.

Take it from an expert: Slamming back shots of tequila is definitely not the way to go. Try slowly sipping tequila with sangrita to really appreciate how delicious a drink tequila can be.

Rompope

This spiked eggnog with the funny name (rohm-POH-peh) is so popular in Mexico that a pasteurized version is sold in liquor stores. You can enjoy it, mostly as an after-dinner drink, any time of year. As an alternative to brandy, you can substitute rum.

Preparation time: *25 minutes, plus chilling*

Yield: *8 to 10 servings (7 cups)*

6½ cups milk	*2 whole cloves*
1½ cups sugar	*5 egg yolks*
2 whole allspice berries	*1 cup brandy*
2 small cinnamon sticks	

1 Combine 6 cups of the milk, 1 cup of the sugar, allspice, cinnamon, and cloves in a saucepan and bring to a boil. Simmer, stirring occasionally, for about 15 minutes.

2 In a bowl, combine the egg yolks with the remaining ½ cup milk and the remaining ½ cup sugar and whisk until smooth. Slowly pour a few cups of the warm milk mixture into the bowl and whisk. Then pour the yolk mixture back into the pan. Simmer, stirring frequently, until the milk is as thick as a thin sauce, for about 4 minutes, being careful not to boil. Stir in the brandy and remove from heat. Pour through a strainer into a pitcher and chill. Serve cold over ice.

TOQUE TIP By combining some of the hot milk into the yolk mixture first, you are slowly heating the eggs to avoid coagulating or cooking them. This step, called *tempering* the yolks, is important in egg cookery because after an egg is cooked, there's no turning back.

What is this thing called mezcal?

As you find out more about tequila, you may start wondering about mezcal — that mysterious beverage with the worm on the bottom of the bottle.

Mezcal, the form of tequila from southern Mexico, hasn't changed much since the Spanish introduced the still to Mexico in 1520. Unlike tequila, which must be made from a specific plant and is produced by large industrial companies, mezcal can be made from several types of agave and is still being made in small batches by tiny distillers. The resulting drink is more rough-hewn and less uniform than tequila.

Mezcal remains a handmade product from start to finish. In rural Oaxaca, *magueros* (maguey gatherers) still gather the hearts of mature plants and carry them on their burros to small outdoor roasting pits. There they are baked over local woods and charcoal for three days under the careful gaze of the supervising *practico*. Then the hearts are shredded, the sap is squeezed out, and the resulting juices are brought to small family-owned distilleries called *palenques,* where the mezcal is distilled.

The worm, or *gusano,* found on the bottle's bottom, is not a worm at all, but a caterpillar. Once, locals may have believed that the gusano was imbued with magical powers. But today, it is merely thought to sell more bottles of mezcal. We recommend avoiding men who brag about eating the worm. They may be suffering from outdated ideas of machismo.

Cruder than tequila, mezcal is an acquired taste — one that we have not acquired yet. The one premium mezcal that we can recommend if you want a taste is Encantado.

Our favorite Mexican beers

The Mexican approach to beer is closer to the American view of soft drinks: bubbly, refreshing beverages meant to be drunk throughout the day to quench a thirst rather than loosen inhibitions. In fact, beers are sold in small 6-ounce bottles for quick snacks, and sometimes they're mixed with half lemonade or limeade for a bubbly morning drink. Beer is always served with a wedge of lime in Mexico, a custom that can be traced back to the Spaniards.

After years of serious study, here are our best beer picks:

- Pacifico is a slightly acidic, light-colored beer, made in an ale style. We like to mix it with half lemonade or half tomato juice for a great summer drink.

- Bohemia, Mary Sue's favorite, is slightly darker than the ales, but still light-colored. This well-crafted, flavorful beer has placed first in blind worldwide beer tastings — no mean feat against all those German brews. Mary Sue appreciates its smooth finish and slight aftertaste, best with just a rub of lime on the rim of her glass.

- Dos Equis, with its amber color, is a nice cross between lighter and darker style beers. The recipe for this 100-year-old beer (named XX for the turn of the century) was created by a German brewmaster.

- Negro Modelo, Susan's favorite, is a dark beer from the Yucatán. It has a hint of molasses, without being too sweet, and a strong flavor. For your complete drinking pleasure, Susan recommends filling a tumbler with crushed ice, coating the rim with salt, pouring in the beer, and squeezing in a few lime wedges. Leave yourself plenty of time to relax and enjoy such a carefully crafted drink.

Chapter 5

Hot Salsas, Cool Dips, and Refreshing Ceviches

In This Chapter

▶ Stirring up salsas

▶ Dishing up dips

▶ Making raw fish cocktails

*W*e love to get a party rolling by serving large bowls of Mexican finger foods. When everyone crowds around and starts reaching into the same bowl, inevitably conversations start flowing.

All the dishes in this chapter are terrific for a party or a buffet. All are easy to prepare and interesting to eat, and most fit well on a chip. So encourage your guests to dig in, dip their chips, and accompany their drinks with any of these enticing salsas, dips, and ceviches.

Scintillating Salsas

Salsas are the heart and soul of the Mexican kitchen. We use them in hundreds of recipes, from soups and stews to casseroles.

With a handful of simple ingredients and no tricky techniques or precise timing, Mexican cooks can toss together sauces as diverse as chunky fresh tomato and onion salsa, smooth, tart green tomatillo sauce, and mysteriously complex dried chile salsa in minutes. In fact, the speed with which delicious salsas are thrown together was the first thing that fascinated us about Mexican cooking.

Since Americans have discovered salsa, making it second only to ketchup in the condiment sweepstakes, hundreds of salsa recipes have been created, featuring everything from strawberries to sun-dried tomatoes. But don't be fooled! The basic Mexican salsas — perfect as chip dips, marinades for grilled foods, bases for stews and soups, and toppings for just about anything — are still the best. Our three favorite salsas, which we serve at our restaurants as table salsas with chips, are Green Tomatillo, Red Roasted Tomato, and Smoked Chile.

Keep a stock of salsas in your refrigerator for maximum flexibility with your recipes and, if you are counting calories, remember that salsas are exceptionally lowfat sauces to use in all your cooking.

Green Tomatillo Salsa

We love the acid bite of raw tomatillos in this quick, uncooked sauce. Use it to counter rich, creamy dishes like tamales, or with any simply grilled fish. (See Chapter 2 for information about tomatillos, the green fruit that resembles a tomato.)

This salsa keeps in the refrigerator, in a covered container, for about 3 days.

Special tool: Blender or food processor

Preparation time: 10 minutes

Yield: 2 cups

¾ pound tomatillos, stemmed, husked, the stem scar cut out, and cut into quarters	1 bunch scallions, white and light green parts, coarsely chopped (about 1 cup)
3 serrano chiles, stemmed, seeded, and coarsely chopped	1 large bunch cilantro leaves and tender stems, roughly chopped (about ½ cup)
⅓ cup cold water	1½ teaspoons salt

Place the tomatillos, chiles, and water in a blender or food processor. Puree just until chunky. Add the scallions, cilantro, and salt and puree about 2 minutes longer, or until no large chunks remain.

For a mellower version of tomatillo salsa, try roasting the tomatillos, chiles, and scallions under the broiler until blackened, about 5 minutes. Then place the roasted items in a blender or food processor with the remaining ingredients and puree.

Red Roasted Tomato Salsa

Roasting the tomatoes until blackened gives this smooth red sauce for the table its distinctive Mexican flavor.

You can store this salsa in the refrigerator for 2 to 3 days, or in the freezer for 2 weeks.

Special tool: *Blender or food processor*

Preparation time: *10 minutes*

Cooking time: *25 minutes*

Yield: *1 quart*

1 pound Roma tomatoes, cored

6 garlic cloves, peeled

2 serrano chiles, stemmed and seeded

1 medium onion, cut into ½-inch slices

2 tablespoons olive oil

1 cup tomato juice

1 teaspoon salt

Pepper to taste

1 Preheat the broiler.

2 Place the tomatoes, garlic, chiles, and onion on a foil-lined baking tray. Drizzle with the olive oil. Broil 6 to 8 inches from the flame for about 12 minutes, turning frequently with tongs, until evenly charred.

3 Transfer the vegetables and any accumulated juices to the blender or food processor. Add the tomato juice, salt, and pepper. Puree, in batches if necessary, until smooth.

4 Pour into a medium saucepan. Bring to a boil, reduce to a simmer, and cook, uncovered, for about 5 minutes. Season with salt and pepper. Cool to room temperature for table salsa, or use warm as an ingredient in rice or chilaquiles (see Chapters 10 and 16).

For the lazy cook's version of this salsa, you can use canned Roma tomatoes and totally skip the broiling part. The salsa still tastes delicious, though definitely not roasted.

These chips are made for dipping

There is a world of difference between a warm, recently fried corn tortilla chip and one that comes from a bag. But sometimes chefs have to be realists. If you're going to buy chips for dipping or including in other dishes, look for corn chips without any added flavor or too much salt to overpower other flavors.

Here are the brands we recommend, as a result of a blind taste test:

✔ Santitas are a thin, white or yellow corn chip with just the right balance of salt and corn, and no other flavors to distract.

✔ Tostitos are a thicker, exceptionally crunchy white corn chip.

✔ Garden of Eatin' is an organic corn chip with a deep-yellow color and strong corn flavor. The perfectly round shape feels too machine-made for our tastes, but the flavor is tops of those we tasted.

✔ Padrino, Restaurant Style, a regional California brand, packs lots of corn flavor into a not-too-salty chip.

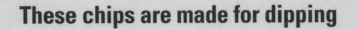

Fresh Salsa

This uncooked table sauce, also known as *pico de gallo, salsa cruda,* or plain old tomato salsa, is probably Mexico's best-known salsa. With its chunks of tomato, chiles, and onion, it's the model for most bottled salsas, but let's face it, how fresh can a sauce from a bottle be?

You can store Fresh Salsa in a covered container in the refrigerator no longer than a day.

Preparation time: *15 minutes*

Yield: *2 cups*

4 medium-size ripe tomatoes, cored, seeded, and finely diced

¼ red onion, minced (¼ cup)

2 jalapeño chiles, stemmed, seeded, and minced

1 bunch cilantro, leaves only, chopped (about ½ cup)

2 tablespoons freshly squeezed lime juice

¾ teaspoon salt

Pinch of pepper

Combine all the ingredients in a mixing bowl. Stir and toss well, and serve.

Freshness makes all the difference in this sauce. Use only the best — and you guessed it — the freshest ingredients and don't make the salsa in advance. After a day, the fresh flavors fade, and the salsa becomes mushy. Avoid the temptation to reach for the food processor to do all this chopping. You want uneven, chunky bits here, not a pureed mush.

Smoked Chile Salsa

This earthy, brown salsa is fragrant with the heat and smoke of good Mexican cooking from the smoked chipotles. It's one of our favorites for chips and has loads of other uses.

This salsa can be stored in the refrigerator up to 5 days, or frozen as long as a month.

Special tools: *Blender or food processor, strainer*

Preparation time: *10 minutes*

Cooking time: *25 minutes*

Yield: *5 cups*

1 medium onion, coarsely chopped

7 dried chipotle chiles, stemmed or 3 canned chipotle chiles, stemmed and rinsed off

8 Roma tomatoes, cored

10 garlic cloves, peeled

3 cups water

2 teaspoons salt

½ teaspoon pepper

1 teaspoon sugar

1 Combine all the ingredients in a medium saucepan. Bring to a boil, reduce to a simmer, and cook, uncovered, for 20 minutes. The liquid should be reduced by one-third, and the tomato skins should be falling off. Set aside to cool.

2 Pour the mixture into a blender or a food processor. Puree until smooth and then strain. Chill until serving time.

 Smoked salsa is terrific on top of a baked potato with sour cream. Or try stirring a spoonful into a bowl of chicken soup for instant Mexican pizzazz. Salsas can give kick to many of your everyday dishes.

Salsas from a bottle

Our hands-down favorites of the prepared salsas we tasted are from restaurant chef Rick Bayless of Chicago. His salsas have a good homemade quality, with charred bits left in for smokiness and no additives or weird ingredients. Two of our favorites are

 ✔ Frontera Chipotle Salsa

 ✔ Frontera Tomatillo Salsa

Most of the commercial tomato salsas are too chunky for our tastes. We recommend pureeing them in the blender before using them in cooking. After giving several a critical tasting, here are our recommendations:

 ✔ Jardine's Cilantro Texasalsa

 ✔ Tostitos Restaurant Style

 ✔ Pace Hot

 ✔ Newman's Own

Roasted Ancho Salsa

We tend to use this smoky, earthy salsa to add a hint of meatiness to vegetarian dishes like red bean stew or chili. It adds the same depth that bacon does — without the animal fat. And like all good salsas, it's great with chips.

You can store this salsa in the refrigerator up to 5 days, or in the freezer as long as a month.

Special tools: *Food processor or blender, baking sheet, strainer*

Preparation time: *10 minutes*

Cooking time: *30 minutes*

Yield: *4 cups*

½ pound Roma tomatoes

¾ pound tomatillos

¼ cup vegetable oil

6 to 8 ancho chiles, stemmed, seeded, and torn into 2-inch strips

1 medium onion, chopped

4 garlic cloves, crushed

1 bunch cilantro leaves, roughly chopped (½ cup)

2 teaspoons salt

1½ cups water

1 Preheat the broiler.

2 Place the tomatoes and tomatillos on a foil-lined baking sheet. Broil 6 to 8 inches from the flame, turning occasionally, until charred all over, about 10 minutes. Then transfer to a medium saucepan and reserve.

3 Heat the vegetable oil in a medium skillet over low heat. Fry the chile strips, a few at a time, for about 15 seconds, or until the flesh bubbles and lightly browns. Drain on paper towels.

4 Add the onion and garlic to the hot oil in the pan, turn up the heat, and sauté for 10 minutes, until golden. Transfer the onion mixture, chiles, cilantro, salt, and water to the saucepan with the tomatoes and tomatillos. Simmer over low heat for 10 minutes.

5 Transfer the mixture to a food processor or blender. Puree and then strain. Serve at room temperature.

Roasted Green Chile Salsa

A chile-intensive sauce such as this one is a terrific complement to any red meat — grilled steaks, lamb chops, or burgers would be great. If all three types of chiles are not available, improvise according to your taste. (See "Chiles 101" in Chapter 2 for details on choosing chiles.)

You can freeze or store Roasted Green Chile Salsa in the refrigerator as long as 4 days.

Special tools: *Food processor, baking sheet*

Preparation time: *15 minutes*

Cooking time: *10 minutes*

Yield: *3 cups*

2 slices red onion, sliced ½-inch thin	*3 poblano chiles, halved and seeded*
4 garlic cloves	*2 tablespoons olive oil*
1 pound medium tomatillos	*Juice of 2 limes*
4 serrano chiles, halved and seeded	*2 teaspoons dried oregano*
12 jalapeño chiles, halved and seeded	*1½ teaspoons coarse salt*

1 Preheat the broiler.

2 Arrange the onion, garlic, tomatillos, and chiles on a baking sheet. Drizzle evenly with the olive oil. Broil 6 to 8 inches from the flame, turning frequently with tongs, until evenly charred, about 12 minutes.

3 Transfer to a food processor and pulse until finely chopped. Add the lime juice, oregano, and salt and process until smooth. Serve at room temperature or chilled.

Maximum Dips

These smooth, rich dips are the opposite end of the spectrum from sprightly salsas. They soothe the nerves, comfort, and balance the typical fiery flavors of the Mexican kitchen.

All of the dips in this section can be scooped up with tortilla chips for a tasty treat, and many of the dips can accompany a wide variety of dishes.

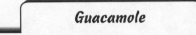

Guacamole

This mashed avocado dip is great for cooling down hot foods or just adding richness to anything it touches (see photo in the color insert). Guacamole is terrific spread on turkey or pork sandwiches, as well as spooned over tacos, burritos, and tostadas.

You can store Guacamole in the refrigerator as long as a day.

Preparation time: *15 minutes*

Yield: *2 cups*

3 ripe avocados, preferably Hass (see Chapter 2)

½ bunch fresh cilantro leaves, chopped (about ¼ cup)

½ medium red onion, diced

3 jalapeño chiles, stemmed, seeded, and finely diced

3 tablespoons freshly squeezed lime juice

1½ teaspoons salt

½ teaspoon pepper

Cut the avocados into quarters. Remove the seeds, peel, and place in a mixing bowl. Mash with a potato masher or fork until chunky. Add the cilantro, onion, chiles, lime juice, salt, and pepper and combine with a fork.

Even though guacamole is such a simple dish, it is often prepared incorrectly. Here are some secrets to making great guacamole. Follow these tips and you'll create guacamole that people can't wait to dip with a chip:

- Do not overmash your avocados. The proper texture is slightly chunky, not liquefied into a paste or filled with air.

- Absolutely no tomatoes are permitted in the land of the perfect guacamole. They add too much liquid.

- Nix on the garlic as well. We don't care what other cookbooks may advise. This luscious green dip is meant to be garlic-free.

Pinto Bean Dip

We add sour cream to our bean dip because its acidity balances the richness of the beans.

Bean dip can be stored in the refrigerator for 2 days, but don't freeze it.

Special tool: *Food processor or mixer*

Preparation time: *10 minutes, plus 2 hours to make Refried Pinto Beans, plus 15 minutes to make Fresh Salsa*

Cooking time: *5 minutes*

Yield: *8 to 12 servings*

2 teaspoons ground cumin	*¾ cup sour cream*
3 cups Refried Pinto Beans (see Chapter 10), or good-quality canned refried beans	*1 cup Fresh Salsa (see the recipe earlier in this chapter)*

1 Toast the cumin in a small, dry frying pan over low heat, frequently shaking the pan, until the cumin is fragrant, about 3 minutes.

2 Place the beans in a food processor with the metal blade or in a heavy-duty mixer with the paddle. Process or mix for about 2½ minutes, until the mixture is fairly smooth. Add the sour cream and toasted cumin. Mix for 1 more minute to blend. Stir in the Fresh Salsa just until combined.

TOQUE TIP

If you don't have the time to make refried beans from scratch, you can purchase them canned, in the Mexican food section of the supermarket. The best ones we've tasted are the Ortega brand.

Queso Fundido

Queso Fundido (KEH-soh fuhn-DEE-thoh), which means melted cheese, is a traditional dish from northern Mexico. The gooey richness of the melted cheese in this dip is irresistible for most of us. We add interest to this recipe by combining three cheeses: Mexican manchego for texture, añejo for salt, and panela for milkiness.

Special tool: *6 (4-ounce) ceramic or glass ovenproof dishes or 1 (1½ quart) casserole*

Preparation time: *15 minutes, plus 10 minutes to make the Green Tomatillo Salsa*

Cooking time: *25 minutes*

Yield: *6 servings as an appetizer*

(continued)

1½ cups (6 ounces) grated Mexican manchego or Monterey Jack cheese

½ cup (2 ounces) grated añejo cheese

½ cup (2 ounces) grated panela cheese

2 poblano chiles, roasted, peeled, seeded, and julienned (see Chapter 3)

½ small red onion, diced (⅓ cup)

Pepper to taste

12 flour or corn tortillas, warmed

Green Tomatillo Salsa for garnish (see the recipe earlier in this chapter)

1 Preheat the oven to 375°.

2 Set six 4-ounce ceramic or glass ovenproof dishes, or one 1½ quart casserole, in the oven for 10 minutes to warm.

3 Mix the manchego, añejo, and panela cheeses in a bowl. Divide the cheese evenly among the warm dishes. Bake for 5 minutes. Arrange the chiles and onion over the warm cheese and return to the oven, until the cheese is completely melted and bubbly, about 6 minutes. Season with pepper and serve immediately with warmed tortillas for dipping and Green Tomatillo Salsa according to taste.

For a crunchy dollop of protein, add 6 ounces of thinly sliced uncooked Spanish chorizo sausage along with the chiles and onion to the melted cheese. Or, if your grill is heated up, you can melt the cheese in aluminum foil packets on the covered grill for an authentic smoky flavor.

Down 'n' Dirty Bean Nachos

After you try this recipe, those fluorescent-orange cheese nachos you eat at football games will never be as satisfying. Go ahead and use the beans of your choice — such as pinto or kidney beans — in this sensational version of nachos.

Preparation time: 10 minutes, plus 35 minutes for Smoked Chile Salsa

Cooking time: 10 minutes

Yield: 8 to 10 servings

3 cups Refried Black Beans (see Chapter 10), or good-quality canned refried beans

¾ cup Smoked Chile Salsa (see the recipe earlier in this chapter)

8 ounces tortilla chips (about 3 large handfuls)

1 cup sour cream, mixed with the juice of 1 lime

1 cup (4 ounces) grated añejo cheese

1 Preheat the broiler.

2 Spread the refried beans in a ¼-inch layer in a 10-inch ovenproof platter or casserole. Spread the Smoked Chile Salsa over the beans. Place 6 to 8 inches under the broiler just long enough to heat through, about 6 minutes.

3 Stand the tortilla chips, their points facing up, in the beans. Using a plastic squeeze bottle, pastry bag, or the tines of a fork, drizzle the sour cream mixture over the chips. Sprinkle with the cheese and return to the broiler for about 4 minutes, just long enough to melt the cheese. Serve hot.

Silky Crab and Cheese Nachos

As upscale as this dish sounds, its consistency bares a striking resemblance to those gooey nachos sold at the movies (see photo in the color insert). Reserve it for a special occasion and wow your crab-loving guests.

At good fish markets, crab is sold already out of the shell, and picked clean. If you can't find it already cleaned for you, you'll need to break up the shells, remove the meat, and then carefully hand-pick any tiny pieces of shell from the meat.

Special tools: *Food processor or blender, strainer*

Preparation time: *20 minutes*

Cooking time: *40 minutes*

Yield: *6 servings*

2 tablespoons butter

2 garlic cloves, peeled and sliced

3 shallots, peeled and sliced

6 mushrooms, trimmed and sliced

Salt and pepper to taste

1 cup dry white wine

1 cup bottled clam juice

1 cup heavy cream

2 canned chipotle chiles, rinsed off

1 cup (4 ounces) grated añejo cheese

1 cup (4 ounces) grated Mexican manchego or Monterey Jack cheese

10 ounces crabmeat, picked clean

8 ounces tortilla chips (about 3 handfuls)

½ bunch cilantro leaves, chopped, for garnish

1 Preheat the oven to 350°.

(continued)

2 Melt the butter in a large skillet over medium-high heat. Sauté the garlic, shallots, and mushrooms, with the salt and pepper, until golden, about 5 minutes. Pour in the wine and boil until the liquid is reduced by half, 2 to 3 minutes. Pour in the clam juice and boil until the liquid is again reduced by half, another 2 to 3 minutes. Strain the liquid into a large saucepan, discarding the solids. Add the cream and cook over high heat until thick enough to coat a spoon. Stir in the chiles and remove from the heat.

3 Transfer the mixture to a food processor or blender and puree. Strain back into a large skillet and stir in ½ cup of the añejo cheese and ½ cup of the manchego cheese.

4 Place the skillet over medium heat, add the crabmeat, and bring to a boil. Stir in the tortilla chips and remove from heat. Pour the mixture into a large casserole, sprinkle with the remaining ½ cup añejo cheese and ½ cup manchego cheese and bake for 5 minutes. Sprinkle with the cilantro and serve with forks.

Snappy Ceviches

Ceviches (she-VEE-chehz) are the raw fish salads of Mexico. Unlike sushi, however, the fish is not completely raw. The quick lime juice bath at the beginning of the recipe technically cooks the outside of the fish (turning it opaque), while the inside remains raw.

TOQUE TIP

Because the center of the fish cubes is still raw in ceviches, be cautious if you are immune-compromised. To eliminate concern, gently poach the cubes of fish in water or clam juice for 2 minutes. Then thoroughly chill and proceed with the recipe.

For a great ceviche, the fish must be of the highest quality and as fresh as possible. (In Mexico, where we have never gotten sick from ceviche, the best ones were always served close to the water's edge, either at little beach shacks or literally on fishing boats.) When shopping for fresh fish fillets, look for glistening, translucent flesh that smells clean, not fishy. Shop the same day for fish for ceviche and store it in the refrigerator in its wrapping.

Basic Red Snapper Ceviche

Feel free to use almost any fresh fish for this crunchy raw fish salad. Just avoid meaty tuna, catfish, and monkfish, and exceptionally delicate fish like trout and whitefish. We love red snapper, but bass, halibut, and grouper are also great.

Preparation time: 5 minutes, plus 15 minutes marinating and 1 hour chilling

Yield: 4 to 6 servings

1 pound fresh red snapper fillets

¾ cup freshly squeezed lime juice

1 large tomato, cored, seeded, and diced

1 small red onion, finely diced

2 bunches cilantro leaves, roughly chopped (about 1 cup)

2 serrano chiles, stemmed and sliced in thin circles

½ cup bottled clam juice

1½ teaspoons salt

Romaine lettuce leaves for garnish

Tortilla chips for garnish

1 Cut the red snapper into ½-inch cubes and place in a glass or ceramic dish. Toss with ½ cup of the lime juice. Cover and marinate in the refrigerator for 15 minutes. Drain and discard the lime juice.

2 Transfer the fish to a medium bowl. Add the remaining ¼ cup lime juice, the tomato, onion, cilantro, chiles, clam juice, and salt and stir to combine. Chill for at least an hour, or as long as a day, to blend the flavors. Serve in tall chilled goblets with spears of romaine lettuce and tortilla chips, or in soup bowls lined with the lettuce leaves.

Ceviche de Veracruz

Flavorful, meaty bits of swordfish or mussels go well with this strong marinade from coastal Veracruz.

Preparation time: 10 minutes, plus 30 minutes marination and 1 hour chilling

Yield: 4 to 6 servings

10 ounces fresh swordfish, cut into ½-inch cubes, or shelled mussels

½ cup plus 1 tablespoon freshly squeezed lime juice

1 small red onion, diced

2 medium tomatoes, cored, seeded, and diced

½ cup freshly squeezed orange juice

½ cup tomato juice

2 jalapeño chiles, stemmed, seeded, and finely chopped

1 bunch oregano, leaves only, chopped (about ½ cup)

¼ cup extra-virgin olive oil

½ cup small green olives, pitted

1 teaspoon salt

½ teaspoon pepper

(continued)

Garnishes: Lettuce leaves, tortilla chips

1 Combine the fish or whole mussels and ½ cup of the lime juice in a glass or ceramic dish and marinate for 30 minutes in the refrigerator. Drain and discard the lime juice.

2 Transfer the fish to a medium bowl. Add the remaining 1 tablespoon of lime juice, the onion, tomatoes, orange juice, tomato juice, chiles, oregano, olive oil, olives, salt, and pepper. Toss well and chill for at least an hour, or as long as overnight. Serve cold in chilled glasses or on lettuce-lined plates, with tortilla chips as garnish.

Be careful not to overmarinate the fish in the initial lime juice. If the fish is left in too long, lime can overcook the fish's fibers, turning them to mush and robbing them of their natural flavors.

Smoked Mussel Ceviche Tostadas

Here is a spectacular fish salad for those who are squeamish about eating raw fish. Smoked, totally cooked mussels are available in vacuum-sealed packages in the refrigerated section of the market, near the smoked salmon.

Special tool: *Baking sheet*

Preparation time: *10 minutes*

Cooking time: *45 minutes, plus 2½ hours chilling*

Yield: *6 to 10 servings*

3 medium-size golden beets, unpeeled and trimmed

1 medium jícama, peeled and cut into ½-inch cubes

1 small red onion, finely diced

2 jalapeño chiles, stemmed, seeded, and minced

12 ounces smoked mussels

¼ cup extra-virgin olive oil

1 bunch cilantro leaves, coarsely chopped (about ½ cup)

¼ cup freshly squeezed orange juice

¼ cup freshly squeezed lime juice

¾ teaspoon salt

½ teaspoon pepper

6 to 10 crispy flat corn tortillas or tostadas

1 avocado, peeled, seeded, and mashed, for garnish

1 Preheat the oven to 350°.

2 Place the beets on a baking sheet and roast until done, about 1 hour. When they are cool enough to handle, remove the skins and cut the beets into ½-inch cubes.

3 Place the beets, jícama, onion, chiles, and mussels in a mixing bowl. Add the olive oil, cilantro, orange juice, lime juice, salt, and pepper and toss well. Refrigerate for 2½ hours to blend the flavors. Divide the ceviche and arrange over crisp tortillas or tostadas. Garnish each with a dollop of mashed avocado. Serve immediately.

 Smoked oysters or clams are good substitutes for smoked mussels. Or if you can't find smoked mussels, substitute 1 pound fresh mussels, scrubbed and debearded. Just steam them open in a large pot that contains a few inches of white wine or water seasoned with salt, pepper, and fresh parsley or cilantro. Bring the pot of mussels to a boil, cover, and cook for about 5 minutes, until the shells are open.

 If you substitute red beets for golden beets, be prepared for bright pink ceviche.

Oysters with Chipotle Vinaigrette

We love ice-cold oysters served with a simple uncooked sauce, such as this vinaigrette. For another Mexican spin, try a spoonful of Fresh Salsa or Green Tomatillo Salsa (both recipes appear in this chapter) with your next batch of fresh oysters.

Special tool: *Blender*

Preparation time: *15 minutes*

Yield: *2 to 4 servings*

½ cup red wine vinegar

2 shallots, peeled and sliced

1 canned chipotle chile, stemmed, rinsed, and seeded

Salt and pepper to taste

½ teaspoon sugar

24 raw oysters in the shell

Crushed ice

Coarse salt

1 Place the vinegar, shallots, chile, salt and pepper, and sugar in a blender and blend well.

2 Shuck the oysters, discarding the half shells that are bare. To shuck, or open, an oyster shell, first scrub the shell under cold running water with a brush to remove the sand. With a towel in the palm of your hand as protection, press the shell against a counter. Insert the tip of an oyster knife or paring knife in the shell's pointy end and gently twist to break the seal. Run the knife around the edges until the shell opens, and pull the shell apart.

(continued)

3 Carefully wipe clean the edges of shells holding the oysters with a damp paper towel. Arrange the oysters on a serving platter lined with crushed ice that has been sprinkled with coarse salt to prevent melting. Spoon a dab of sauce over each oyster and serve.

Mexican Shrimp Cocktail

You were expecting boiled shrimp in your shrimp cocktail, weren't you? Just to make sure that you don't fall asleep at the table, we thought we'd surprise you with this double whammy of flavor: quickly seared, spice-coated shrimp and a homemade spicy dipping sauce to boot. Bring on the margaritas and dig in!

Preparation time: *15 minutes*

Cooking time: *5 minutes*

Yield: *4 servings*

¼ teaspoon salt

½ teaspoon pepper

2 teaspoons ground cumin

1 teaspoon paprika

½ teaspoon cayenne

12 ounces medium shrimp (about 30), peeled and cleaned with tails on

2 tablespoons olive oil

Juice of ½ lime (1 tablespoon)

Spicy Cocktail Sauce for dipping (see the following recipe)

1 Combine the salt, pepper, cumin, paprika, and cayenne in a medium bowl. Add the shrimp and toss to evenly coat.

2 Heat the olive oil in a large skillet over high heat. Sauté the shrimp for about 1 minute on each side. Remove from heat and stir in the lime juice. Transfer to a platter and serve at room temperature, or chilled, with Spicy Cocktail Sauce for dipping.

TOQUE TIP The black vein that runs through shrimp is edible. The choice to remove it is entirely aesthetic. To remove the vein, first peel the shell. Then, holding the shrimp in one hand, run a sharp paring knife along the outside curve and slice about ¼-inch down. Scrape out the vein with the tip of the knife.

Spicy Cocktail Sauce

This hot and chunky cocktail sauce is great for dipping your favorite cold seafood.

Preparation time: *10 minutes*

Yield: *1 cup*

¾ *cup ketchup*

2 serrano chiles, minced, with seeds

3 tablespoons chopped fresh cilantro leaves

3 tablespoons minced red onion

2 tablespoons freshly squeezed lime juice

½ *teaspoon salt*

½ *teaspoon pepper*

Tabasco to taste

Mix all the ingredients together in a bowl. Store in the refrigerator as long as 2 days.

Chapter 6

Foods from the Mexican Marketplace

In every place we visit, we are always drawn to the marketplace first. The museums and monuments can wait because first we want to soak up some food ambience. The market gives us an immediate sense of a region's products, its people, and the cooking style. In Mexico's vibrant markets, the brilliantly colored fruits, tomatoes, and peppers; the smoky dried spices and chiles; the stacks of fresh corn tortillas in baskets; and the sizzling sounds of griddled meats always inspire us. We like to leave with full stomachs and heads swimming with ideas for the kinds of rustic, full-flavored foods that we love to re-create at home.

The foods in this chapter are sold and eaten at the local markets or informal stands scattered all over Mexico. People usually eat these foods as small snacks, sometimes even for breakfast, while they're out conducting their business. But in our homes, they fit in perfectly with the way we try to eat and feed our families. They make excellent use of leftovers, offer well-balanced servings of small portions of meat combined with vegetables and grains, and taste terrific.

As an added benefit, tacos and tortas make excellent, informal party foods. You can arrange all the fixings on a buffet table, along with chips and salsas, cold drinks, and maybe something easy for dessert, like cookies, so that everyone can just dig in, relax, and have fun. (For more complete directions for setting up a taco party, see Chapters 16 and 18.)

Getting Stuffed on Quesadillas

Quesadillas (keh-sah-DEE-yahz) are the Mexican answer to the grilled cheese sandwich or pizza. They are a versatile dish of flour tortillas, usually stuffed with cheeses and one or two other ingredients, cooked quickly enough to just melt the cheese and marry all the flavors. What makes a quesadilla rise to greatness, however, is the quality of those few simple ingredients and the care taken in cooking them.

Paying attention to your ingredients

Quesadillas contain very few ingredients; however, things can literally fall apart on you if the ingredients aren't brought together in the right proportions and handled properly. Here are some pitfalls to avoid when creating your own melted cheese creations:

- **Too much cheese:** Strive for a balance between tortilla and cheese so that one ingredient doesn't overwhelm the other. A quesadilla should taste of more than cheese.

- **Raw vegetables:** Each component of the quesadilla should be seasoned and cooked before being added. If you want to add a vegetable (or meat), remember that once a quesadilla is tossed into the oven or pan, you are cooking it quickly, just long enough to melt the cheese. Uncooked ingredients in the center will remain uncooked, and they won't be nearly as delicious as cooked and seasoned vegetables.

Making your own flour tortillas

In Mexico, tortillas are often made by hand and are present at almost every meal in some form or another. Flour tortillas are eaten in northern Mexico, while corn tortillas are favored in the south. (Chapter 10 tells you about making corn tortillas.)

The taste of a good homemade flour tortilla adds an extra dimension to any dish; however, if you're pressed for time, you can substitute good store-bought tortillas (with or without the lard).

Flour Tortillas

Ever wonder what to do on one of those afternoons when it seems like there's nothing going on? Why not gather the kids together and roll out a batch of unbelievably delicious homemade tortillas? They're easier to make than bread (see Figure 6-1), and the rewards are immediate. Children love them slathered with butter and honey for breakfast.

You can store tortillas in the refrigerator for a few days or in the freezer for as long as a month.

Special tools: *Wooden spoon, baking tray or cutting board*

Preparation time: *25 minutes, plus 15 minutes resting time for dough*

Cooking time: *15 minutes*

Yield: *12 8-inch tortillas*

3½ cups flour plus extra for dusting

½ cup plus 1 tablespoon vegetable shortening

1½ teaspoons salt

1 cup plus 2 tablespoons lukewarm water

1 Place the flour, shortening, and salt in a bowl and lightly rub the ingredients together with your fingers until evenly mixed. Pour in the warm water and stir with a wooden spoon. Then gather the dough together and knead a few times by hand until a smooth dough is formed.

2 Divide the dough into 12 equal-sized pieces. Roll each piece into a ball and place on a baking tray or cutting board. Cover with a tea towel and let rest at room temperature for at least 15 minutes, or up to 1 hour.

3 Cut out 12 10-inch squares of waxed or parchment paper for stacking the tortillas. On a lightly floured board, roll each ball into an 8-inch circle and transfer to a paper square. Stack the tortillas on a baking tray or platter and refrigerate until cooking time. You can keep uncooked tortillas in the refrigerator for up to 2 days if they're well wrapped with paper squares between the layers.

4 To cook, heat a dry griddle or 12-inch nonstick skillet over medium heat. Carefully peel the paper from the tortillas and cook them, one at a time, until they're puffy and slightly brown, about 40 seconds per side. Set aside to cool slightly on a paper towel-lined platter. Bring them to the table wrapped in a towel for warmth, or wrap well and store.

 Flour tortillas can be crisped in the oven for a delicious, nutritious treat. Brush the tortillas with melted butter, sprinkle with a mixture of cinnamon and sugar, and arrange them in a single layer on an uncoated baking sheet. Bake in a 350° oven until crisp, about 10 minutes. For a savory version, brush with olive oil, sprinkle with savory seeds and spices like cumin, sesame, and chiles, and bake until crisp, about 10 minutes.

How to Make Your Own Flour Tortillas

1. Place flour, shortening and salt in a bowl. Lightly rub together with fingers until evenly mixed.

Pour in warm water. Stir with a wooden spoon until a smooth dough has formed.

2. Divide the dough into 12 pieces. Roll each piece into a ball and place on a baking tray. Cover with a towel. Let rest at room temperature, 15 minutes to 1 hour.

3. Cut out parchment paper squares for stacking the tortillas. On a lightly floured board, roll each ball into an 8" circle. Transfer to a paper square.

Stack on a baking tray or platter. Refrigerate till cooking time.

4. To cook, heat a dry griddle or skillet over medium heat....

Carefully, peel off paper. Cook tortillas one at a time till puffy, slightly brown, about 40 seconds per side. Set aside to cool on towel lined platter.

Figure 6-1: Making flour tortillas.

Quintessential quesadillas

TOQUE TIP

In the following recipes, we have you put the quesadillas in the oven for the final bring-it-all-together stage. However, there is more than one way to cook a quesadilla, especially if you are cooking at home for just one or two people. You can prepare quesadillas quickly on the stovetop, using our quick and easy method: Heat the tortilla on both sides in a lightly oiled or buttered skillet over low heat. Then sprinkle on and lightly melt the cheese, scatter on the toppings, and fold. Cook, turning once or twice, until the cheese is completely melted.

Poblano Quesadillas

A great quesadilla depends on just the right balance of soothing cheese and other, livelier flavors. In this recipe, roasted peppers, tart salsa, and more than one cheese keep things interesting.

Special tools: *Pastry brush, baking sheet*

Preparation time: *20 minutes, plus 15 minutes for the Green Tomatillo Salsa*

Cooking time: *15 minutes*

Yield: *6 servings*

2 cups (8 ounces) grated Mexican manchego cheese

1 cup (4 ounces) grated añejo cheese

6 8-inch flour tortillas

4 poblano chiles, roasted, peeled, seeded, and julienned (see Chapter 3)

2 tablespoons butter, melted

Green Tomatillo Salsa for garnish (see Chapter 5)

1 Preheat the oven to 350°.

2 In a bowl, mix together the manchego and añejo cheeses.

3 Place the tortillas on a work surface. Divide the cheese mix into 6 equal portions and spread over half of each tortilla. Arrange the chile strips evenly over the cheese. Fold the tortillas over to enclose the filling, and brush the tops of the folded tortillas with the butter.

4 Place a dry griddle or cast-iron skillet over medium-high heat. Place the tortillas, one or two at a time, buttered side down in the pan. Cook until very light golden, about 1 minute. Then brush the uncoated sides with butter, flip the tortillas over, and cook the second side. Transfer to a baking sheet and bake for 10 minutes, until the cheese begins to ooze. Serve hot, whole or cut into wedges, with Green Tomatillo Salsa.

For an added dollop of flavor, drizzle some Smoked Chile Salsa (Chapter 5) inside the quesadilla before cooking. Substitute canned roasted jalapeños if fresh poblanos aren't available.

Grilled Vegetable Quesadillas

Here is a great use for leftover grilled or roasted vegetables. You'll need to start out with about 2½ cups of whatever veggie mix you choose to use.

Special tools: *2 baking sheets*

Preparation time: *20 minutes*

Cooking time: *15 minutes*

Yield: *6 servings*

¼ cup olive oil

2 tablespoons red wine vinegar

1 teaspoon salt

½ teaspoon pepper

(continued)

2 cloves garlic, minced

½ bunch fresh oregano or marjoram leaves, coarsely chopped (¼ cup), or ½ tablespoon dried oregano or marjoram leaves

2 small zucchini, ends trimmed

2 small yellow crookneck squash, trimmed

1 large red bell pepper, stemmed and seeded

1 medium red onion

3 jalapeño chiles, stemmed and seeded

Butter for greasing baking sheets

6 8-inch flour tortillas

2 cups (8 ounces) grated Mexican cheeses such as Mexican manchego, panela, and añejo

1 Prepare a medium fire in a grill or preheat the broiler.

2 In a large bowl, whisk together the olive oil, vinegar, salt, pepper, garlic, and oregano or marjoram.

3 Cut the zucchini, squash, red pepper, onion, and chiles into quarters lengthwise. Place them in the bowl with the olive oil mixture and mix to evenly coat. Grill or broil slowly, turning frequently, until lightly golden and soft, about 10 minutes. Cool slightly and cut all the vegetables into 2-inch pieces. Transfer to a bowl and set aside.

4 Adjust the oven temperature to 350°. Lightly butter 2 baking sheets and arrange the tortillas in a single layer. Spread equal amounts of the grated cheese mix over each tortilla and bake for 5 minutes, until melted. Spoon equal amounts of the grilled vegetable mixture over the cheese, fold over to enclose, and return the tortillas to the oven just to heat through, about 4 minutes. Serve hot, whole or cut in wedges.

If you're firing up the gas grill for the veggies, you can make your quesadillas on the grill as well. Turn the heat down to medium-low and place a cookie sheet, or sheet of foil, over the grate to avoid messy cheese drops.

Smoky Chicken Quesadillas

This authentic spicy quesadilla is a big seller at the Border Grill (see photo in the color insert). All those greens and chiles counterbalance the richness of the cheese.

Preparation time: *15 minutes*

Cooking time: *25 minutes*

Yield: *6 servings*

3½ cups shredded, roasted chicken

3 canned chipotle chiles, seeded and thinly sliced

½ bunch cilantro leaves, chopped (¼ cup)

3 scallions, trimmed and thinly sliced at an angle

4 tablespoons butter, melted

6 8-inch flour tortillas

2 cups (about 8 ounces) grated Mexican cheese mix (see "The cheese mix" in Chapter 2)

1 Preheat the oven to 350°.

2 In a large bowl, combine the chicken, chiles, cilantro, and scallions.

3 Brush one side of each tortilla with the butter and place, buttered side down, on a baking sheet. Brush the tops with butter. Spread equal amounts of the grated cheese mix over each tortilla and bake for 5 minutes, until melted.

4 Spoon equal amounts of the chicken mixture over half of the cheese, fold over to enclose, and return to the oven just long enough to heat through, about 5 minutes. Serve hot, whole or cut in wedges.

Quesadilla riffs

Like other great melted cheese dishes, quesadillas lend themselves to improvisation. Here are a few alternative ideas for topping our standard cheese mix (see "The cheese mix" in Chapter 2). Regardless of what kind of cheese you use, the technique remains the same: First top the tortilla with grated cheese, melt slightly, scatter on toppings, and bake until melted through.

✔ Mashed, roasted garlic and shredded, roasted, or barbecued pork

✔ Sautéed whole zucchini blossoms, seasoned with salt and pepper

✔ Sautéed, sliced mushrooms (the wilder the better), with garlic and herbs

✔ Fresh Salsa (Chapter 5) over cheese

✔ Sautéed small shrimp and Green Tomatillo Salsa (Chapter 5)

✔ Sautéed corn kernels, avocado slices, and Fresh Salsa (Chapter 5)

✔ Crumbled blue cheese or cream cheese (instead of the cheese mix) with guava jelly or plum jelly

✔ Thinly sliced, cooked steak with Smoked Chile Salsa (Chapter 5) and onions, raw (according to Mary Sue) or caramelized (according to Susan)

✔ Caramelized onions with basil or thyme, and Red Roasted Tomato Salsa (Chapter 5)

Transforming Tortillas into Tacos

Ever since we started hanging out at Los Angeles's taco stands in search of authentic snack foods, we've been taken with the taco's ability to satisfy like very few fast foods.

The foundation of a taco is two warmed, soft corn tortillas, stacked. These are topped with a savory filling like meat or fish and then sprinkled with spicy, crunchy garnishes and salsas to taste. The resulting package is tender and juicy. Our mouths water at the thought of those little bits of grilled or stewed meats, chunks of crunchy onion, cabbage, or lettuce, and soothing avocado, all doused with spicy salsa and sloppily tucked into fragrant, soft, corn tortillas. Yummm — sure beats a hot dog on a stick and those crisp tacos sold at fast food joints.

If you don't have all the suggested toppings in the house, don't let that come between you and a good taco. After all, tacos were created to make good use of leftovers. Almost anything that you can wrap in a tortilla and bring to your mouth qualifies as a taco. Chopped fresh onion, cilantro leaves, lime wedges, sour cream, and bottled salsa make great authentic toppings for most fillings. And tacos are terrific interactive party foods. Just place some grilled, sliced meats out on a buffet table with an assortment of salsas and toppings and watch your guests improvise. (See Chapter 16 for tips on throwing a taco party.)

Warming the tortillas and building a taco

A good taco is a well-balanced meal in a package. It can be as simple or as complex as you like, but here are some blueprints (also consult Figure 6-2):

1. **Warm the tortillas by quickly dipping each in a shallow pan of water and placing them on a grill or hot dry sauté pan for 30 seconds on each side to soften. Stack and wrap in a damp tea towel and then in aluminum foil. Set the tortillas aside in a warm place for up to 30 minutes.**

2. **Stack two warm, soft corn tortillas together.**

   Chapter 10 tells you how to make your own corn tortillas at home and also gives you some tips on purchasing corn tortillas at the store.

3. **Top with warm, well-seasoned meat, either chopped or shredded.**

4. **Add some spicy salsa.**

5. **Sprinkle with a variety of garnishes.**

   For crunch, add chopped onion, shredded cabbage, sliced radish, or Fresh Salsa (Chapter 5). For creaminess add Crema (see Chapter 15), Guacamole (see Chapter 5), chopped avocado, sour cream, or shredded cheese.

6. **Fold to enclose and carry to your mouth quickly for instant ingestion.**

Choosing a taco joint

In places with large Mexican communities, like Los Angeles, the best tacos and snack foods are available at makeshift operations. They're either on wheels — on trucks with portable kitchens — or they're tiny storefront stands with walkup counters. Because they often are in the same (Spanish-speaking) neighborhood, we've devised a plan for scoping out the best taco joints. All your senses should come into play when making such important decisions. Here are our tips:

✔ First, use your eyes: Walk past all the joints and look for the busiest one. The one with the longest line is probably the best. Also look for cleanliness and, most importantly, if the taco stand is a truck, look for one that has no storage and must cook each day's fixings fresh.

✔ Next, read the menu. Look for a small menu — a place that specializes in doing a few things well, like all stewed meat or all fish, is usually better. Also, we find that places that list exotic meats like tongue are usually excellent because they are catering to homegrown tastes. Family-owned is a plus, of course, because the cooks use their own tried-and-true family recipes.

✔ Open up a dialogue. The people serving you should be friendly and willing to help, even if your Spanish stopped at *Sesame Street*. Smiles are a very good sign. We like to check out what other people are eating. If everyone's chowing down on something you don't recognize, simply point and express yearning with your eyes. You may run into order takers who refuse to serve you something that they assume you won't like. Put down your foot, and insist. They'll respect you more for it. Besides, how else are you ever going to get a taste of stewed pig intestines? Another good thing to discuss is what the order taker is eating for lunch that day. It's a clue to what's great.

✔ A great taco stand should smell like corn from the soft corn tortillas, and the griddle should smell like sizzling meat. The best stands heat up each order right next to the tortillas on the griddle. The salsas should be fresh and offered freely, and the chopped garnishes like cabbage and onion should look bright, as though they were just cut.

✔ Taste and enjoy the results of your research. Then dream of coming back.

Figure 6-2: Assembling a taco.

How to Build a Taco.

Stack 2 warm corn tortillas back to back.

Top with chopped or shredded meat.

Spoon on a spicy salsa.

Sprinkle on a few garnishes.

Fold over and EAT immediately!

Making tasty tacos

The best tacos probably don't start with a recipe at all. They spring from surprising sources — like the leftovers in the back of your refrigerator. Here are some likely inspirations:

- Holiday turkey
- Roasted chicken or last night's Mexican takeout chicken
- Leg of lamb
- Steak
- Picadillo (see the Empanadas recipe in Chapter 7)
- Pork, roasted or barbecued
- Brisket
- Fish fillets
- Cold, poached shrimp, lobster, or crabmeat

The following recipes aren't quite as adventurous as the previous suggestions, but they'll give you a great place to start experiencing the taco.

Grilled Steak Tacos

Fabulous *tacos al carbon,* or grilled tacos, are sold on the streets in Mexico by vendors pushing charcoal-burning pushcarts. (To find out how to make homemade corn tortillas, turn to Chapter 10.)

Special tool: *Gas or charcoal grill*

Preparation time: *10 minutes, plus 15 minutes for Fresh Salsa*

Cooking time: *15 minutes*

Yield: *4 to 6 servings*

1 pound, skirt or tri-tip steak, trimmed of fat and silverskin

Salt and pepper to taste

2 cloves garlic, minced

1 teaspoon dried oregano

1 tablespoon olive oil

Juice of ½ lime (1 tablespoon)

12 (4 ½-inch) or 8 (6-inch) corn tortillas

1 bunch coarsely chopped cilantro leaves (about ½ cup)

2 peeled, seeded, and sliced avocados

1 bunch diagonally sliced scallions

Garnishes: Lime wedges, ¼ head shredded white cabbage or lettuce, Fresh Salsa (see Chapter 5)

1 Prepare a hot fire in a gas or charcoal grill.

2 Half an hour before grilling, season the steak evenly with salt and pepper. Rub with the garlic and oregano and evenly drizzle with the olive oil and lime juice. Turn to evenly coat steak and refrigerate.

3 Grill the steak over high heat for 1½ minutes per side, or until it's caramelized on the outside and pink in the center. Let sit for 5 minutes, before slicing into ¼-inch strips across the grain (at a right angle to the way the meat's fibers are running). Serve immediately with warmed tortillas, garnishes, and plenty of Fresh Salsa.

 For grilled chicken tacos, season the meat with plenty of salt and pepper or marinate in your favorite marinade. Grill about 1¼ pounds of chicken thighs or breasts, on the bone, for 30 minutes over medium heat, turning frequently. Remove the meat from the bones, cut into ¼-inch strips, and use as a filling with the same garnishes suggested in the recipe for Grilled Steak Tacos.

Cactus Tacos

These refreshing tacos make a great little meal for the adventurous vegetarian — or a hungry person lost in the desert (see photo in the color insert). Cactus has a lemony flavor and a texture like okra.

Look for fresh cactus paddles or *nopales* (noh-PAHL-az) at your local farmers market or in ethnic markets. If you're purchasing corn tortillas, buy the small (4½-inch) size for authentic taco making.

Preparation time: *15 minutes, plus 15 minutes for Fresh Salsa*

Cooking time: *15 minutes*

Yield: *6 servings*

3 tablespoons olive oil

½ small red onion, diced

2 cloves garlic, minced

1 pound (3 cups) fresh or prepared cactus paddles, needles removed, skins on and cut into ¼-inch cubes (see Chapter 2 for tips on working with cactus paddles)

2 serrano chiles, stemmed, seeded, and finely diced

1 teaspoon salt

1 teaspoon pepper

2 tablespoons red wine vinegar

½ cup (2 ounces) finely grated añejo cheese

12 4½-inch corn tortillas, warmed

Garnishes: Avocado slices, Fresh Salsa (see Chapter 5)

(continued)

1 Heat the olive oil in a large skillet over moderate heat. Sauté the onion for 2½ minutes. Add the garlic and cook for an additional minute or until aroma is released. Add the cactus and cook over high heat, tossing or gently stirring frequently, until the cactus is tender and all the juices have thickened, about 10 minutes.

2 Transfer the mixture to a large bowl. Add the chiles, salt, pepper, vinegar, and cheese and stir well. Serve in warm tortillas with the Fresh Salsa and avocado slices on top.

At a cactus farm I visited on a trip to Mexico, I watched workers harvest the smallest paddles from giant cactus that were 6 feet tall. Just like baby vegetables, the tiniest, newest paddles are the most prized.

Fish Tacos

We like our fish tacos soft, juicy, and overflowing with luscious chunks of fish and bits of vegetables (see photo in the color insert). If you don't have time to make the special Cucumber Salsa that we suggest to go along with these tacos, you can just add chopped cucumbers, chiles, and tomatoes, along with a squirt of lemon or lime juice and some olive oil.

Special tool: *Charcoal or gas grill*

Preparation time: *10 minutes, plus 50 minutes for the Cucumber Salsa*

Yield: *3 servings*

1½ pounds salmon, snapper, bass, or halibut fillet	*6 lettuce leaves*
Extra-virgin olive oil for drizzling	*Cucumber Salsa (see the following recipe)*
Salt and pepper to taste	*Lime wedges for squeezing*
12 6-inch corn tortillas, warmed	*Garnishes: Avocado, radish slices*

1 Prepare a medium-hot fire in a charcoal or gas grill.

2 Drizzle the fish with olive oil, season with salt and pepper, and grill until barely done, for 2 to 5 minutes per side, depending on the thickness. Remove the fish from the grill, let cool slightly, and then pull apart into large flakes.

3 Place the tortillas on a work surface. Line each with a piece of lettuce and top with chunks of fish. Top each with a generous spoonful of Cucumber Salsa, a squirt of lime, and a drizzle of olive oil. Garnish with avocado and radishes and serve.

You don't have to start this recipe with uncooked fish. Tacos are a terrific way to use leftover fish. Just warm the fish first and then pull the flesh apart into large flakes.

Cucumber Salsa

You can store this salsa in the refrigerator up to 48 hours.

Preparation time: *20 minutes, plus 30 minutes marination*

Yield: *3 cups*

4 pickling cucumbers, diced

½ small red onion, diced

¼ bunch cilantro, chopped (⅓ cup)

1 small tomato, seeded and diced

3 tablespoons freshly squeezed lime juice

3 tablespoons freshly squeezed orange juice

1 teaspoon salt

½ teaspoon pepper

2 serrano chiles, stemmed and sliced in thin rounds

Place all the ingredients in a bowl, combine well and let stand, covered, for at least 30 minutes.

Rajas and Egg Tacos

Creamy scrambled eggs and roasted pepper strips, or *rajas* (RA-has), tucked into warm tortillas are perfect for breakfast the morning after a late night.

Preparation time: *15 minutes*

Cooking time: *20 minutes*

Yield: *4 servings*

2 tablespoons olive oil

1 medium onion, halved crosswise and cut into ¼-inch slices lengthwise

Salt and pepper to taste

3 red bell peppers, stemmed, roasted, peeled, seeded, and julienned

(continued)

3 poblano chiles, stemmed, roasted,
peeled, seeded, and julienned

½ cup cream

½ cup (2 ounces) grated Mexican
manchego cheese or Monterey Jack cheese

3 eggs, beaten

8 (5-inch) corn tortillas, warmed

1 Heat the oil in a large skillet over medium heat. Sauté the onion with the salt and
pepper until it begins to wilt and brown, about 10 minutes. Stir in the red peppers and
chiles. Pour in the cream, bring to a boil, and reduce to a simmer. Cook for 4 minutes or
until the cream is reduced by half.

2 Reduce the heat to low. Stir in the grated cheese and beaten eggs and cook, stirring constantly, until soft curds form. Remove from heat and serve immediately in the stacked
warm tortillas.

For an even more fortifying breakfast, add a boiled, diced potato to the pan
with the onions. Doing so will increase the bulk of the filling, so keep additional tortillas at hand!

Entertaining with Enchiladas

Authentic enchiladas are not at all like the heavy, goopy concoctions, overbur-
dened with cheese and swimming in sauce, found on most combination plates
in Mexican restaurants in the United States. In Mexico, enchiladas are a dish of
day-old tortillas, lightly coated with sauce, filled with small bits of meat or
vegetables, rolled up, and then baked to meld the flavors. At home, they make
a terrific inexpensive, healthful, small meal to serve at informal gatherings.

Rolling an enchilada

The rolling involved in assembling enchiladas can sometimes frustrate beginning cooks. For perfectly rolled enchiladas every time, make sure that your
tortilla is properly soaked and soft (see the following recipes for the details
on what to soak them in) and then follow these steps (see Figure 6-3):

1. **Place 1 tortilla flat on your work surface. Place the enchilada filling in
the center of each tortilla, spreading it evenly from edge to edge.**

2. **Fold ⅓ of the tortilla over the center.**

3. **Fold the other ⅓ of the tortilla over to enclose the filling.**

4. **Place the enchilada in a casserole dish with the seam side down.**

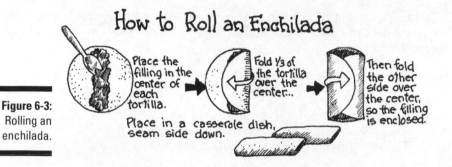

Figure 6-3:
Rolling an
enchilada.

How to Roll an Enchilada

Place the filling in the center of each tortilla.

Fold ⅓ of the tortilla over the center...

Then fold the other side over the center, so the filling is enclosed.

Place in a casserole dish, seam side down.

Amazing enchiladas

Enchiladas are great for weeknight entertaining. Just assemble the casserole
in the morning and store it in the refrigerator. When you get home at night,
pop the enchiladas in the oven to heat through and serve. Tortillas, by the
way, will last in the refrigerator as long as a week.

Green Enchiladas with Pork

Rich pork and tangy light green salsa are a natural combination in the Mexican kitchen.
Add the earthiness of toasted corn from the tortillas and you've got a winning dish.

Preparation time: 5 minutes, plus 15 minutes for Green Tomatillo Salsa

Cooking time: 1 hour and 30 minutes

Yield: 6 servings as an appetizer, 4 as an entrée

1¼ pounds boneless stewing pork butt or
shoulder, cut into 2-inch chunks

Salt and pepper to taste

3 cups Green Tomatillo Salsa (see
Chapter 5)

1 cup vegetable oil

12 6-inch corn tortillas

4 ounces panela cheese, crumbled

½ red onion, cut into rings

1 Preheat the oven to 350°.

2 Season the pork all over with salt and pepper and place in a small ovenproof casserole.
Pour on 1 cup of the Green Tomatillo Salsa. Cover with foil and bake for 1 hour, until
tender. Let the pork cool and then shred it, reserving it in the sauce.

3 Pour the vegetable oil into a large skillet and place over medium heat. One at a time, dip
the tortillas in the hot oil, and fry for about 10 seconds on each side. Drain on a rack.

(continued)

4 Pour the remaining 2 cups of salsa into a shallow bowl or pie dish. Dip each tortilla into the salsa to lightly coat and place them on your work surface. (Reserve the remaining salsa for the next step.)

5 Divide the meat into 12 servings, and spoon into the center of each tortilla. Roll to enclose the meat in the tortilla.

6 Arrange the enchiladas in a single layer in a medium casserole, seam side down, and pour the remaining salsa over the top, discarding the fatty juices in the bowl. Bake for 15 minutes, until heated through. Sprinkle with the cheese and onions and serve.

Chicken Poblano Enchiladas

If you love poblano chiles as we do, you can get a double dose of your favorite chile in this rich, rustic enchilada (see photo in the color insert). Brick red anchos are the dried form of poblanos.

Special tool: *Blender*

Preparation time: *20 minutes, plus 15 minutes soaking*

Cooking time: *30 minutes*

Yield: *4 to 6 servings*

3 cups shredded roasted chicken

3 poblano chiles, roasted, peeled, seeded, and julienned (see Chapter 3)

Salt and pepper to taste

4 ancho chiles, stemmed, seeded, and lightly toasted

1½ cups hot water

1 teaspoon salt

½ teaspoon pepper

1 teaspoon sugar

¼ medium yellow onion, coarsely chopped

2 cloves garlic, peeled and chopped

½ teaspoon ground cumin

2 tablespoons white vinegar

1 teaspoon dried oregano

2 tablespoons olive oil

⅔ cup vegetable oil for frying

12 6-inch corn tortillas

Garnishes: 1 cup (4 ounces) grated añejo cheese, 1 small red onion, sliced in rings

1 For the filling, mix the chicken and poblanos together in a large bowl, season with salt and pepper, and set aside.

2 For the sauce, cover the ancho chiles with hot water and let them soak for 15 minutes. Transfer the chiles and their water to the blender and add the salt, pepper, sugar, onion, garlic, cumin, vinegar, and oregano. Puree until smooth and then strain into bowl.

3 Heat the olive oil in a heavy medium-size saucepan over medium heat. Pour in the strained ancho mixture and cook, stirring frequently, about 5 minutes, until slightly thickened.

4 Preheat the oven to 350°.

5 Heat ¼ inch of vegetable oil in a small skillet over moderate heat. Fry the tortillas, one at a time, about 20 seconds per side, until wilted but not crisp. Drain well on paper towels. One at a time, dip each limp tortilla in the sauce and place it on your work surface. Fill each tortilla with the chicken mixture. Roll to enclose the meat in the tortilla.

6 Arrange the stuffed tortillas in a single layer in a medium-size glass or ceramic casserole. Top each with a few spoonfuls of extra sauce and bake for about 10 minutes to warm through. Sprinkle with the cheese and onion and serve immediately.

Enmoladas

Wondering what to do with that tub of leftover *mole* (MOH-leh) in your freezer? (Chapter 11 tells you all about mole.) Here is a creative way to make a meal with old tortillas and leftover sauce without the rolling involved in enchiladas. Just serve with a salad and soup, or with rice and beans for a typical Mexican home-cooked meal.

Cooking time: *20 minutes*

Yield: *4 to 6 servings*

⅔ cup vegetable oil for frying

12 6-inch corn tortillas

2 ½ cups Mole Sauce (see Chapter 11)

¾ cup (3 ounces) crumbled Queso Fresco, Ranchero, or Cotija cheese

½ red onion, sliced into rings

1 Preheat oven to 350°.

2 Heat ¼ inch vegetable oil in a small skillet over moderate heat. Fry the tortillas, one at a time, about 30 seconds per side, until wilted but not crisp. Drain well on paper towels. Dip the tortillas in the mole to evenly coat. Fold them in half and then in half again to form a wedge.

3 Arrange the tortillas, slightly overlapping, in a medium-size casserole or on a baking tray. Pour remaining mole over the tortillas. Bake for 10 minutes, just to heat through. Top with the cheese and onion and serve immediately.

(continued)

Use this same technique with leftover black beans to make *enfrijoladas* (en-free-hoh-LAH-thahs), a tortilla and bean snack. Dip tortillas in a pot of boiled beans pureed with their liquid to coat and then arrange tortillas in a casserole as described in the preceding recipe. Bake for 10 minutes to heat through.

Snacking on Tortas

In addition to fabulous tacos for snacking anywhere, Mexican cooks also make delectable sandwiches called *tortas*. These small, overstuffed sandwiches, served on hollowed-out crusty rolls called *bolillos* (boh-LEE-yohs), are generally found at small stands specializing in tortas.

We first tasted a torta after waiting in line outside a small shack in Mexico City. Sampling one of these well-packed, warm little bundles, served with its requisite selection of pickled vegetables, was well worth the wait.

Torta stands may be rare in your hometown (there are a few in Los Angeles), but you can taste the real thing in your own kitchen with any of these easy recipes.

Bolillos

Bolillos are a plain, crisp, white roll that you can use to make sandwiches or to eat with butter and jam at breakfast in Mexico. They are a delight to have in the house, but if you don't have the time, a good substitute is a small, crisp French roll or a light sourdough roll.

Always pull out the doughy filling of these rolls with your fingers before making tortas.

Special tools: *Electric mixer, pastry brush*

Preparation time: *25 minutes mixing, plus 30 minutes sitting and 1 hour and 30 minutes rising*

Cooking time: *25 minutes*

Yield: *12 6-inch rolls*

2 cups lukewarm water

2 ¼ ounce packages dry yeast

1 tablespoon sugar

¼ cup vegetable shortening

7 cups flour plus flour for coating work surface

1 tablespoon salt

½ cup milk

2 tablespoons vegetable oil for coating the bowl

1 tablespoon salt dissolved in ½ cup water for brushing

1 Preheat oven to 375°.

2 In a large mixing bowl or bowl of an electric mixer with a paddle, combine the water, yeast, and sugar. Stir to dissolve the yeast. Add the shortening and 2 cups of the flour and mix until smooth. Set aside at room temperature for 30 minutes.

3 Stir the salt into the milk and add to the flour mixture. With the machine running, gradually add the remaining 5 cups of flour until the dough pulls away from the sides of the bowl. Switch to the dough hook and knead at low speed for an additional 15 minutes. Transfer the dough to a lightly oiled bowl and turn to coat all sides of the dough. Cover with a damp towel and set aside to rise in a warm place until doubled in bulk, about 1 hour.

4 Punch down the dough and briefly knead on a lightly floured surface. Divide the dough into 12 portions. Roll each portion into a ball, or shape into a flat oval and pinch the ends. Place the balls on baking sheets with 2 inches between each, cover with a damp towel, and let rise, about 30 minutes, or until the dough holds a fingerprint when poked.

5 Brush the salt water over the rolls and bake for 20 to 30 minutes, until the crusts are golden brown. Cool and serve, or wrap well and freeze.

Barbecued Pork Torta

Roasted chicken or turkey is also delicious in this traditional barbecued sandwich (see photo in the color insert). If you prefer smoky, messy, meaty sandwiches, you'll love this one.

Preparation time: *5 minutes*

Cooking time: *10 minutes*

Yield: *4 sandwiches*

1 tablespoon vegetable oil

1 medium yellow onion, julienned

1 teaspoon salt

½ teaspoon pepper

2 poblano chiles, roasted, peeled, seeded, and julienned (see Chapter 3)

1 cup Adobo Sauce (see Chapter 14)

2 cups shredded or chopped roast pork

(continued)

4 bolillos, cut in half lengthwise and excess dough removed from both halves (see the recipe earlier in this chapter)

4 tablespoons mayonnaise

4 lettuce leaves

8 tomato slices

1 Heat the oil in a medium saucepan over medium-high heat. Sauté the onion with the salt and pepper until translucent. Add the chiles, Adobo Sauce, and pork. Cook, stirring well, just to heat through, about 3 minutes.

2 Spread the inside of each bolillo half with the mayonnaise. Line one half of each bolillo with a lettuce leaf and the other half with tomato slices. Spoon in the warm pork mixture, press together, and serve.

Chicken Black Bean Torta

A warm chicken sandwich such as this, served with interesting garnishes, is so much more satisfying than an ordinary cold meat sandwich.

Preparation time: *5 minutes*

Cooking time: *5 minutes*

Yield: *4 sandwiches*

2 tablespoons butter for spreading

4 bolillos, cut in half lengthwise and excess dough removed from both halves

1 cup Refried Black Beans (Chapter 10), or good-quality canned refried black beans

8 tablespoons (2 ounces) grated añejo cheese

1 chicken breast, cut into 4 thin slices crosswise and pounded to ⅛-inch thickness

Salt and pepper to taste

Olive oil for coating

1 cup Pickled Red Onions (see Chapter 14)

Freshly cracked black pepper

1 Preheat the broiler or prepare a medium-hot fire in a charcoal or gas grill.

2 Lightly butter both halves of the bolillos. Toast on the hot grill or under the broiler until golden, about 3 minutes. Spread the bottom halves with the black beans, sprinkle with cheese, and warm on a tray in the oven for about 5 minutes.

3 Season the chicken all over with salt and pepper. Lightly coat a skillet with the olive oil and place over high heat. Sauté the chicken for about 30 to 45 seconds per side, until cooked through. Place the chicken on the top halves of bread. Top with Pickled Red Onions and plenty of fresh cracked pepper. Close with the bean-lined halves of the bolillos and serve.

For a turkey torta, purchase thinly sliced, uncooked turkey breast slices and substitute for the chicken.

Vegetarian Torta

We've always taken great care in developing vegetarian recipes for our restaurants. In California, so many people want to eat vegetables that coming up with interesting ways to serve them is a pleasure and a challenge. This sandwich is a great place to use left-over grilled or roasted vegetables.

Preparation time: *5 minutes*

Cooking time: *10 minutes*

Yield: *4 sandwiches*

3 tablespoons vegetable oil for frying

2 medium boiled potatoes, cut in ¼-inch slices

4 bolillos, cut in half lengthwise and excess dough removed from both halves

4 tablespoons mayonnaise

1 cup Refried Black Beans (see Chapter 10), or good-quality canned refried beans

2 cups (8 ounces) grated Mexican manchego or Monterey Jack cheese

2 poblano chiles, roasted, peeled, seeded, and julienned

1 avocado, peeled, seeded, and sliced

2 cups shredded cabbage

4 tablespoons Crema (see Chapter 15)

Lime wedges for squeezing

1 Preheat the broiler.

2 Heat the vegetable oil in a medium-size skillet over medium-high heat. Fry the potato slices until golden brown on both sides, 2 to 3 minutes per side; drain on a paper towel lined plate.

3 Toast the bolillo halves under the broiler. Then coat both sides with mayonnaise. Spread the beans over the bottom halves, sprinkle with the cheese, and place on a baking tray. Place under the broiler just long enough to heat the beans and melt the cheese, about 3 minutes.

(continued)

4 Top the beans with the roasted chile strips, fried potato slices, avocado, and cabbage. Drizzle with Crema and the juice of a lime wedge. Cover with the top halves of the bread and serve.

One of my pet peeves is uncooked vegetables in a sandwich or a pizza. Vegetables, like everything else, need to be seasoned and cooked to develop their flavors. The only exceptions I can think of are lettuce, tomatoes, radish, and cucumbers. Okay, you caught me. Raw onion on a hamburger has also been known to pass my lips.

Part III
Enjoying an Extended Tour

The 5th Wave   By Rich Tennant

"Let me know when you've got enough lettuce on that taco."

In this part . . .

This is the meat of our book — a whole host of our tried and true recipes. You'll find recipes, tips, and hints for all sorts of food in this part, including traditional tamales and moles, our progressive salads and soups, and some all-time classic desserts.

Chapter 7

Stuffed Treats

- -

In This Chapter

▶ Snacking on savory empanadas

▶ Trying your hand at tamale making

▶ Stuffing chiles with success

- -

The foods in this chapter are among the most traditional and beloved in Mexico. All the recipes take some extra time to prepare because of the many steps and the handwork involved in wrapping the foods. But just like any carefully chosen gift, they are more special because of all that work.

Mexican cooks are expert at stuffed foods. For example, they know how to make hundreds of variations of tamales. They are skilled at stuffing flavored corn masa (corn dough enriched with lard) into corn husks, banana leaves, avocado leaves, or Swiss chard. They also are adept at folding the food wrapper into an ordinary rectangle, a trickier triangle, or a giant log shape that is later served in slices. The common quality that these inventive dishes share is the element of surprise that the package creates. Opening a corn husk, inhaling the spicy aroma, and then taking a bite is intrinsically more interesting than digging into the much more obvious steak on a plate.

In Mexico, specialty cooks often sell stuffed treats in the marketplace or at street stands. Typically, a woman who is known in her village for a specific tamale or empanada sells them each day at the market. Mexicans bring home empanadas and tamales as takeout foods, just as Americans stop at a deli counter to pick up something for dinner on the way home. These stuffed treats are considered too informal to be served in restaurants in Mexico, but in the United States, a dish that requires so much work ordinarily qualifies as restaurant food.

Tamales and empanadas, with their air of mystery and delicious savor, make great party foods. And chiles rellenos is one of the best known Mexican restaurant specialties. All are so special that they don't need much to accompany them. In their homelands, stuffed treats like these that take so much care and time to make often are served at holiday feasts.

Empanadas: Little Pies Full of Flavor

If you explore your local Spanish-speaking neighborhood and wander into a few small grocery stores or bakeries, you are sure to spot a fragrant stack of *empanadas* behind the counter. Sometimes they're big overstuffed half moons (see Figure 7-1), and sometimes they're delicate miniature pastries, but whatever shape they take, they have usually been crafted at home by a local cook.

Figure 7-1:
Bite into an
empanada
and find out
what's
inside.

With their irresistible savory fillings and neat handheld size, these little pastries are a popular snack food in most Latin American communities. In addition to making wonderful, interesting appetizers for a party at home, empanadas make a terrific lunch and are naturals for packing into picnic baskets and lunch boxes.

Empanadas de Picadillo

Picadillo is a dish from Spain. It contains highly seasoned, slightly sweetened, ground fried meat. In addition to making an excellent stuffing for these little turnovers, you also can use picadillo to stuff chiles for baking, to fill tacos, or to simply serve alongside rice and beans. You can make the dough recipe (which follows) a few days ahead and refrigerate it.

Special tools: Baking sheet, pastry brush

Preparation time: 20 minutes, plus 30 minutes chilling and 60 minutes to make the salsas

Cooking time: 35 minutes

Yield: 15 empanadas

1 pound lean ground beef	¼ teaspoon ground cloves
1 medium yellow onion, chopped	1 tablespoon brown sugar (optional)
2 cloves garlic, peeled and chopped	½ cup Red Roasted Tomato Salsa (see Chapter 5), or store-bought salsa
½ cup raisins, chopped	
½ cup green olives, chopped	Empanada Dough (see following recipe) or 1 pound frozen pie dough
1 teaspoon salt	
1 teaspoon pepper	1 egg combined with 2 tablespoons milk, lightly beaten for brushing on dough
2 teaspoons ground cumin	Garnish: Roasted Green Chile Salsa (see Chapter 5)

1 Brown the ground beef in a large heavy skillet over medium-high heat, stirring frequently, about 7 minutes. Drain off and discard the excess fat. Add the onion and sauté for 5 minutes. Then add the garlic, raisins, olives, salt, pepper, cumin, cloves, and brown sugar, if desired. Cook until their aromas are released, about 2½ minutes. Stir in the Red Roasted Tomato Salsa, bring to a boil, and set aside to cool.

2 Roll out the dough and cut into circles as described in the following recipe.

3 Place a generous tablespoon of the beef filling in the center of each pastry round. Fold over and press the edges together to seal. Transfer to a baking sheet and chill for a half hour, or wrap and freeze. (You don't have to defrost frozen empanadas before baking.)

4 Preheat the oven to 400°.

5 Brush the pastries all over with the egg wash and arrange in a single layer on a baking sheet. Bake until golden, about 15 minutes. Serve hot with the Roasted Green Chile Salsa.

For cocktail-size servings, we sometimes make empanadas into tiny bite-sized pieces. When cutting out the dough, make sure that each circle is large enough to stuff. You want each bite to contain both meat and pastry. We find a 3-inch circle is just the right size.

Empanada Dough

Feel free to substitute frozen pie dough from the supermarket for this recipe.

Preparation time: *20 minutes, plus 1 hour chilling*

2 cups flour plus additional for dusting

12 tablespoons cold butter

½ teaspoon salt

1 teaspoon sugar

¼ cup water

1 Combine the flour and butter in a large bowl. Lightly blend with your fingertips until the butter is evenly distributed in chunks. Dissolve the salt and sugar in the water and stir into the flour mixture.

2 On a lightly floured surface, turn out the mixture and lightly knead the dough until it forms a ball, adding a bit more water if necessary. Knead by pushing the ball of dough away from you with the heel of your hand, and then gathering it up, and making a quarter turn before repeating. Wrap in plastic and refrigerate for at least 1 hour or freeze as long as a week. Return to room temperature before rolling.

3 Divide the dough in half. On a floured board, roll out half the dough to a thickness of ⅛ inch. With a cookie cutter or a drinking glass, cut out 4-inch circles. Gather the scraps, add to the remaining dough, and reroll and cut out circles until all the dough is used.

Mushroom Empanadas

Mushrooms are a popular ingredient in Mexico. We love combining them with earthy corn dough rather than plain pastry, rich cheese, and a tart green salsa in these — our favorite empanadas (see photo in the color insert). The trick here is to roll the dough fairly thin and make sure that the filling has plenty of oomph! Epazote, a strong-tasting wild herb, can be found in Mexican markets. (See Chapter 2 for more information on epazote.)

Special tool: *Baking sheet*

Preparation time: *20 minutes, plus 30 minutes refrigeration and 15 minutes to make the Green Tomatillo Salsa*

Cooking time: *20 minutes*

Yield: *16 empanadas*

2 tablespoons butter

1 small yellow onion, diced

2 cloves garlic, peeled and minced

1 pound white or oyster mushrooms, cleaned, trimmed, and coarsely chopped

1½ teaspoons salt

½ teaspoon pepper

2 arbol chiles, stemmed, seeded, and finely ground, or ½ teaspoon cayenne pepper

1 bunch epazote or parsley, leaves only, coarsely chopped (½ cup)

1 cup (4 ounces) grated ranchero or Monterey Jack cheese

1 recipe Corn Tortilla dough (see Chapter 10)

¾ cup vegetable oil for frying

Garnishes: 1 cup Green Tomatillo Salsa (see Chapter 5), 1 cup shredded cabbage, and 1 cup Crema (see Chapter 15)

1 Melt the butter in a medium skillet over medium heat. Sauté the onions until they just begin to brown. Then stir in the garlic and cook until the aroma is released, about 1 minute. Add the mushrooms, salt, pepper, and chiles or cayenne. Continue cooking until the mushrooms soften, about 5 minutes. Stir in the epazote and cook briefly, about 1 minute. Set aside to cool. Stir in the cheese.

2 Divide the corn tortilla dough into 16 balls and flatten, between sheets of plastic wrap, to ¼-inch-thick circles that are 3 inches in diameter. Divide the cooled mushroom mixture into 16 portions.

3 Place one portion of the mushroom mixture in the center of each circle. Fold over to enclose the filling and tightly pinch the edges together to seal. Transfer to a baking sheet, cover with plastic wrap and refrigerate for a minimum of 30 minutes or up to 2 days.

4 Pour the oil into a medium saucepan to a depth of 1 inch. Heat over medium-high heat to 375°. When the oil is hot, fry the empanadas, a few at a time, until they color slightly and rise to the surface, about 4 to 5 minutes. Transfer to paper towels to drain.

5 Split each empanada open along the seam and top with 1 tablespoon each salsa, cabbage, and Crema. Serve hot.

In making any empanada or turnover, press the edges of the dough together carefully so that no filling peeks out. Otherwise, the package can spring a leak when it's frying or baking. Another trick to keep the pastry sealed is to chill empanadas before frying them.

Hot tamale hijinks

The best way to approach your first tamale-making experience is to draw up a game plan. First, call for a family powwow to discuss the advantages of teamwork or send out a desperate e-mail message suggesting that hungry friends join you in a wild culinary adventure. Then plan on making the filling and its sauce a day ahead. You also want to have the masa and corn husks ready just as your workers — oops! we mean guests — arrive.

When your team is in place, organize a space for all the assembling and divide the chores. Have someone cut the aluminum foil squares. Ask somebody to keep an eye on the water level in the steamer and check to see when the tamales are done. Keep the diagram for basic tamale folding (conveniently located in this chapter) posted for all to see. Then select someone to turn to Chapter 4 for expert advice on mixing the drinks.

Tamales: Feast-Day Treats

Tamale-making, like tamale-eating, is an activity meant to be shared. In Mexico, where tamales have been a fiesta food since the Indians first offered them to the gods, these labor-intensive stuffed and steamed packages are traditionally prepared by groups, in a sort of preparty party. The holiday they are most closely associated with in Mexico is All Saints' Day, while in America, tamales are a Christmas tradition.

We've tasted so many wonderful tamales in our travels, but two unusual ones really stand out. One tamale — called *brazo de reina,* or queen's arm — is an oversized tamale from the Yucatán that's made of ground pumpkin seeds and herbs mixed with masa and stuffed into a long banana leaf. We saw it served in slices for a special gathering. And the other tamale, which impressed us with its pre-Hispanic origins, was a simple tamale of rich, flavorful black beans and corn.

Wrapping a tamale

Before you can unwrap and enjoy the delicious filling of a tamale, you first need to create the tidy corn-husk packages. Just follow these steps (and have a look at Figure 7-2):

1. **Soak the dried corn husks in hot water for 2 hours or overnight.**

2. **Drain the corn husks on paper towels. Cut out 9-inch squares of aluminum foil. You'll need one for each tamale.**

3. **To wrap the tamales, spread 1 or 2 husks lengthwise on the counter with the narrow end pointing away from you. Spread about 2½ table-spoons of filling down the center, leaving about 2 inches bare at the top of the husk.**

4. **Fold over the sides and then the ends to enclose the filling. Place the folded tamale on a square of foil and fold over the foil to enclose the package. (You can also close the tamale with a strip of corn husk; see the recipe for Green Corn Tamales for instructions.) Repeat with the remaining filling and additional corn husks.**

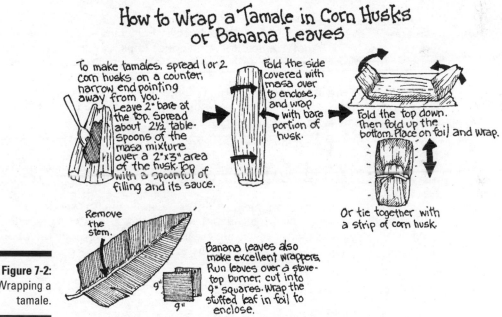

How to Wrap a Tamale in Corn Husks or Banana Leaves

To make tamales, spread 1 or 2 corn husks on a counter, narrow end pointing away from you. Leave 2" bare at the top. Spread about 2½ table-spoons of the masa mixture over a 2"x3" area of the husk. Top with a spoonful of filling and its sauce.

Fold the side covered with masa over to enclose, and wrap with bare portion of husk.

Fold the top down. Then fold up the bottom. Place on foil and wrap.

Or tie together with a strip of corn husk.

Remove the stem.

Banana leaves also make excellent wrappers. Run leaves over a stove-top burner, cut into 9" squares. Wrap the stuffed leaf in foil to enclose.

9"
9"

Figure 7-2: Wrapping a tamale.

Banana leaves also make excellent wrappers for tamales. To use, holding them in your hands, run the leaves directly over a stovetop gas or electric burner on low heat or place in a dry skillet for a few seconds. This process softens the leaves, makes them fragrant, and brightens the green color. Cut them into 9-inch squares, trimming out the tough center stem, and wrap the stuffed banana leaf in foil to enclose.

Steaming the tamales

Small batches of tamales can fit into a vegetable steamer basket, but for larger quantities, you need a steamer, which is a large pot with a perforated portion on top for the tamales.

Mexican corn tradition

Corn has been the symbol of sustenance since ancient times for the Mexican people. The Indian word for corn, *maiz,* means "sacred mother," or "giver of life." Among the legends surrounding this ancient source of nourishment is the belief that corn wasted or scattered on the ground complains to God. Another legend says that corn is afraid to be cooked, so a woman must warm the corn with her breath before it is cooked. And cornmeal sprinkled across the doorway reportedly keeps enemies out.

If you don't have a steamer, you can improvise by balancing a rack or colander on top of one or two empty cans or inverted coffee cups that are set in a large pasta or soup pot. Make sure that the water doesn't touch the rack's bottom.

Always keep an eye on the pot while the tamales are steaming so that the water doesn't get too low or entirely evaporate. And always line the steamer tray with extra husks to cushion the cooking process.

Tamales for every occasion

We've included some great tamale recipes for beginners in this section. Don't be daunted by a recipe's length or unfamiliar ingredients. Mastering tamale making is really just a matter of getting organized and setting aside the time, preferably with a group of friends, to dig in and cook.

Green Corn Tamales

The corn harvest is celebrated all over Latin America with different versions of these simple packets of sweet, fresh corn wrapped in corn husks. They're a good choice for the beginning tamale maker because they don't contain masa. These tamales are also a great choice for a party because everybody loves them. The flavors are simple and sweet. We've been serving them at a rapid clip for many years at our restaurants.

The *green* in Green Corn Tamales means that the corn is fresh rather than dried. It doesn't refer to the color of the corn, although fresh husks are green.

Special tool: *Steamer or pot fitted with a rack*

Preparation time: *15 minutes, plus 15 minutes to make the Fresh Salsa (does not include time to soften the corn husks)*

Cooking time: *1 hour and 15 minutes*

Yield: *10 to 12 tamales, or 6 servings*

3 tablespoons butter

½ cup hominy grits

3 cups canned corn, undrained (2 12-ounce cans)

½ teaspoon salt

¼ teaspoon pepper

Pinch of sugar, if necessary

½ cup milk

1 teaspoon baking powder

1 8-ounce package dried corn husks, softened (see "Wrapping a tamale" earlier in this chapter)

Garnishes: 1 recipe Fresh Salsa (see Chapter 5) and sour cream

1 Melt the butter in a large skillet over moderate heat. Add the grits and cook for about 4 minutes, until golden. Add the corn and its juices, the salt, pepper, the sugar if the corn isn't sweet, and the milk, and simmer until the mixture is thick as oatmeal, about 7 minutes. Set aside to cool until touchable. Then stir in the baking powder and reserve in the refrigerator.

2 Wrap the tamales in corn husks according to the instructions in "Wrapping a tamale" earlier in this chapter. You can skip the step of wrapping the package in foil. Instead, make ties for the tamales by cutting a few of the moistened husks into 6 by ¼-inch strips. Use the strips to tie the "package" closed with a double knot.

3 In a steamer or a pot fitted with a rack, make a bed for the tamales by laying the remaining corn husks on the bottom of the rack. Layer the tamales upright and steam over low heat for 1 hour. Remove from the steamer and let rest 10 minutes. Serve hot with the garnishes in bowls at the table.

 For sweetened fresh corn tamales, add ½ teaspoon ground cinnamon, ¼ teaspoon cloves, ¼ teaspoon nutmeg, and ½ cup raisins to the skillet when you add the corn. For a savory touch and some color, stir roasted and diced red or green bell peppers into the corn.

 Celebrate your own corn harvest by substituting 10 ears of fresh corn, with the kernels scraped off the cob and uncooked, in the Green Corn Tamales. Add about ½ cup cream. Save the green husks for wrapping, and then you'll realize how these tamales got their name.

All about masa

Masa means dough in Spanish. The masa used for making tamales, *masa para tamales,* is sold in the refrigerated section of supermarkets with a large Spanish clientele, or in ethnic markets. For this type of masa, dried corn is cooked with limestone and water and then coarsely ground for tamales. It resembles thick, light yellow, damp hominy grits and is packaged in plastic bags.

Lard realities

The rich, distinctive flavor of lard is an intrinsic part of the tamale experience. We understand that some of you may have hard and fast rules about eating that particular type of fat, but unless you are a vegetarian or don't eat pork for religious reasons, we want to argue for giving lard a chance, just this once. One-half cup of it beaten into 12 tamales is certainly no worse for you than eating a piece of bacon. And you'll be experiencing tamales as they were meant to be eaten.

Basic Masa Tamales with Fillings

Our basic masa tamale recipe is built for flexibility. First, we explain the technique for beating the masa, filling the corn husks, and then steaming. We follow that recipe with four options for savory fillings to flavor the masa — chiles and cheese, chicken and salsa, pork in adobo sauce, and leftover mole.

The salsas or sauces that go with the fillings are used in three ways: ½ cup gets beaten into the masa, ½ cup gets mixed into the filling, and the remaining ½ cup is served with the finished tamales.

Tamales as delicious as these deserve to be the main focus of a meal. The traditional accompaniments are rice and beans, but we prefer to serve them with something lighter. A trio of interesting salads, like the Fiesta Bean, Cactus Paddle, and Caesar Salads from Chapter 9, would be terrific, as would any big green salad.

You can store leftover tamales in the refrigerator as long as 4 days, or you can freeze them. Reheat for about 30 minutes in the steamer.

Special tools: Electric mixer, steamer or pot fitted with a rack

Preparation time: 30 minutes (not including the preparation time for the filling and sauce and softening time for corn husks)

Cooking time: 1 hour and 15 minutes (not including the preparation time for the filling and sauce)

Yield: 12 to 14 tamales

½ cup sauce from one of the filling recipes that follow this recipe

1 cup chicken stock (see Chapter 8), at room temperature

1 teaspoon baking soda

1½ teaspoons salt

1 pound cold prepared ground masa for tamales, or 1¾ cup dry masa harina, moistened with 1 cup warm water and then chilled

½ cup vegetable shortening or cold lard

1 8-ounce package dried corn husks, soft-ened (see "Wrapping a tamale" earlier in this chapter)

Fillings and sauces (see the following recipes)

Garnish: Sour cream

1 Mix together ½ cup of the salsa or sauce from one of the fillings, the chicken stock, baking soda, and salt and set aside.

2 Place the masa in the bowl of an electric mixer and beat at medium speed until light in texture, about 6 minutes. Slowly add the chicken stock mixture while beating continu-ously at medium-high speed. Turn the mixer speed up to high and add the shortening or lard, a tablespoon at a time, beating well after each addition. Continue beating and scraping down the bowl until the mixture is light and fluffy, about 15 minutes total. Test for lightness by dropping 1 tablespoon of masa into cold water: If it floats, the mixture is light enough. If not, continue beating at high speed a few minutes longer.

3 Wrap the tamales according to the instructions in "Wrapping a tamale" earlier in this chapter, spreading about 2½ tablespoons of the masa mixture over a 2-by-3-inch area of husk. Top with a spoonful of filling and its sauce.

4 To cook, line a steamer with corn husks and fill with tamales, upright in layers. Cook over simmering water for 1 hour and 15 minutes, until the husks just pull away from the masa without sticking. Serve hot with the remaining sauce and sour cream. (Cold tamales can be reheated in a steamer over simmering water for 30 minutes.)

Green Chile Cheese Filling

If you like chile rellenos, you'll love this similar combination of roasted green chiles and luscious rich cheese (see photo in the color insert). It's amazing that all it takes is a great cheese and a great salsa to make a terrific tamale.

Preparation time: *15 minutes, plus 15 minutes to make the Green Tomatillo Salsa*

Yield: *12 to 14 tamales*

1½ cups Green Tomatillo Salsa (see Chapter 5)

4 poblano chiles, roasted, peeled, seeded, and cut into ½-inch strips

1 pound Mexican cheese, such as Ranchero, queso fresco, panela, or manchego, cut into ½-inch cubes (about 3 cups)

In a large mixing bowl, combine ½ cup of the salsa, the chiles, and the cheese. (Reserve ½ cup of the salsa to incorporate into the masa.) Serve the remaining ½ cup of salsa alongside the finished tamales.

Roasted Tomato Chicken Filling

Olives and raisins add sweet and salty accents to this easy chicken filling.

Preparation time: *5 minutes, plus 35 minutes to make the Red Roasted Tomato Salsa*

Cooking time: *15 minutes*

Yield: *12 to 14 tamales*

1½ cups Red Roasted Tomato Salsa (see Chapter 5)

2 cups shredded cooked chicken

½ cup green olives, pitted

½ cup golden raisins

In a medium saucepan over medium heat, combine ½ cup of the salsa, the chicken, olives, and raisins. Simmer for about 15 minutes, until heated through. (Reserve ½ cup of the salsa to incorporate into the masa.) Serve the remaining ½ cup salsa alongside the finished tamales.

Pork and Green Chile Adobo Filling

Rich pork and spicy green chiles on a steaming bed of corn masa are a tough combination to beat.

Preparation time: *5 minutes, plus 1 hour 20 minutes to make the Adobo Sauce*

Cooking time: *15 minutes*

Yield: *12 to 14 tamales*

1½ cups Adobo Sauce (see Chapter 14)

2 cups shredded, cooked pork

1 poblano chile, roasted, peeled, seeded and cut into ½-inch wide strips

In a medium saucepan over medium heat, combine ½ cup of the Adobo Sauce, the pork, and the chile. Simmer for about 15 minutes, until heated through. (Reserve ½ cup of the sauce to incorporate into the masa.) Serve the remaining ½ cup sauce alongside the finished tamales.

Chicken Mole Filling

Serve these festive, rich tamales at holiday time when you need a make-ahead menu for a buffet.

Preparation time: *5 minutes, plus 2 hours 10 minutes to make the Mole Sauce*

Cooking time: *15 minutes*

Yield: *12 to 14 tamales*

1½ cups Mole Sauce (see Chapter 15) or store-bought mole sauce

1½ cups cooked shredded meat from mole recipe in Chapter 11

In a medium saucepan over medium heat, combine ½ cup of the mole and the shredded meat. Simmer for about 15 minutes, until heated through. (Reserve ½ cup of the mole to incorporate into the masa.) Serve the remaining ½ cup of mole alongside the finished tamales.

Chiles Rellenos

If your guests are full-fledged chile fanatics, you can't go wrong with a dish featuring whole stuffed chiles, known as *chiles rellenos* (CHEE-lehs reh-YEH-nohs).

Both of the recipes in this section are a bit fancier than tamales or empanadas (they are sit-down, rather than stand-up, foods). But, like other stuffed treats, they also derive much of their savor from the blending that occurs when a food is wrapped and then cooked. The edible wrapper, in this case the smoky, roasted poblano, seals in and intensifies the flavor of the stuffing, while its own juices soak in and enrich the final product.

Classic Chiles Rellenos

These crisply coated, deep-fried chiles are a standby at any good Mexican restaurant. Stuffed chiles can be made and refrigerated up to a day in advance for easy preparation. If you find the filling too rich, feel free to add some other vegetables like corn kernels or peas to the cheese.

(continued)

Special tool: *Baking sheet*

Preparation time: *45 minutes, plus 50 minutes to make the salsas*

Cooking time: *30 minutes*

Yield: *4 servings, 8 chiles*

3 cups (12 ounces) grated Mexican manchego or Monterey Jack cheese

½ cup (2 ounces) grated panela cheese

½ cup (2 ounces) grated añejo cheese

8 medium poblano chiles, roasted and peeled

⅓ cup flour for coating the chiles

4 eggs, separated

½ teaspoon salt

½ teaspoon pepper

Vegetable oil for frying

1 cup Red Roasted Tomato Salsa (see Chapter 5)

1 cup Green Tomatillo Salsa (see Chapter 5)

Garnish: 6 tablespoons Crema (see Chapter 15)

1 Combine the cheeses in a large bowl and divide into 8 equal portions.

2 With a sharp paring knife, carefully make a lengthwise slit in each chile. Cut out and discard the stems, seeds, and veins. Mold the cheese mixture portions into torpedo shapes and place one inside each chile. Roll each chile to completely enclose the cheese and reserve in the refrigerator for up to 8 hours.

3 Preheat the oven to 350°.

4 On a counter near the stovetop, spread the flour on a plate or a piece of wax paper. In a clean bowl, whisk the egg whites with the salt until stiff. In another large, wide mixing bowl, beat the yolks with the pepper until smooth. Fold the beaten whites into the yolks and place near the flour.

5 Dip each stuffed chile in the flour, taking care to coat completely. Thoroughly pat off any excess flour with your hands.

6 Pour about 1 inch of vegetable oil into a wide cast-iron skillet. Place over moderate heat until almost smoking, about 350°. Dip two chiles at a time in the beaten eggs and roll them around in the eggs until entirely coated. (No green should be showing.)

7 Gently lift the chiles out with the palm of your hand, one at a time, and holding your hand just above the oil, slide the chile into the pan. Fry until lightly browned, and then turn with a slotted spoon and brown the other side. Lift from the oil with a slotted spoon and drain on a paper towel-lined baking sheet. When all 8 chiles are cooked, remove the paper and transfer to the oven for 5 minutes or until the cheese is entirely melted.

8 To serve, coat 4 plates with half red and half green salsa and place 2 chiles on each plate. Top with Crema and serve immediately.

Because roasted peppers are slippery to handle, at our restaurants we place the chiles on a kitchen towel for easier rolling.

Finding poblano chiles for stuffing is worth the search. Not only do they have the best flavor, but their wide shoulders and thick flesh make them easier for stuffing. Remember that a chile's spiciness varies according to growing conditions. Turn to Chapter 2 for an in-depth discussion on chiles.

Corn-and-Cheese-Stuffed Chiles in Red Rice

We prefer a lighter, unfried, easier stuffed chile like this for weeknight entertaining. You can avoid last-minute jitters by putting the casserole together in the morning or the night before and then just placing it in the oven right before your guests arrive.

Preparation time: *15 minutes, plus 35 minutes to make the Red Roasted Tomato Salsa, 20 minutes to roast the chiles, and 50 minutes to make the rice*

Cooking time: *35 minutes*

Yield: *6 servings*

4 tablespoons butter or oil

1 medium yellow onion, chopped

2 cloves garlic, peeled and minced

3 cups fresh or thawed frozen corn kernels (about 6 ears fresh corn or 2 10-ounce packages, frozen)

1½ teaspoons coarse salt

1 teaspoon pepper

1 cup (4 ounces) grated manchego or Monterey Jack cheese

6 large poblano chiles, roasted and peeled (see Chapter 3)

4 cups cooked white rice

1 cup Crema (see Chapter 15)

1 cup Red Roasted Tomato Salsa (see Chapter 5)

½ cup (2 ounces) grated añejo cheese

1 Preheat the oven to 350°.

2 Melt the butter in a medium saucepan over medium heat. Sauté the onion for about 5 minutes until translucent. Add the garlic and cook for 1 minute longer. Add the corn, salt, and pepper, and sauté until tender, about 2½ minutes. Transfer to a bowl and cool. Stir in the manchego or Monterey Jack cheese and set aside.

(continued)

3 Carefully slit the chiles lengthwise, removing the seeds and veins, leaving the stems and tops intact if possible. Stuff the chiles with the corn mixture.

4 Arrange the rice in a shallow buttered roasting pan or casserole. Nestle the chiles in the rice in a single layer. Mix together the Crema and Red Roasted Tomato Salsa and pour over all. Sprinkle with the añejo cheese and transfer to the oven. Bake for about 25 minutes, until heated through. Serve hot.

In any stuffed chile dish, start with well-roasted chiles. If they are not thoroughly roasted, they won't be pliable, which makes stuffing the chiles difficult, plus you'll miss out on the important roasted flavor.

Chapter 8

Soulful Soups

• •

In This Chapter

▶ Making soup, Mexican style

▶ Hearing the garnishing truth

▶ Stock-making and freezing tips

▶ Discovering sopas, posoles, and caldos

• •

*T*here is nothing complicated about making Mexican soups. No silky smooth bisques require multiple strainings, no expensive ingredients like lobster or crab make you check your credit card balance, and no delicate techniques set your teeth on edge. With just a few simple ingredients and the push of a blender button, you'll be making the kind of flavorful, satisfying soups that mean pleasure in any language.

Setting Your Sights on Mexican Soups

Mexican soups are a snap to prepare, once you have the right tools and a few tips under your cooking belt.

Putting all your soup in the right pot

Any large cylindrical pot will do for making Mexican soup, but here are some pointers if you're in the market for a new pot:

▸ Bigger is better when choosing pots for making soup. If you're going to splurge on a new stockpot, go for the 12-quart size for maximum versatility. You may never fill a large pot, but the good news is that you'll rarely have to worry about overflows onto your sparkly clean stovetop.

- Aluminum is fine for a soup pot. It conducts heat well and is less expensive than stainless steel. Just make sure that the pot is heavy-bottomed or lined with copper on the bottom so that it doesn't warp over time.

- You want a soup pot to be heavy, but not too heavy. A 12-quart pot made of enameled cast-iron could be a problem to lift once it's full of liquid.

- Handles on either side for easy lifting and a tight-fitting lid are lovely features of a soup pot.

And don't forget to have a ladle — the stockpot's best friend — for gracefully transferring liquids.

Discovering the art of the garnish

As chefs, we've had to face the cold hard facts. Probably some people do not follow our recipes exactly, especially when it comes to that long list of garnishes at the end of our soup recipes. Some of you may even ignore garnishing altogether — a thought we prefer not to entertain.

Here's how we feel about garnishes: All these soups can be served without any garnish — they will still taste terrific. We develop the garnishes to enhance the look of a dish and add contrasting tastes and textures. The garnish elevates the soup from something simple to something exquisite. To us, garnishes are so integral to the dish that it pains us to see people garnishing improperly. (Susan has been known to scowl at bad garnishers and fix their soup bowls for them.) We add salsa to earthy bean soup for a fresh note of acidity and a bright dash of color, and we arrange strips of avocado on lime soup to mellow out the acidity. And garnishes of corn chips add crunch to many types of soup.

At home, we know that you need to stay flexible so that cooking isn't a chore. Use the garnishes you have on hand and substitute where possible. Here are some good standbys for common garnishes:

- Crushed corn chips for fried tortilla strips

- Lemon or vinegar for lime

- Parsley or basil for cilantro (although the taste of cilantro is unique)

- Jack, feta, and Parmesan cheese for Mexican cheeses (see Chapter 2 for more on Mexican cheeses and substitutions)

Freezing soups

Most soups are ideal for freezing. You can make soup whenever you have the time and then freeze it and serve it later — without any loss of quality.

A squirt of lime

The one ingredient essential to Mexican soup making is that final wedge of lime, squirted and then tossed into the bowl right before serving. That splash of fresh acidity freshens all the other flavors and brings them up a note. Try a wedge of lime in your next winter vegetable soup or bowl of chili for a Mexican twist.

It's best to cool a pot of soup down before storing it in your freezer or refrigerator so that the heat from the soup doesn't lower the temperature inside the freezer.

Here's an easy way to cool your soup: Fill a sink with iced water and lower the hot pot into it. Stir occasionally until the entire soup is cool to the touch. Then store the soup in plastic containers, with an inch of air at the top, and freeze as long as 2 months.

Creating your own stock

If you want to taste the difference between good and great, compare a soup made with homemade stock with a soup made with canned stock or bouillon cubes. Wow!

Good stock recipes are available in any all-purpose cookbook, but here are some general guidelines for the two we use most often.

Chicken stock

To make about 3 quarts (12 cups) of chicken stock, just follow these steps:

1. **Combine about 2½ pounds chicken bones (or backs and wings, including turkey wings, with the meat attached are great), 1 coarsely chopped celery stalk, 1 onion, and 2 carrots in a stockpot.**

2. **Add enough water to cover generously, along with ½ bunch fresh or 1 tablespoon dried parsley or thyme, 1 tablespoon salt, ½ tablespoon peppercorns, and 4 bay leaves.**

3. **Bring to a boil, reduce to a simmer, and cook, uncovered, about 1½ hours. Check the pot occasionally and skim and discard the foam from the top.**

4. **Let the stock cool in the pot and then pour through a strainer, discarding the solids.**

You can store this chicken stock in sealed containers in the refrigerator for up to 5 days or in the freezer as long as 3 months. Remove the layer of fat from the top and discard, or save for sautéing.

Vegetable stock

To make about 2½ quarts (10 cups) vegetable stock, follow these steps:

1. **Combine chopped vegetables such as 2 onions, 1 parsnip, 2 celery ribs, 2 carrots, and 1 fennel bulb in a large pot. Add 2 chopped tomatoes, 6 corn cobs (without the kernels), 6 garlic cloves, 1 bunch of parsley or thyme, 2 bay leaves, 3 cloves, and plenty of black peppercorns and salt.**

2. **Add enough water to cover, bring to a boil, reduce to a simmer, and cook, uncovered, about 1½ hours. Check the pot occasionally and skim and discard the foam from the top.**

3. **Let the soup cool in the pot and then pour through a strainer, discarding the solids.**

Using canned stocks

When you just don't have the time or energy to make stock from scratch, use canned chicken or vegetable broth and add some water to dilute the salty taste.

The typical can of chicken broth contains 14½ ounces, so, by pouring the contents of the can into a 2 cup measure and then adding water to the 2 cup level, you can get about 2 cups of stock from each can.

Soup is for tasting

Taste, taste, taste your soup before adjusting seasonings with salt and pepper at the end of the cooking time. The saltiness of any finished soup depends on the saltiness of the broth you used for cooking. Because canned stock and bouillon cubes are quite salty to begin with, and boiling intensifies flavors, you may not need salt at all at the end of cooking.

So Many Sopas, So Little Time

Mexican cooks make several types of brothy dishes, but the most popular are the thinner broths referred to as *sopas* (Spanish for "soups"). They run the gamut from rich creamed vegetable soups, to cold gazpacho, to the thin and familiar tortilla soup, but the unifying thread is that all are light enough to be eaten as a first course.

Sopa secas are leftover sopas in which the liquid has been absorbed enough for the dish to be eaten as a side dish or starter, with a fork.

Tangy Cold Avocado Soup

We don't often use water in our soup making, but this velvety green soup doesn't need the enhancement of a stock. It is full of flavor and richness from the avocado and has just the right note of tartness from the tomatillos. (Chapter 2 tells you everything you need to know about tomatillos.) This is a good dish to make in the summertime when your avocados are just the other side of ripe.

Special tool: *Blender or food processor*

Preparation time: *15 minutes*

Yield: *6 servings (8 cups)*

8 tomatillos, roughly chopped (about 2 cups)

2 jalapeño chiles, roasted and seeded (see Chapter 3)

Juice of 1 lime (2 tablespoons)

Juice of ½ orange (¼ cup)

1 teaspoon salt

½ teaspoon black pepper

1 cup cold water plus enough ice cubes to bring water to 2 cups in a liquid measure

2 ripe avocados, peeled and seeded

Garnish: 1 bunch scallions, thinly sliced (⅔ cup)

Combine the tomatillos, jalapeños, lime and orange juices, salt, pepper, and a tablespoon or two of the ice water in a blender or food processor. Puree until smooth. Add the avocados with the remaining water mixture and puree briefly, just until smooth. Serve in chilled bowls with the scallions scattered on top.

 Watch that trigger finger when you push the puree button! This recipe calls for just a few seconds or pulses. Lengthy processing incorporates too much air, giving the soup a frothy head, which is great for a beer but not desirable in a soup.

 To accessorize this acidy green soup for a party, try a dollop of your favorite red salsa in the center or, better yet, drizzle it freehand from a spoon. Chopped tomatoes or strips of roasted red pepper also add a nice spot of color. Or for a lovely rich, green salad dressing, omit the ice cubes and use less water — about ½ cup.

Tomatillo and Chicken Chilaquiles

Chilaquiles (chee-lah-KEE-lehs), a homey dish of day-old tortillas and salsa, is eaten all over Mexico as a hearty breakfast or light midday meal. This version is wet enough to serve as a soup, but if you wait a day, the tortillas absorb enough liquid to turn it into a sopa seca, or dry soup.

This recipe provides a great use for leftover chicken meat. Just start the cooking at Step 2 with ½ pound of cooked, shredded chicken.

Preparation time: *10 minutes, plus 15 minutes for the Green Tomatillo Salsa*

Cooking time: *30 minutes*

Yield: *4 servings*

6 cups chicken stock (see the "Chicken stock" section in this chapter)

½ pound boneless, skinless chicken breasts

Salt and pepper to taste

2 tablespoons vegetable oil

1 medium yellow onion, thinly sliced

3 cloves garlic, crushed and peeled

2 cups Green Tomatillo Salsa (see Chapter 5)

7 small (6-inch) corn tortillas, or about 3 dozen tortilla chips

½ bunch cilantro leaves, chopped (½ cup)

Garnishes: ¼ cup (1 ounce) grated añejo cheese, ½ cup diced onion, and ½ cup Crema (see Chapter 15)

1 Bring the chicken stock to a boil in a deep skillet. Sprinkle the chicken breasts with salt and pepper and add to the stock. Simmer, covered, for 8 to 10 minutes. (Don't boil the stock to avoid toughening the meat.)

2 Remove the chicken breasts from the skillet, wrap them in a damp tea towel, and set aside to cool. When they're cool enough to handle, shred the chicken into long strips. Reserve the stock.

3 Heat the oil in a stockpot over medium heat. Sauté the onion with salt and pepper until soft. Add the garlic and cook for about 3 minutes, until the aroma is released. Add the salsa and bring to a boil. Pour in the reserved chicken stock and simmer for 10 minutes.

4 Cut fresh tortillas into ½-inch strips and fry according to the instructions in Chapter 10.

5 Add the shredded chicken to the stock pot and season with salt and pepper. Bring to a boil and stir in the cilantro and fried tortilla strips or chips. Simmer 5 minutes longer. Ladle into 4 bowls. Garnish with the cheese, onion, and a dollop of Crema. Serve hot.

For breakfast chilaquiles, top each serving with a fried egg.

Gazpacho

Gazpacho is a perfect first course for just about anything you choose to serve in the heat of the summer — except for a tomato-based entrée.

Gazpacho is one of those simple uncooked dishes where a quality olive oil makes a great deal of difference. So haul out that expensive extra-virgin olive oil you got as a present for your last birthday and let it pour. You won't regret it.

This soup keeps in the refrigerator up to 2 days.

Special tool: *Blender or food processor*

Preparation time: *20 minutes, plus 2 hours chilling time*

Yield: *4 to 6 servings*

1 slice white bread, crusts removed	*2 cloves garlic, peeled*
2 tablespoons red wine vinegar	*½ cup extra-virgin olive oil*
3 cups tomato juice, plus more if needed to thin the soup	*3 jalapeño chiles, stemmed, seeded, and chopped*
6 pickling cucumbers, peeled, seeded, and diced	*1 teaspoon sugar*
	¾ teaspoon salt
4 scallions, thinly sliced	*½ teaspoon black pepper*
1 red bell pepper, seeded and diced	*Garnish: Sliced chives*

1 Place the bread on a plate, sprinkle it with the vinegar, and let sit until thoroughly moistened, 5 minutes.

2 Combine the tomato juice, cucumbers, scallions, and red pepper in a large bowl.

3 Transfer about one-fourth of the vegetable mixture to a blender or food processor. Add the moistened bread, garlic, olive oil, jalapeños, sugar, salt, and pepper. Puree until smooth.

4 Pour the puree into the bowl with the vegetables. Stir to combine. Thin with more tomato juice if desired and adjust seasonings. Chill for at least 2 hours. Serve cold and garnish with chives.

 Because the taste of tomato juice is so dominant in Gazpacho, the juice you choose is important. As a serious tomato juice sipper, I advise you to read the labels carefully before purchasing a juice. Briskly reject any juices with weird ancillary ingredients. If nature intended bisulfates to be in tomato juice, she would have put them in tomatoes. Don't even think about buying any tomato juices containing sugar or Bloody Mary spices. No way — not in this delicious soup. Tomatoes and salt are all you really want to see on that label.

(continued)

To turn this refreshing soup into a meal, try placing a pile of cold Aztecan Quinoa Salad (see Chapter 9) in the center of a shallow soup bowl and pouring the soup around it (see photo in the color insert). At the restaurant, we mold the quinoa in a *timbale* (a small ceramic mold) or custard cup and invert it onto the dish for a more polished look. If you like rice in your soup, you'll love this soup and grain combination.

I'm a gazpacho nut. I've tasted gazpacho all over Spain and Mexico, and believe me, this recipe is the best. It tastes as though it's loaded with cream, though it doesn't contain any, and it feels sophisticated, though it's easy to prepare. It's great for summer picnics and barbecues!

Corn and Chile Chowder

You can make this lovely corn soup all year-round if you use an excellent canned or frozen corn. It makes a nice first course for a dinner party with a grilled meat entrée.

To make the Corn and Chile Chowder or any milk-based soup in advance and freeze, cook until the end of Step 1. Then freeze. To defrost and finish, warm the corn mixture in a soup pot and continue the recipe at Step 2.

Special tool: *Blender or food processor*

Preparation time: *20 minutes*

Cooking time: *40 minutes*

Yield: *4 to 6 servings (6 cups)*

2 tablespoons olive oil

1 medium yellow onion, diced

1 teaspoon salt

4 cups fresh or canned corn kernels, drained (8 ears fresh corn, 2½ 12-ounce cans, or 3 10-ounce packages, frozen)

2 to 3 cloves garlic, peeled and minced

1 teaspoon ground cumin

3 poblano or Anaheim chiles, roasted, peeled, seeded, and diced (see Chapter 3)

2 cups milk or half-and-half

2 cups chicken stock (see the "Chicken stock" section in this chapter)

Garnish: ½ bunch chives, thinly sliced diagonally (¼ cup)

1 Heat the olive oil in a large stockpot over medium heat. Sauté the onion with the salt until golden brown, about 15 minutes. Add the corn, turn the heat to high, and cook for 5 to 7 minutes, until slightly browned. Stir in the garlic and cumin and cook, stirring frequently, 2 minutes longer. Reduce the heat to low, stir in the chiles, and cook for 2 to 3 more minutes.

2 Pour in the milk and chicken stock. Bring to a simmer over low heat, being careful not to boil. Gently simmer, uncovered, for 15 minutes.

3 Pour one-third of the soup into a food processor or blender and puree. Stir back into the stock pot and simmer for 5 minutes longer. Serve hot, garnished with chives.

If you can't get your hands on the more exotic chiles, substitute 2 green bell peppers and 2 jalapeño chiles, both roasted and diced. (Remember that you can order some chiles from many of the Web sites mentioned in Chapter 21.)

Tortilla Soup

Tortilla soup, probably the best-known of the Mexican soups, is a brilliant use of two common Mexican leftovers — tortillas and salsa.

If you don't feel like making the Red Roasted Tomato Salsa first, you can substitute a favorite bottled smooth red salsa. You can also simply puree the following ingredients in the blender: 1½ pounds of Roma tomatoes, 6 cloves garlic, 1 small yellow onion, and ½ cup water and add to the pot along with the stock.

Preparation time: *15 minutes, plus 15 minutes for Red Roasted Tomato Salsa*

Cooking time: *1 hour*

Yield: *6 servings*

3 tablespoons olive oil

1 large yellow onion, diced

3 cloves garlic, peeled and minced

2 cups Red Roasted Tomato Salsa (see Chapter 5)

5 cups chicken stock (see the "Chicken stock" section in this chapter)

1 dried chipotle chile, stemmed and seeded (optional)

1 teaspoon salt

¾ pound fried tortilla chips (see Chapter 10)

Garnishes: 1 bunch cilantro leaves (½ cup); 1 avocado, peeled, seeded, and coarsely chopped; ½ cup Crema (see Chapter 15); 2 limes, cut in wedges

(continued)

1 Heat the olive oil in a large stockpot over low heat. Add the onion and cook, stirring frequently, until pale brown and caramelized, 10 to 15 minutes. Stir in the garlic and cook 10 minutes longer.

2 Pour in the tomato salsa, chicken stock, chipotle chile (if desired), and salt. Bring to a boil, reduce to a simmer, and cook, uncovered, for 20 minutes. Stir in the fried tortilla chips and cook 10 minutes longer, until the chips soften. Remove and discard the chile. Serve hot, topped with cilantro, avocado, Crema, and lime wedges.

Toasted Angel Hair Soup

In this classic soup, called *fideo* (fee-DEH-oh) in Spanish, the noodles are toasted to bring a typical Mexican smokiness to the broth. You can use any thin pasta in small pieces. Mary Sue recommends orzo, the tiny rice-shaped pasta, as one of her favorites.

Special tool: *Blender*

Preparation time: *10 minutes*

Cooking time: *30 minutes*

Yield: *6 servings*

⅓ cup olive oil

8 ounces dried angel hair pasta, broken into 1-inch pieces

3 dried chipotle chiles

1½ pounds Roma tomatoes

6 cloves garlic, peeled

1 medium yellow onion, coarsely chopped

½ cup water

2 teaspoons salt

6 cups chicken or vegetable stock (see the "Creating your own stock" section in this chapter)

Garnishes: 1 avocado, peeled, seeded, and sliced, and 1 bunch chopped cilantro leaves (½ cup)

1 Heat the olive oil in a large stockpot over medium-low heat. Sauté the pasta, stirring frequently, until golden brown, being careful not to burn. Then stir in the chiles and cook for 2 minutes longer.

2 Meanwhile, combine the tomatoes, garlic, onion, water, and salt in a blender. Puree until smooth.

3 Add the tomato puree and chicken or vegetable stock to the stockpot. Bring to a boil and reduce to a simmer. Cook until the noodles soften and the flavors meld, about 15 minutes. Remove and discard the whole chiles. Serve hot, garnished with avocado and cilantro.

To totally demystify Toasted Angel Hair Soup, which is my favorite Mexican soup, I like to describe it as Mexican Chicken Noodle Soup. It's similar to brand-name soups but just a bit deeper and spicier.

Do not, we repeat, *do not* shortchange the all-important sautéing step at the beginning of this recipe. If you do, you might as well be eating any old chicken noodle soup. Susan will be disappointed. Anyway, you bought a Mexican cookbook to cook Mexican style, and that's what the browning step is all about.

Creamed Summer Squash Soup

Smooth creamed soups, such as this lovely one for summer, aren't often associated with the Mexican-American kitchen. But in Mexico they are common and delicious first courses. This soup is great for summer gardeners, who just may find that they have more squash on hand than they bargained for in the springtime.

Special tools: *Blender or food processor, strainer*

Preparation time: *10 minutes*

Cooking time: *40 minutes*

Yield: *8 servings (8 cups)*

4 tablespoons butter

1 large yellow onion, sliced

1 teaspoon salt

½ teaspoon black pepper

2 cloves garlic, peeled and sliced

6 cups vegetable stock or water (see the "Vegetable stock" section in this chapter)

1 pound small zucchini or pattypan squash, thinly sliced

2 cups half-and-half

Salt and pepper to taste

Garnishes: ½ cup (2 ounces) grated añejo cheese and 1 lime, cut in wedges

1 Melt the butter in a stockpot over moderate heat. Sauté the onion with the salt and pepper for about 5 minutes. Add the garlic and cook 1 to 2 minutes longer. Pour in the vegetable stock or water. Bring to a boil, reduce to a simmer, and cook for 10 minutes. Stir in the squash and cook for 5 minutes longer.

2 Transfer the soup to a blender or food processor and puree until smooth. Strain back into the stockpot. Add the half-and-half and bring to a boil. Season with salt and pepper. Serve hot, garnished with the cheese and the lime wedges.

(continued)

To cut calories, use half the butter called for in the recipe and substitute 1 percent nonfat milk for the half-and-half. If you garden or visit a farmer's market in the summer, you may want to try this soup with the flowers of the zucchini plant, or zucchini blossoms, as it might be made in Oaxaca; the flavor of flowers is like essence of zucchini. Substitute about 8 cups of flowers for the zucchini or squash, and use the flowers exactly as you would the squash. Carefully open and examine blooms for bugs before cooking.

I'll try almost anything once (see Chapter 1 for proof), but when it comes to bugs, I pass. There's such a thing as too much protein. Always rinse all fruits and vegetables well to remove any garden critters before cooking.

Pinto Bean Soup with Fresh Salsa

This wholesome bean soup doesn't contain a lot of distractions. It derives its creamy, luxurious texture from the beans themselves. If you don't have time to make the Fresh Salsa, bottled salsa will do just fine.

Special tool: *Blender*

Preparation time: *15 minutes*

Cooking time: *1½ hours for beans, plus an additional 45 minutes*

Yield: *8 servings (8 cups)*

1½ cups dry pinto beans	*3 cloves garlic, peeled and minced*
7 cups water	*6 cups chicken or vegetable stock (see the "Creating your own stock" section in this chapter) or water*
¼ cup olive oil	
1½ medium yellow onions, diced	*Garnishes: Fresh Salsa (see Chapter 5) and Crema (see Chapter 15)*
Salt and pepper to taste	

1 Combine the beans and water in a large pot over high heat and bring to a boil. Reduce to a simmer and cook, covered, until the beans are tender but still firm, about 1 hour and 15 minutes. Stir the pot occasionally. Remove from heat.

2 In another large saucepan, heat the olive oil over medium heat. Sauté the onions with the salt and pepper until lightly browned, about 10 minutes. Then add the garlic and cook a few minutes longer. Add beans and their liquid, and the stock or additional water. Bring to a boil and reduce to a simmer. Cook, uncovered, stirring occasionally, 25 minutes longer.

3 Transfer to a blender and puree in batches until smooth. Return to the pot and warm over low heat, stirring frequently, until ready to serve. Serve hot with the salsa and Crema as garnish.

Boiling the beans before soup making replaces the overnight soaking stage that a lot of old bean recipes call for. After the beans have been softened by boiling, you can set them aside in their water and cook the soup a few hours later or the next day. Refrigerate the beans if saving them overnight. (See Chapter 3 for more about bean cookery.)

Bean soups need lots of stirring so that the same beans don't sit at the bottom and scorch, so stay nearby.

How we fell in love (with Mexican soups)

We first fell in love with the big, bracing soups of Mexico because they offered a change. After years of fine dicing and straining vegetables into oblivion to make classic French soups, we found that the rustic Mexican sopas with their rough-hewn chunks of *chayote* (chah-YOH-the), a common Mexican squash, and large shreds of chicken were just what we craved. But now, after cooking and eating them for years, our attraction is more than mere infatuation.

We love the roasty, toasty fragrance that permeates so many of these soups. We love the play of textures when crunchy tortillas, sharp raw onions, fragrant cilantro, spicy jalapeños, buttery avocados, and citrusy lime all mingle a while in a big bowl of rich chicken broth. We love the elegance of Mexico's creamed soups, which highlight one simple ingredient like squash. And finally, we are suckers for the more complex *posoles* (poh-SOH-lehs), in which long-cooked meat and vegetables are contrasted with the crisp freshness of chopped salad.

The Caldo Connection

Caldos (KAHL-dohs) are hearty broths filled with large enough chunks of meats and vegetables to make them a meal. Chicken soup, or *caldo de pollo* (KAHL-doh deh POH-yoh), is often such a light meal, eaten with toasted tortillas. What could be finer than a nice, bubbling hot caldo waiting on the stove after a day spent outdoors in the cold?

Lime Soup

If chicken soup can cure a cold, then this bracing chicken and lime broth from the Yucatán is like a double dose of goodness.

When we first tasted this caldo, called Sopa de Lima in Mexico, it made such a big impression on us that we knew we had to re-create it at home. Now it is Mary Sue's son's first choice when he is home sick with a cold. As his mom says sympathetically, "What could be more miserable than not being able to taste?"

Special tool: *Strainer*

Preparation time: *15 minutes*

Cooking time: *1 hour and 10 minutes*

Yield: *6 to 8 servings*

1 2-pound chicken, cut into medium pieces

12 cups chicken stock (see the "Chicken stock" section in this chapter)

2½ teaspoons salt

1½ teaspoons black peppercorns, cracked

1½ teaspoons dried oregano

½ head garlic (8 cloves), separated and crushed (unpeeled)

2 tablespoons olive oil

1 medium yellow onion, halved and sliced

Black pepper to taste

1 poblano or Anaheim chile, cored, seeded, and julienned

2 medium tomatoes, cored, seeded, and julienned

Juice of 3 limes (½ cup)

Garnishes: 3 limes, cut in wedges; 3 serrano chiles, seeded and minced; 1 cup crushed corn chips; 1 avocado, peeled, seeded, and chopped

1 Combine the chicken and stock in a large stockpot. Bring to a boil and skim and discard the foam. Add 1½ teaspoons of the salt, the cracked peppercorns, oregano, and garlic. Reduce to a simmer and cook for 35 minutes, until the meat is tender. Remove the chicken, transfer to a platter, and cover with a damp tea towel.

2 Strain the stock, discarding the solids. Skim and discard the layer of fat that settles on the top.

3 When the chicken is cool enough to handle, remove the skin and pull the meat from the bones. Shred the meat into strips and set aside.

4 Heat the olive oil in a large stockpot over medium-low heat. Cook the onion with the remaining 1 teaspoon salt and ground pepper until translucent, about 10 minutes. Stir in the chile and cook for 5 minutes longer. Add the tomatoes, shredded chicken, reserved chicken stock, and lime juice. Bring to a boil, reduce to a simmer, and cook, uncovered, for 12 minutes. Serve hot with the garnishes scattered on top.

A caldo such as this lends itself to innumerable variations. For example, you can add large chunks of peeled potato, carrot, and chayote to the broth at the end and simmer for about 20 minutes. Or if you like some rice in your chicken soup, add about ½ cup of leftover rice along with the chicken.

To re-create the taste of Seville oranges (see "The orange of Seville" in this chapter), try combining the juices of grapefruit, orange, and lime in a ratio of 2 tablespoons grapefruit juice, to 1 tablespoon orange juice, to 2 tablespoons lime juice. Try it in place of the lime juice in Lime Soup for a taste of the real thing.

Possibly the Best Posole

Posoles, more like stews than soups, are even heartier than caldos, thanks to the key starch ingredient of hominy, a form of corn (see the "Homily on hominy" sidebar in this chapter for more on hominy). These heavy hitters are a whole meal — like a crunchy salad served over a thick meaty broth. See the variations in this section for posole possibilities.

The orange of Seville

In the Yucatán peninsula, where Sopa de Lima (Lime Soup) comes from, it isn't made from limes but with Seville oranges — the same oranges used to make the famous marmalade from Spain.

Also known as bitter oranges or *naranja agria*, this small fruit has thick, green, bumpy skin and is less juicy than an ordinary orange. Its potent sour juice replaces vinegar in typical Yucatecan marinades and seasoning pastes. Although bitter oranges are also found in Puerto Rico and Cuba, only Mexicans prize the juice more than the fleshy skin. At Mexican markets, the fruit is sold with the top layer of skin removed so that the bitter oils don't seep into the juice.

Chicken Posole

Although there is no one correct way to cook a posole, traditionally this stewy dish contains pork and hominy. However, because southern Californians prefer their meat white, we created this lighter version for our restaurant. We did draw the line, however, at breast meat. Dark thighs and legs are so much tastier.

If you don't have time to prepare all the garnishes, don't be deterred. The most important ones are fresh crunchy onions, lime, and oregano.

You can make posole (except for the garnishes) in advance and freeze it. Prepare the garnishes while the soup is reheating.

Special tools: *Blender, strainer*

Preparation time: *20 minutes*

Cooking time: *1½ hours*

Yield: *8 servings (10 cups)*

1 pound boneless, skinless chicken thighs, cut in 1-inch cubes

½ teaspoon salt

4 cups water

4 ancho chiles, stemmed and seeded

5 cloves garlic, peeled

1½ teaspoons dried oregano

2 tablespoons vegetable oil

1 large yellow onion, diced

2 cups canned white hominy, drained

3 Roma tomatoes, cored, seeded, and diced

4 cups chicken stock (see the "Chicken stock" section in this chapter)

Salt and pepper to taste

Garnishes: 1 cup sliced radishes, shredded lettuce, 1 cup diced onion, 2 cups fried corn tortilla strips or crushed corn chips, 1 cup diced avocado, ¼ cup dried oregano, and 10 lime wedges

1 Combine the chicken, salt, and water in a pot. Bring to a boil, reduce to a simmer, and cook, uncovered, until barely done, about 15 minutes. Let cool and then strain, reserving the broth. Cover the chicken with a wet tea towel and set aside.

2 Soak the chiles in the reserved warm broth for 20 minutes. Add the garlic and oregano, transfer to a blender, and puree until smooth.

3 Heat the oil in a medium stockpot over medium-high heat. Sauté the onion until lightly golden, about 10 minutes. Add the pureed chile mixture, hominy, tomatoes, 4 cups of chicken stock, and chicken. Bring to a boil, reduce to a simmer, and cook, uncovered, until the chicken is tender, about 30 minutes longer. Stir occasionally to prevent the hominy from sticking to the bottom of the pan.

4 Season with salt and pepper and serve in large soup bowls. Bring the garnishes to the table for sprinkling to taste.

To taste the more traditional version of posole, substitute 2½ pounds of trimmed, cubed pork butt for the chicken. For green posole, you can substitute 4 jalapeños for the anchos and 8 tomatillos for the tomatoes. Garnish with cilantro.

When I throw a party at home, this is my approach: Keep a big pot of posole simmering on the stove, arrange the garnishes nearby on a counter, and have enough beer on ice to keep everyone happy. No sweat!

Homily on hominy

You can find canned hominy in the international or canned vegetable section of the supermarket. Hominy is made from dried white field corn that has been cooked with powdered lime until its skin falls off. Then the kernels' eyes are removed, and the kernel blossoms — resembling a moist piece of popped corn.

Chapter 9

Border Salads

Salad does not play the same part in the Mexican meal plan as it does in other parts of the world. Mexican cooks use so many fresh vegetables in their garnishes and salsas that serving a bowl full of chopped lettuce and tomato as an accompaniment just doesn't make sense. Instead, they top tacos with chopped onion, cilantro, and tomato; generously garnish posoles with shredded cabbage, radishes, and avocado; and sell sliced cucumbers, roasted corn, and fresh fruit on the street as snack foods.

One interesting thing we noticed when we opened our first Border Grill was that the produce bill went up 50 percent from our previous restaurant, where we served European-based cuisine. Our produce costs didn't increase because people were ordering more salads. They went up because good Mexican cooking calls for loads of fresh vegetables.

Without a native tradition to fall back on, we gathered inspiration from the Mexican marketplace and combined it with our veteran salad-making skills in creating this selection of Mexican-style salads. As Los Angeles restaurateurs, we are always on the lookout for fresh salad ideas because 40 percent of our lunch guests order salad.

In this chapter, we include the well-loved tostada and Caesar salads, healthful starch-based bean, bread, and quinoa salads for larger appetites, and even a marinated cactus salad for those who are ready to expand their culinary experiences.

Preparing the Greens

Always wash and dry your salad greens (see Figure 9-1). To wash a large quantity of greens, first cut away the cores and stems of the leaves. Then fill a clean sink or large bowl with cold water, add the lettuce leaves, and soak for 10 minutes so that the sand sinks to the bottom. Lift out the leaves, shake off the excess water, and pat the leaves dry with paper towels or spin them dry with a salad spinner.

Washing Greens in a Sink

Figure 9-1:
Cleaning
your greens.

Fill the sink with **cold** water.

Cut away the cores and stems, separate the leaves and swish around in the water. Then let sit for 10 minutes. The grit will fall off to the bottom. Shake out excess water.

rub a dub dub!

Dry in a salad spinner, or roll loosely between paper towels.

ready for salad!

MARY SUE SAYS

If you like to have a salad every day like I do, here is a time-saving tip: Wash and dry your lettuce as much as one week in advance. Just slip the well-dried leaves into a plastic bag with a piece of paper towel and store in the veg-etable bin of the refrigerator. Also, the prewashed, bagged salads sold in the supermarket are fine substitutes for the time-pinched home cook. When I'm on the road and just can't stand another hotel or fast food meal, I sometimes cruise by a local market and pick up a bagged salad and a crusty loaf of bread for lunch.

TOQUE TIP

Crazy for croutons

As crouton fanatics, we recommend making your own with leftover bread or bread you may be saving in the freezer. Homemade tastes so much better than prepared! A great crouton should supply taste and several textures, not just crunch, to a salad. You'll never go back to those wimpy, little boxed croutons after you've tasted these jumbos.

When making your croutons, cut the bread into cubes of a substantial size so that you can still taste the dough as well as the crust. If you don't want to fire up the oven to make croutons, just toss the oiled and salt and peppered bread cubes in a skillet and sauté them over low heat, shaking the pan frequently to avoid scorching.

Dressing the Greens

For us, a dry salad is up there with tepid soup — something that makes us miserable! Follow these tips to turn out successful salads:

- ✔ Mix your salad in a bowl that's twice as large as what you appear to need. The bigger, the better for carefree tossing.

- ✔ Generally, dressings are made with three parts oil to one part vinegar or lemon. But we agree with Mexican cooks who favor a 50/50 split — nice and sour! To our cooking colleagues, we're known as the acid queens!

- ✔ The salad fixings (except for the onions which lose their fresh flavor quickly once cut) and dressing can be made in advance and chilled.

- ✔ If you make your dressing ahead, store it in a bottle that holds twice the volume of the dressing. Then you can give the bottle a good shake to completely mix it before drizzling it over the vegetables.

- ✔ After you place all the ingredients in the bowl, start adding the dressing about 2 tablespoons at a time, tossing and tasting between additions. Less is best to begin with because you can always add but you can't subtract dressing. Your ultimate goal should be to thinly coat each ingredient, without a pool of dressing remaining on the bottom of the bowl.

- ✔ The all-time best tool for tossing salad is your hands. Because you can spread your fingers wider than a fork, and your hands are more flexible, you can truly lift and separate the ingredients. So keep 'em clean, dig into that salad bowl, and stir and toss with abandon. It's even okay to take a bite. How else can you tell if the dressing is right?

Whoa! Before tossing out that leftover salad, place it back in the fridge. Soggy salad is delicious the next day if you mound it on toast and top it with a hot fried egg for breakfast.

The Tostada: A Salad in Disguise

Tostadas are wonderful, healthful salads served on edible fried tortilla plates (see Figure 9-2). With their small meat portions, they make terrific all-in-one suppers. You also can think of them as healthful sandwiches because they combine carbos (corn), veggies, and a little bit of meat.

Figure 9-2:
Tostadas make salad eating fun!

tostada

TOQUE TIP

The key to a terrific tostada is to season each part separately and well. The chicken or meat, as well as the salad, should be moistened and seasoned with dressing so that every bite is moist and flavorful. You almost force people to eat the perfect balance of foods by putting something with acidity and texture on top of something rich like the beans. If you serve salad on the side, people tend to eat it separately.

SUSAN SAYS

In a tostada, spread the beans out to all the edges and scatter the other components evenly. Each bite should deliver a combination of flavors. Who wants a mouthful of plain tortilla with those wonderful tastes congregating in the middle?

The versatile tostada

Like tacos and enchiladas, tostadas are perfect for using up leftovers. They're a good supper to serve toward the end of the week, when the refrigerator is brimming with odds and ends and everyone is ready for the fun of something light, crunchy, and unexpected.

Leftover beef, fish, chicken, and turkey are perfect for tostadas. Just shred or julienne the meat or fish and serve hot or cold, according to your taste. A can of refried beans in the cupboard is a good staple for last-minute tostada making. And if avocados are on hand, mash them with salt and pepper and a squeeze of lemon or lime and spread the mixture to the edges over the beans.

If you can't find tostada shells in the market and you don't have the time to make your own, you can line a plate with tortilla chips and dollop on the beans. Or you can break a crisp taco shell in half and use that as your crisp component.

The other, all-important crisp element is the lettuce. Any sturdy, crisp green will do. Snappy iceberg lettuce or shredded cabbage is excellent on tostadas.

See Chapter 10 for instructions on how to fry a tortilla for tostada-making.

Chicken Tostada Salad

Preparation time: *25 minutes*

Cooking time: *15 minutes*

Yield: *4 servings (8 tostadas)*

¾ pound cooked, shredded chicken

1 small red onion, diced

1 bunch cilantro leaves, chopped (about ½ cup)

1 small or ½ large head romaine lettuce, finely shredded

1 medium tomato, cored, seeded, and diced

½ cup (2 ounces) grated añejo cheese

½ cup red wine vinegar

¾ cup olive oil

Salt and pepper to taste

¾ cup vegetable oil for frying

8 large (6-inch) corn tortillas or 8 prepared tostada shells

1 cup Refried Black Beans (see Chapter 10) or good-quality canned refried beans

Garnishes: 3 tablespoons Crema and 1 large avocado or 2 medium avocados, peeled, seeded, and thinly sliced

1 Combine the chicken, onion, and cilantro in a medium bowl.

2 In another bowl, combine the lettuce, tomato, and cheese.

3 To make the dressing, combine the red wine vinegar, olive oil, and salt and pepper in a small jar or bottle. Cover and shake vigorously to combine, or whisk the ingredients together.

4 Pour the vegetable oil to a depth of ½ inch in a small frying pan. Heat the oil over moderate heat. Fry the tortillas on both sides until crisp and drain on paper towels. (See Chapter 10 to find out how to fry tortillas.)

5 Heat the beans through in a small pot over low heat, stirring often to prevent sticking. Add some water if beans are dry.

6 To assemble, spread a thin layer of beans on each crisp tortilla. Drizzle with about 1 teaspoon Crema and top with a few avocado slices. Pour enough dressing on the reserved chicken mixture to coat generously and toss well. Scatter over the tortillas. Toss the remaining dressing with the lettuce mixture and generously cover each tostada with it.

Don't cry over oxidized onions

For salad making, always use recently purchased fresh onions and cut them just before adding them to the salad. Because onions turn sharp and acrid as soon as their liquid is released and they begin to oxidize, do not prepare them in advance.

All-Star Side Salads

Although I know that "salad" means leafy greens for lots of people, I look for salads packed with interesting, contrasting elements and don't worry too much about the lettuce. For example, Mexican Chopped Salad (see the following recipe) has so much going for it — refreshing green apples, salty chips, rich nuts, and fragrant spice — that lettuce never really enters my mind at all.

Mexican Chopped Salad

This unusual chopped salad of tart green apples, corn, and pine nuts is a best-seller at our Santa Monica Border Grill and appeals especially to the advanced salad maker and eater (see photo in the color insert). The broken tortilla chips supply the crunch ordinarily delivered by salad croutons.

Make sure not to get stuck on these particular ingredients. Almonds can stand in for the pine nuts, jícama for the apple — you get the idea. Whatever you have in the house will be perfect.

Preparation time: *20 minutes*

Cooking time: *5 minutes*

Yield: *4 servings*

⅓ cup pine nuts

1 teaspoon ground cumin

Salt and pepper to taste

¼ cup red wine vinegar

½ cup extra-virgin olive oil

1 small or ½ large head romaine lettuce, cut into ½-inch strips

2 medium tomatoes, cored, seeded, and diced

1 small red onion, diced

1 medium green apple, peeled, cored, and diced

½ cup fresh corn kernels (cut from 1 ear of corn)

1½ cups crushed tortilla chips

Garnish: 1 avocado, peeled, seeded, and thinly sliced

1 To make the dressing, toast the pine nuts in a small dry frying pan over medium heat for 2 minutes, shaking frequently. Add the cumin and continue toasting and shaking the pan, 1 minute longer. Remove from heat. Add the salt and pepper, vinegar, and olive oil to the pan and whisk until the ingredients blend. Let cool.

2 In a large bowl, combine the lettuce, tomatoes, onion, apple, corn kernels, and tortilla chips. Toss well. Drizzle with dressing. Toss until well-coated. Top with avocado slices and serve.

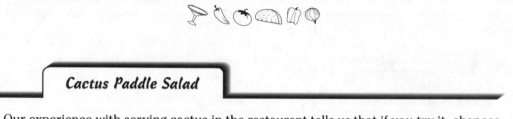

Cactus Paddle Salad

Our experience with serving cactus in the restaurant tells us that if you try it, chances are you'll like it — especially if you don't know what you're eating. So stop being a food wimp and let a little cactus into your life! (Check out Chapter 2 for more information on the cactus paddle.)

This is our most authentic Mexican salad because cactus is such a popular ingredient there — it's served all over the country.

Preparation time: *20 minutes, plus 2 hours chilling*

Cooking time: *5 minutes*

Yield: *4 to 6 servings*

1½ pounds fresh or prepared cactus paddles, or nopales, needles removed (see Chapter 2 for more information on preparing cactus paddles)

¾ cup olive oil (or ½ cup if you're using canned cactus)

½ teaspoon salt

4 Roma tomatoes, cored, seeded, and diced

½ small red onion, diced

2 serrano chiles, finely diced

1 bunch cilantro leaves, chopped (½ cup)

½ cup finely grated añejo cheese

¼ cup red wine vinegar

Salt and pepper to taste

4 to 6 red lettuce leaves

Garnish: 1 avocado, peeled, seeded, and thinly sliced

1 Preheat the grill medium hot or heat the broiler.

(continued)

2 For fresh cactus, place the cleaned paddles in a large bowl and toss with ¼ cup of the olive oil and the ½ teaspoon salt. Grill or broil the paddles until grill marks appear on both sides, or until the paddles turn dark green with black patches, about 4 minutes total. Set aside to cool to room temperature. Cover and chill for at least 2 hours or overnight. If using canned cactus, simply drain well and skip the grilling, omitting the ¼ cup of olive oil used for grilling.

3 Cut the cactus into ½-inch pieces. In a large bowl, combine the cactus, tomatoes, onion, chiles, cilantro, and cheese with the remaining ½ cup oil, vinegar, and salt and pepper. Toss well. Serve on plates lined with lettuce leaves and garnish with avocado slices.

If you can't get cactus, try this salad with sliced grilled chayote or winter squash in place of the cactus. See Chapter 2 for the lowdown on chayote, a very versatile vegetable.

Watercress and Radish Salad

The idea for this simple but vibrant combination came from a Mexico City marketplace. That's where we saw radishes ranging from white to pink, purple, and red in a wide variety of shapes displayed right next to bushels of brilliant green watercress — one of our favorite tart greens. We were surprised to learn that watercress is a popular ingredient in Mexico. It's used for green moles, salsas, and garnishes.

Preparation time: *10 minutes*

Yield: *6 servings*

2 bunches red radishes (12 to 15), washed and trimmed

4 bunches watercress, washed and 1-inch stems trimmed

⅓ cup olive oil

3 tablespoons freshly squeezed lime juice

Salt and pepper to taste

1 Thinly slice the radishes into half moons. Combine the radishes and watercress in a large bowl.

2 To make the dressing, in a small bowl whisk together the olive oil, lime juice, and salt and pepper. Pour over the salad and toss well to coat. Serve immediately on chilled plates.

Cracked black pepper is the perfect salad accompaniment. I adore pepper and often use fresh cracked peppercorns moistened with olive oil to sprinkle over a sliced avocado half on my salads. For a fuller-bodied watercress salad, fan avocado slices across the top and give them the cracked pepper treatment.

Watercress is a great little green to work with. Although it often gets over-looked in our rush to embrace the new, it has a similar bite to more expensive greens like arugula and is easy to find. Even the stems are edible. We just trim the woody, bottom part.

Caesar Salad

Are you surprised to see this recipe for Caesar Salad included in a book on Mexican cooking? Although most people associate this salad with Italian cooking, its true origins are in Mexico. Read the sidebar "All hail, Caesar" in this chapter for the details.

The Caesar salads served in restaurants are often just too rich for our tastes. This one has just the right balance of lime juice and vinegar to the rich combination of egg, salty anchovy, and cheese.

Preparation time: *20 minutes*

Cooking time: *15 minutes*

Yield: *6 servings*

1 egg, refrigerated

3 cloves garlic, crushed and peeled

5 canned anchovy fillets, not rinsed

2 teaspoons Dijon mustard

1 teaspoon celery salt

Salt

½ teaspoon pepper

½ cup extra-virgin olive oil

3 tablespoons red wine vinegar

2 tablespoons lime juice

3 dashes of Tabasco sauce

3 dashes of Worcestershire sauce

3 tablespoons olive oil

½ loaf (8 ounces) sourdough or hearty French or Italian bread, with crust, cut in ¾-inch cubes for large croutons (3 to 4 cups)

2 medium heads romaine lettuce

⅔ cup freshly grated añejo cheese

1 Bring a small saucepan of water to a boil. Place a refrigerated egg on a slotted spoon and gently lower into boiling water. Cook for 1½ minutes, remove, and reserve.

2 To make the dressing, place the garlic and anchovies in a large bowl and mash with a fork until smooth. Add the mustard, celery salt, salt, pepper, ½ cup olive oil, vinegar, lime juice, Tabasco, and Worcestershire sauce. Crack open the egg and, with a spoon, scrape out all the egg, including the uncooked parts, into the bowl. Whisk until well combined. The dressing may be refrigerated at this stage.

(continued)

All hail, Caesar

It's difficult to separate fact from folklore when it comes to tracing the bloodlines of such a popular and idiosyncratic dish as the Caesar salad. However, we do know that the Caesar salad was invented in Mexico during the Prohibition era when Americans would drive over the border for a drink with dinner. The creators, Tijuana restaurateurs Alex and Caesar Cardini, perfected it as a main course with whole lettuce leaves, no anchovies, and two barely-cooked eggs. To enhance its allure, each signature salad was assembled tableside.

We can easily imagine these inventive brothers with a restaurant full of hungry, thirsty visitors from Los Angeles. As they searched for inspiration among the condiments and spices, they eventually created a salad dressing so special that all it needed was some lettuce and croutons to be a complete dish. In Los Angeles, a bottled Caesar salad dressing bearing the Cardini name is still sold in the markets.

3 Heat the 3 tablespoons olive oil in a large cast-iron skillet over medium-low heat. Add the croutons and cook, stirring constantly, until golden and crisp, about 10 minutes.

4 Wash and dry the lettuce and break it into bite-sized pieces. Place in a salad bowl, along with the dressing and grated cheese, and toss well. Add the toasted croutons, toss again, and serve.

TOQUE TIP

Although the egg may still look runny or even completely raw after you cook it, you needn't worry. One minute of cooking time is long enough to kill any bacteria. By cooking the egg for more than a minute, any threat of salmonella has been eliminated. Use this technique in any recipe calling for raw egg if you are concerned with safety.

Corn and Pepper Compote

Serve this strongly flavored, bright little compote as you would a relish, alongside a sandwich or grilled steak or underneath a slice of grilled fish.

Corn and Pepper Compote can be stored, tightly covered, in the refrigerator up to a day. To make this dish 2 to 3 days in advance, mix all the ingredients except the avocado and store in the refrigerator. Toss in the avocado shortly before serving.

Preparation time: 15 minutes, plus 25 minutes marination

Cooking time: 5 minutes

Yield: 4 servings

¾ cup olive oil

4 cups fresh corn kernels (cut from about 5 ears)

1 teaspoon salt

¾ teaspoon pepper

2 avocados, peeled, halved, and seeded

1 large red bell pepper, cored and seeded

4 poblano chiles, roasted, peeled, and seeded (see Chapter 3)

4 scallions, white and light green parts, thinly sliced on the diagonal

½ cup red wine vinegar

1 Heat ½ cup of the olive oil in a large skillet over high heat. Sauté the corn with the salt and pepper in the oil, about 5 minutes. Transfer to a large mixing bowl and set aside to cool.

2 Dice the avocados, bell pepper, and chiles into ¼-inch pieces. Add to the sautéed corn along with the scallions, red wine vinegar, and remaining ¼ cup olive oil. Mix well and let sit about 25 minutes to blend the flavors. Serve at room temperature.

To complement the chiles with more smoky flavor, grill the corn and remove the kernels before combining them with the salad ingredients. Use ¾ cups oil to make the dressing.

I'm a big fan of the salad that pretends it's a sauce. I like to take a combination of chopped marinated vegetables, like this Corn and Pepper Compote, and tuck it under or place it over my grilled chicken in place of a sauce. A tasty salad can provide the moisture and contrast of a sauce without as much fat.

The miraculous cactus

Since ancient times, the parts of the cactus have served many purposes in Mexican life. Prickly spines were used as fish hooks, needles, and even toothpicks by the Aztecs. Tall, columnar stems are still in use today to construct fences, while green paddles are chopped for animal fodder and munched on by wild animals.

Cactus's curative powers are legendary. Tiny cactus paddles are said to help cure coughs, diabetes, stomach ailments from ulcers to diarrhea and constipation, and inflammation of the molars.

The fruit is used to produce candy, syrups, marmalades, and a brilliant red dye, and the roots of this desert plant also help prevent soil erosion.

Bean and Grain Salads

Making the salads in this section will be a snap if you keep these tips in mind:

✔ As much as we love our beans, nothing is worse than under- or over-cooked beans in a salad. Always test beans for doneness by biting into the smallest, densest one. The center should be creamy, and all the beans should hold their shape.

✔ Any time you're dressing beans or lentils for a salad, they will absorb the dressing better if you coat them while they are still slightly warm.

Fiesta Bean Salad

We jazz up a typical American-style bean salad with three different beans and a colorful confetti of diced peppers. This versatile salad is a great choice for a buffet table or picnic because it can remain out without wilting. Or serve it as an accompaniment to a full-flavored entrée like ribs or fried chicken.

Preparation time: 10 minutes, plus 2 hours chilling

Yield: 4 to 6 servings

1 red bell pepper	*1 small red onion, finely diced*
1 yellow bell pepper	*1 cup canned, drained black beans*
1 poblano chile	*1 cup canned, drained pinto beans*
½ cup olive oil	*1 cup canned, drained red beans or kidney beans*
¼ cup red wine vinegar	
1 teaspoon salt	*½ bunch cilantro leaves, coarsely chopped (¼ cup)*
½ teaspoon pepper	

1 Core and seed the bell peppers and poblano and cut them into ¼-inch cubes. The pepper and chile cubes should be similar to the size of the cooked beans.

2 To make the dressing, in a large bowl whisk together the olive oil, vinegar, salt, and pepper. Toss in the diced peppers, chile, onion, beans, and cilantro, and mix well. Refrigerate for 2 hours or overnight before serving.

If you have a smoker, try smoking the beans for Fiesta Bean Salad. A chipotle chile pureed into the dressing emphasizes the smokiness of the beans, giving the whole salad a heartier taste.

Aztecan Quinoa Salad

Quinoa, a "new" ingredient that has been around for thousands of years, is a tiny, high-protein grain from South America. It's nicknamed the "wonder grain" because it cooks more quickly than rice, is virtually foolproof, and is lighter and more nutritious than other grains. See the sidebar "Keen on quinoa" for more information on this grain, including the pronunciation.

Special tool: Strainer

Preparation time: 15 minutes

Cooking time: 15 minutes

Yield: 6 to 8 servings

12 cups water

1½ cups quinoa, rinsed

5 pickling cucumbers, peeled, ends trimmed, and cut into ¼-inch cubes

1 small red onion, cut into ¼-inch cubes

1 medium tomato, cored, seeded, and diced

1 bunch Italian parsley leaves, chopped (½ cup)

1 bunch cilantro leaves, chopped (½ cup)

½ cup olive oil

¼ cup red wine vinegar

Juice of 1 lemon

1½ teaspoons salt

¾ teaspoon pepper

6 romaine lettuce leaves

1 Bring the water to a boil in a large saucepan. Add the quinoa, stir once, and return to a boil. Cook, uncovered, over moderate heat for 12 minutes. Strain and rinse well with cold water, shaking the sieve well to remove all moisture.

2 When dry, transfer the quinoa to a large bowl. Add the cucumbers, onion, tomato, parsley, cilantro, olive oil, vinegar, lemon juice, salt, and pepper and toss well. Serve on lettuce-lined plates or chill.

For a good vegetarian cocktail party tidbit, fill small romaine spears with the Aztecan Quinoa Salad. Even meat eaters will enjoy this delicious, and healthy, appetizer. Or, serve the salad in a bowl of Gazpacho (Chapter 8) for a summertime treat (see photo in the color insert).

Keen on quinoa

It's hard to feel cozy about an ingredient that you can't even pronounce, so we want to get that out of the way right now: KEEN-wah is the way you say it.

Quinoa is a tiny, bead-shaped, cream-colored, plain-tasting grain similar to couscous. When boiled in water, it expands to four times its size.

Quinoa is a complete protein. It's high in unsaturated fats and low in carbohydrates and is a more balanced source of nutrients than any other grain. An added bonus is its ease of preparation. Unlike rice, quinoa is impossible to mess up — it never turns out too watery or gooey or clumpy.

Look for quinoa in your health food store and try to purchase the organic variety. This is one ingredient where the taste of organic makes a big difference.

Bread Salad

Here is a great summer salad to make when tomatoes are in season and you're wondering what to do with yesterday's bread (see photo in the color insert). We think of it as a sandwich in a bowl.

Special tool: *Baking sheet or cookie tray*

Preparation time: *15 minutes*

Cooking time: *20 minutes*

Yield: *4 to 6 servings*

¼ loaf crusty (1 pound) Italian bread

⅓ cup plus 2 tablespoons olive oil

Salt and pepper to taste

¼ cup red wine vinegar

½ bunch cilantro leaves, chopped (¼ cup)

3 cloves garlic, crushed and peeled

¾ teaspoon salt

½ teaspoon black pepper

6 pickling cucumbers, peeled and cut into ¾-inch chunks

1 small red onion, thinly sliced

3 Roma tomatoes, chopped

½ cup Spanish green olives, pitted and cut in half

Romaine lettuce leaves for serving

1 Preheat the oven to 300°.

2 Cut the bread, with crusts, into ¾-inch cubes. Spread on a baking sheet or cookie tray and drizzle with 2 tablespoons of the olive oil and salt and pepper to taste. Bake for 20 minutes, shaking the pan occasionally, until golden. Set aside to cool.

3 To make the dressing, in a small bowl whisk together the ⅓ cup of the olive oil, vinegar, cilantro, garlic, ¾ teaspoon salt, and ½ teaspoon black pepper.

4 Mix the cucumbers, onion, tomatoes, and olives together in a large bowl. Add the dressing and the bread cubes. Toss well. Serve immediately on lettuce-lined plates.

Six ounces of ½-inch cubed Panela or another favorite cheese you have on hand is a good addition to mix in for a more substantial bread salad. (Chapter 2 tells you about all sorts of cheeses used in the Mexican kitchen.)

Cruising for cucumbers

With so many choices on the market, it pays to be picky about cucumbers. Generally speaking, the smaller varieties like pickling or Kirbies, Japanese, English, and Middle Eastern are sweeter and less watery than the larger, supermarket cuke.

At the height of the season, late spring through early fall, big, old-fashioned American cukes can still be terrific. One sign of freshness to look for are those tiny, prickly brown hairs on the skin.

Whatever cucumber you use, always trim and discard ½-inch off the ends first, where bitter juices collect. Then peel if desired.

Chapter 10

The Essential Sides: Rice, Beans, Tortillas, and Vegetables

In This Chapter

▶ Frying rice Mexican-style
▶ Enjoying beans for all seasons
▶ Making tortillas and chips at home
▶ Varying the menu with veggie sides

*N*o matter how much time we spend in the professional kitchen, we are always awed by the inventiveness of Mexican cooks, who create a healthful and exciting cuisine with such a simple handful of ingredients. Thanks to the creativity of Mexican cooks, meager ingredients like rice and beans are elevated to complex, sensual foods.

In these delicious side dishes, salsa, chiles, and herbs bring rice to a whole new level of interest. Beans are mashed and enriched with fat to make luxuriously creamy refried beans. Old tortillas never die or get thrown out; instead, they are reborn as crispy, scrumptious tortilla chips and tostadas.

In addition to their ability to breathe new life into simple ingredients, some of these side dishes are also very healthy. Remember that combining beans (without lard, of course) and rice forms a full protein.

This chapter focuses on the simple, inexpensive side dishes that most Mexican meals are built around. In most Mexican homes, a pot of beans is always bubbling on a burner, there's rice in the fridge for reheating, and tortillas are always present.

Getting the Rice Spirit

The Mexican method for cooking rice is a great example of how the simplest foods can become a special occasion in the hands of gifted cooks. Frying the rice to develop a toasty flavor and then infusing it with salsa to give it color, flavor, and pizzazz is one of the most exciting techniques we've learned from the Mexican kitchen. Although cooking rice the Mexican way takes more time than the ways you may be used to cooking rice, these special rice dishes are well worth the extra effort.

To get the most from your Mexican rice, you need to start with the right ingredients and treat them right during preparation. Follow these tips to increase your success:

✔ Start with well-rinsed long-grain rice. We always rinse rice before cooking to remove the excess starch that causes gumminess. To rinse the rice, place it in a large bowl, not a colander, and rinse under cold running water for 5 minutes, or until the water runs clear. Keep stirring the grains with your hand to loosen starch particles.

✔ If your recipe calls for you to toast the rice (which is done on the stove top in a skillet, rather than in the oven), go for a full golden color and roasted aroma.

✔ Always let your rice rest before serving it. Doing so allows the rice to finish cooking and cool slightly.

✔ Stirring rice with a spoon to cool it down can break delicate grains. Instead, use a fork to gently separate the rice and cool it down before serving it. Cool overcooked or mushy rice by emptying it out onto a baking sheet and spreading it thinly so that air can circulate.

✔ For an interesting twist, try tossing some broken, dry spaghetti or tiny, whole orzo into the pot along with the rice and fry until golden. If you want to add the spaghetti, use the thin-style spaghetti and break it into small pieces of about ¼ inch.

✔ More is always better than less when adding chiles and salsas to these rice dishes. Creating a full-flavored rice takes a gutsy dose of spice and salsa. (Chapter 2 tells you all about chiles, and Chapter 5 can get you up to speed with all sorts of salsas.)

White Rice

We like to serve white rice with heavily spiced foods that benefit from something sooth-ing for balance. For example, serve this rice with the Dark Mole with Turkey or Chile Braised Lamb Shanks in Chapter 11.

Preparation time: *5 minutes*

Cooking time: *45 minutes*

Yield: *6 to 8 servings*

3 tablespoons vegetable oil

1½ cups long-grain white rice, rinsed

½ medium onion, diced

1 clove garlic, peeled and minced

Salt and pepper to taste

3½ cups chicken stock, vegetable stock, or water (see Chapter 8 for the stock recipes)

Heat the oil in a medium saucepan over medium-low heat. Sauté the rice and onion, stir-ring constantly, until a very light golden color, about 5 minutes. Add the garlic and salt and pepper and cook 1 minute longer. Pour in the stock or water and bring to a boil. Reduce to a simmer, cover, and cook for 20 minutes. Add a bit more liquid if longer cooking is necessary. Let rest 10 minutes, fluff with a fork, and serve.

Green Rice

Don't be shy about the amount of greens in this flavorful side dish. Our favorite rice is definitely not the kind to fade into the background. This tomatillo-infused rice makes a great sidekick to Citrus Chicken (Chapter 13) or Cumin and Chile Marinated Skirt Steak (Chapter 14).

Special tool: *Food processor or blender*

Preparation time: *15 minutes*

Cooking time: *45 minutes*

Yield: *6 to 8 servings*

(continued)

½ cup cold water

2 poblano chiles, roasted, peeled, and seeded (see Chapter 3 for tips on working with chiles)

2 romaine lettuce leaves

1 bunch cilantro, stems and leaves, coarsely chopped (½ cup)

2 scallions, white and green parts cut into 1- to 2-inch pieces

2 cloves garlic, peeled

6 tomatillos, coarsely chopped

1 teaspoon salt

1 to 1½ cups chicken stock, vegetable stock, or water (see Chapter 8 for the stock recipes)

3 tablespoons vegetable oil

1½ cups long-grain rice, rinsed

1 Pour the ½ cup water into a food processor or a blender. Add the chiles, lettuce leaves, cilantro, scallions, garlic, tomatillos, and salt. Puree until liquefied, adding enough stock or water to bring to 3½ cups. (If using a blender, work in batches.) Set aside.

2 Heat the oil in a medium-size heavy saucepan over medium-low heat. Sauté the rice, stirring constantly, until golden and crackling, about 5 minutes. Pour in the reserved green puree and stir to combine. Bring to a boil, reduce to a simmer, cover, and cook until the liquid is absorbed and the rice is tender, about 20 minutes. Let rest 10 minutes. Fluff with a fork and serve hot.

Red Rice

This is the basic tomato-tinged rice that accompanies so many Mexican dishes (see photo in the color insert). You can make the Red Roasted Tomato Salsa, which gives the rice its color, as long as a week in advance. Red Rice is delicious with Cochinita Pibil (Chapter 14) or Chipotle Glazed Chicken (Chapter 13).

Preparation time: *5 minutes, plus 35 minutes for the Red Roasted Tomato Salsa*

Cooking time: *45 minutes*

Yield: *6 to 8 servings*

3 tablespoons vegetable oil

1½ cups long-grain rice, rinsed

½ medium yellow onion, chopped

2 cloves garlic, peeled and chopped

Salt and pepper to taste

5 serrano chiles, or to taste, stemmed, seeded if desired

2 cups chicken stock, vegetable stock, or water (see Chapter 8 for the stock recipes)

1½ cups Red Roasted Tomato Salsa (see Chapter 5)

1 Heat the oil in a medium-size heavy saucepan or skillet over medium-low heat. Sauté the rice, stirring constantly, until golden brown and crackling, about 5 minutes. Add the onion and sauté just until soft. Stir in the garlic, salt and pepper, and chiles and sauté until the aroma is released.

2 Pour in the stock or water and the salsa, mixing well to combine. Bring to a boil, reduce to a simmer, cover, and cook for 20 minutes. Let rest 10 minutes. Fluff with a fork and serve hot.

Beautiful, Beautiful Refried Beans!

With their dollop of richness from lard or other fat, refried beans are an inexpensive way to satisfy the universal need to feel full and happy. Refrieds are a little more special than ordinary beans, and they're typically served alongside small snacks like tacos or enchiladas to round out the meal.

In Mexico, small black beans are more popular in the south, while pink pintos are favored in the north. Any kind of bean can be fried in fat and mashed.

Bean dips and nachos are a great way to use leftover refried beans! See Chapter 5 for dipping suggestions.

In this section, we give you recipes for making refrieds with both black and pinto beans. Regardless of which color you decide to go with, follow these tips as you prepare your beans:

✔ Wash and pick over your beans before cooking. Wash them in a colander with cold water and then spread the beans out on a cookie sheet or counter. Pull out and discard any stray dirt, stones, or shriveled beans.

✔ Both of our refried bean recipes ask you to use lard because that is the most typical Mexican fat for beans and it adds a hint of pork flavor that makes the dish delicious. You can't fry beans without fat, but you can use different fats if lard is not to your liking. In place of the lard, you can substitute bacon drippings, vegetable oil, or half butter and half olive oil in the same quantity as specified.

Chapter 3 offers some additional tips for working with beans.

Refried Black Beans

Frying beans with a bit of fat and onion accentuates their rich, creamy quality (see photo in the color insert). Our own tastes tend toward even more lard than the following recipes calls for, but we don't want to scare away the faint-hearted. Feel free to increase the lard for a richer, more authentic refried bean. Remember that if you don't eat refried beans with lots of meat or protein, the overall proportion of fat in the meal is not unhealthy. Serve these fantastic beans with any of the tacos in Chapter 6.

Special tool: *Potato masher*

Preparation time: *10 minutes*

Cooking time: *1 hour and 30 minutes*

Yield: *4 to 6 servings*

2 cups dried black beans, washed and picked over	*1 large onion, diced*
	1½ teaspoons salt
8 cups water	*½ teaspoon freshly ground black pepper*
⅓ cup lard or vegetable oil	

1 Place the beans and water in a large pot and bring to a boil. Cover, reduce to a simmer, and cook for 1 hour and 15 minutes, or until the beans are tender and creamy in the center. (To test for doneness, taste 3 or 4 of the smaller beans.) Crush the beans in their liquid with a potato masher or the back of a wooden spoon.

2 Heat the lard or vegetable oil in a large saucepan over medium heat. Sauté the onion with the salt and pepper until golden, about 10 minutes. Add the beans and their liquid and continue cooking over medium heat, stirring frequently, until the liquid evaporates and the beans form a creamy mass that pulls away from the bottom and sides of the pan, about 15 minutes. Serve immediately.

If you are lucky enough to find epazote (see Chapter 2), a sprig or two added to the pot of the refried beans for the last 15 minutes gives the beans an authentic flavor. Epazote has also been known to counteract the unpleasant side effect of beans on the digestive system!

Refried Pinto Beans

Though black beans are fashionable these days, we still love big, creamy, crushed pintos alongside a bowl of Carnitas Norteñas or Cumin and Chile Marinated Skirt Steak (both in Chapter 14).

Special tool: *Potato masher*

Preparation time: *10 minutes*

Cooking time: *2 hours*

Yield: *4 to 6 servings*

8½ cups water

2 cups dried pinto beans, washed and picked over

½ cup lard or vegetable oil

1 large yellow onion, diced

1 teaspoon salt

½ teaspoon pepper

1 Bring the water to a boil in a medium saucepan. Add the beans, reduce to a simmer, cover, and cook, skimming foam from the top occasionally, approximately 1 hour and 45 minutes. (To test for doneness, taste 3 or 4 of the smaller beans. They should be cooked through and creamy inside.) Mash the beans, along with the liquid in the pot, with a potato masher or the back of a wooden spoon until creamy.

2 Heat the lard or vegetable oil in a medium saucepan over medium-high heat. Sauté the onion with the salt and pepper until golden brown, about 10 minutes. Add the mashed beans and continue cooking, stirring occasionally, until the liquid evaporates and the beans form a mass that pulls away from the sides and bottom of the pan, about 10 minutes. Serve immediately.

If you prefer your beans boiled, "in the pot" as they are known in Mexico, just skip the mashing and ladle the boiled beans with their liquid into bowls to serve. Sprinkle with diced fresh onion, jalapeño, and cilantro.

Reheating refrieds

Refried beans can be kept in the refrigerator three or four days. You also can freeze them for a month or two in a sealed container.

When you want to reheat the beans, add water or chicken stock to thin them out so that they are soupier than the end product. That way, when you reheat and moisture is absorbed, they won't dry out.

Beans can be reheated in the following ways:

✔ In a 350° oven in a covered casserole.

✔ In a container placed in a larger roasting pan filled with an inch or two of water, in a 350° oven. By protecting the beans with the surrounding water, the heat will be evenly distributed and gentler.

✔ In a skillet over low heat. Stir the beans frequently.

Making Your Own Corn Tortillas

Handmade corn tortillas have a pebbly texture and a definitive, earthy corn flavor. They're a wonderful addition to a Mexican-themed party, where their heavenly aroma is sure to draw guests into the kitchen to start the nibbling. In the Mexican home, fresh tortillas are bought daily, as the French buy baguettes.

One of the first things that hits you when you walk into Border Grill is the earthy sweet smell of handmade tortillas. I like to eat them hot off the comal (a term explained in the sidebar "The comal") when racing between appointments.

Corn Tortillas

The Quaker Oats brand of masa harina or the Aztec Milling Company's deep yellow masa harina works well in this recipe (see photo in the color insert). (See Chapter 2 for more about masa harina.)

Special tool: Tortilla press (see Chapter 3 for more information on this tool)

Preparation time: 15 minutes

Cooking time: 20 minutes

Yield: 12 to 18 6-inch tortillas

2 cups masa harina   *1 to 1½ cups lukewarm water*

Pinch of salt

1 Combine the masa harina and salt in a large mixing bowl and add the lukewarm water while stirring, until smooth. The dough should be slightly sticky and form a ball when pressed together. To test, flatten a small ball of dough between your palms or 2 sheets of plastic wrap. If the edges crack, add more water a little at a time until a test piece does not crack.

2 Divide the dough into 12 to 18 pieces depending upon the size you prefer for your tortillas. Roll each piece into a ball and place the ball on a plate covered with a damp cloth towel.

3 Heat a dry cast-iron or nonstick frying pan or a stovetop griddle over medium heat. Flatten each ball of dough between 2 sheets of heavy plastic wrap either in a tortilla press (see Figure 10-1) or on a counter by using your hands or with a rolling pin. Remove the plastic from the top and, holding the tortilla with your fingertips, peel off the bottom sheet of plastic. Lay the tortillas, one by one, on the griddle and cook for about 1 minute and 15 seconds per side, gently pressing the top of the second side with your fingertips to encourage the tortilla to puff. Use tongs or a spatula to turn.

4 Cool the hot tortillas in a single layer on a towel. When they are still warm, but not hot, stack and wrap in the towel. Serve immediately or let cool, wrap well in plastic, and store in the refrigerator up to 1 week. Corn tortillas can be frozen for 2 weeks.

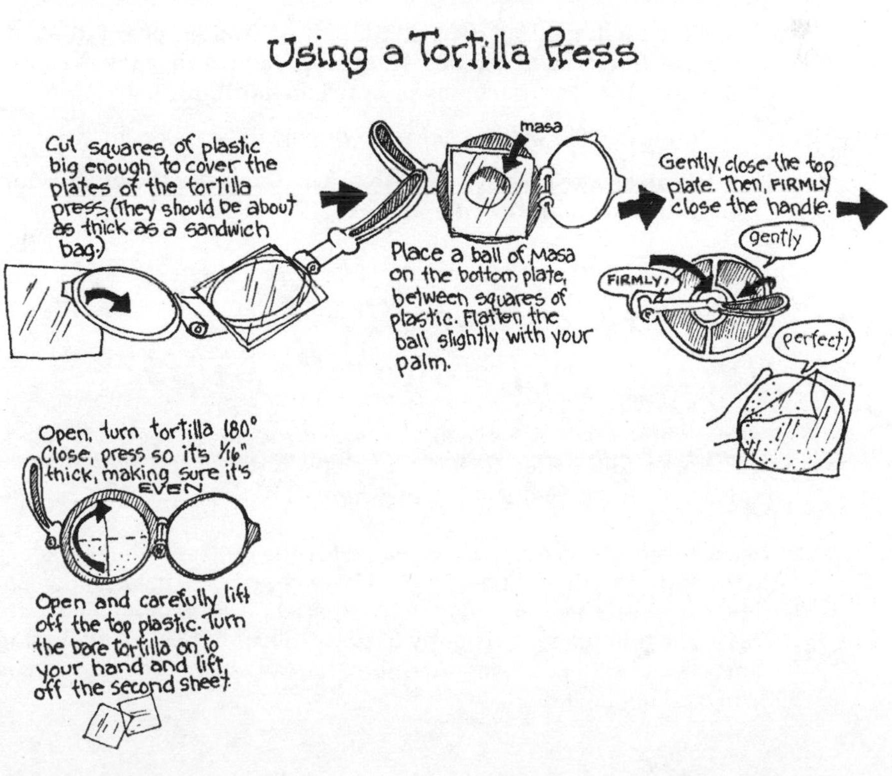

Using a Tortilla Press

Cut squares of plastic big enough to cover the plates of the tortilla press. (They should be about as thick as a sandwich bag.)

masa

Place a ball of masa on the bottom plate, between squares of plastic. Flatten the ball slightly with your palm.

Gently, close the top plate. Then, FIRMLY close the handle.

gently

FIRMLY!

perfect!

Open, turn tortilla 180°. Close, press so its 1/16" thick, making sure it's EVEN

Open and carefully lift off the top plastic. Turn the bare tortilla on to your hand and lift off the second sheet.

Figure 10-1: Shaping a tortilla by using a tortilla press.

The comal

When we opened our first Border Grill in Santa Monica, we wanted the sight, sound, and fragrance of earthy corn tortillas to greet people as soon as they stepped inside. To us, that was the best way to signal to our guests that they were about to experience absolutely fresh, handmade Mexican food.

In Mexico, a station of women patting and pressing out dough and frying fresh tortillas in a central spot in a restaurant is not an unusual sight. The traditional pan, called a *comal,* is a large, round, flat cast-iron griddle, perfect for flipping tortillas. Any well-seasoned cast-iron skillet works just fine, but the beauty of the comal (if you can find one) lies in its low sides.

Reheating tortillas

To reheat refrigerated corn or flour tortillas, just follow these steps:

1. **Heat the oven to 200°.**

2. **Warm a tea towel by placing it on a baking sheet and putting it in the oven briefly.**

3. **Place a dry skillet over medium heat. Warm the tortillas in the skillet, one at a time, about 30 seconds per side, and stack them, covering them with the warm towel between additions.**

   If the tortillas are dry, sprinkle them with water before reheating.

4. **Wrap stacked tortillas in the towel, wrap the towel with foil, and place in the oven until ready to serve.**

Frying a corn tortilla (and turning it into a tortilla chip)

Fried whole tortillas serve as the base for tostadas (see Chapter 9), or you can break up the fried tortilla into chips to be served with all manner of salsas. Strips of fried tortillas are often used as garnishes.

Sure, there are plenty of serviceable tortilla chips on the market (see our recommendations in Chapter 5), but if you're going to master Mexican cooking at home, you owe it to yourself to experience some homemade chips and taste the difference. A recently fried tortilla chip has so much more character and crispness that it becomes more than a vehicle for other flavors. It's delicious all by itself.

Our homemade corn tortillas are great for chip making because they have less moisture to fry out than bagged tortillas. But, of course, you don't have to start absolutely from scratch. Stale, old tortillas that have been lurking in your refrigerator for longer than you care to remember are ideal for chip making.

Whatever you start with, leave the tortillas out on a counter to dry before frying. Then follow these steps to fry them (and see Figure 10-2):

1. **For strips, cut the tortilla in half and then thinly slice across the width. For chips, cut in half and cut each half into 4 wedges. For tostadas, keep the tortilla whole.**

2. **Pour vegetable oil into a large pot or skillet to a depth of about 2 inches. Place over medium-high heat and heat to 375°, or until a piece of tortilla, when dropped in the oil, bubbles and rises to the surface.**

3. **Fry wedges and strips a handful at a time, stirring with a slotted spoon to separate, until very lightly browned all over. If frying whole tortillas, use tongs to turn.**

4. **Transfer to paper towels to drain. Sprinkle with salt while warm and serve in bowls for munching. When completely cooled, store in resealable plastic bags or any airtight container at room temperature.**

Figure 10-2: Frying up a batch of homemade corn tortilla chips.

Spicing Things Up with Veggie Sides

We love to eat our veggies. In fact, if we weren't chefs, we just might cross the line and become vegetarians.

So many of our customers in Los Angeles want to eat light and healthy that we always take special care with our vegetable dishes so that they're as special as everything else on the menu. These Mexican sides are so rich-tasting and flavorful you'll wonder how you ever settled for steamed vegetables.

Mashed Yams with Sour Cream and Honey

We love to add something sour to sweet yams to offset their candylike quality. If you prefer to avoid the calories of sour cream, feel free to substitute the juice of one lime. What a great beta carotene-packed treat at Thanksgiving dinner! (See the sidebar "I'm yam I am" in this chapter for more information on this delightful vegetable.)

Special tool: *Potato masher*

Preparation time: *15 minutes*

Cooking time: *1 hour and 45 minutes*

Yield: *6 to 8 servings*

6 small or medium yams (about 4 pounds)	*Salt and pepper to taste*
3 tablespoons butter, room temperature	*2 tablespoons honey or to taste (optional)*
½ cup sour cream	

1 Preheat the oven to 350°.

2 Wash the yams and prick all over with a skewer or fork. Place on a baking tray. Bake until they are soft all the way through and the skins are puffy and oozing, about 1 hour and 30 minutes. Set aside to cool slightly, leaving the oven on.

3 When the yams are cool enough to handle, peel them and place in a medium baking dish. Add the butter, sour cream, and salt and pepper. Stir and mash well with a potato masher. Drizzle the top with honey, if desired, and return to the oven for 15 minutes, until heated through and browned on top. Serve hot.

Avoid cooking with fresh sweet potatoes or yams in June or July. Those still on the market have been in cold storage eight months or more and will be dry, stringy, and sometimes wrinkled from shrinkage.

When I don't have sour cream in the house to dress these potatoes, I mix cream cheese with milk or a little plain yogurt until it's the consistency of pancake batter and use that instead.

I'm yam I am

We come down on the side of yams in the great sweet potato versus yam debate. But just to get our terminology straight, the tuber we all recognize as a yam, is in fact a darker-skinned, orange-fleshed variety of the sweet potato. The true yam, which can be found in Latin American markets, is a thick tropical-vine tuber used throughout Latin America and the Caribbean but seldom found in American markets.

Now that you're really confused, what is sold in the supermarket as yams is what we recommend — especially the Jewel or Garnet varieties. Yams are sweeter and moister than sweet potatoes. If you mistakenly purchase sweet potatoes, you'll know it when they bake up pale, dry, and flaky like a baking potato and have only a smidgen of sweetness. Just add more butter and sour cream or increase their juiciness with a splash of apple juice.

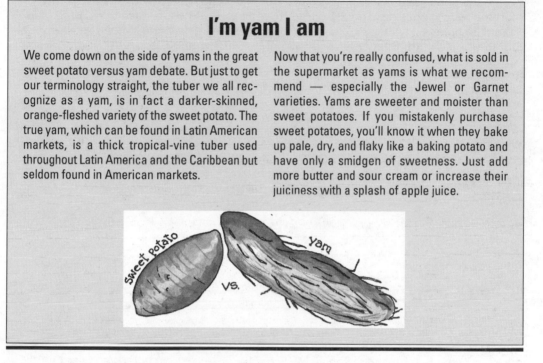

Poblano Mashed Potatoes

These spicy, rich potatoes are one of the most frequently requested recipes at our restaurants. Serve with an entrée of equal heft — like a juicy grilled Chile and Garlic Stuffed Rib Eye or Cumin Pepper Lamb Chops (both in Chapter 14).

Special tool: *Potato masher or food mill*

Preparation time: *15 minutes*

Cooking time: *35 minutes*

Yield: *6 servings*

2½ pounds baking potatoes, peeled and quartered

1½ tablespoons salt

1 cup sour cream

½ cup olive oil

5 poblano chiles, roasted, peeled, seeded, and diced (see Chapter 3 for more information on working with chiles)

Salt and pepper to taste

(continued)

1 Place the potatoes in a large saucepan. Pour in enough water to cover and add the 1½ tablespoons salt. Bring to a boil, reduce to a simmer, and cook, uncovered, until soft, about 25 minutes. Drain well, return the potatoes to the pan, and, while still warm, mash with a potato masher or food mill until slightly chunky.

2 In a small pot, combine the sour cream, olive oil, and chiles and warm over low heat just until warm to the touch. Too much heat causes the sour cream to separate.

3 Add the sour cream mixture to the potatoes and gently stir just to combine. Season with salt and pepper and serve immediately.

The worst thing you can do to these mashed potatoes is overmix them. Gently combine them with the sour cream mixture just until mixed. Overzealous mixing and mashing lead to gummy, starchy potatoes.

Fried Plantains

When ripe plantains are fried, they turn into the most delectable, slightly sweet side dish. We love them for breakfast; in fact, fried plantains served over a bowl of white rice is a very common breakfast item in Mexico. They also go great with Cochinita Pibil (Chapter 14) and Grilled Red Snapper Tikin-Chik (Chapter 16), both dishes from the Yucatán. (Chapter 2 tells you more about plantains and how to work with them.)

Preparation time: *5 minutes*

Cooking time: *10 minutes*

Yield: *6 servings*

3 ripe plantains	*4 tablespoons butter*

1 Peel the plantains and cut into ¼-inch slices on the diagonal.

2 Melt the butter in a large skillet over medium heat. Sauté the plantains until golden brown and soft, about 2 to 3 minutes per side. Serve hot.

Use plantains to make south-of-the-border banana pancakes. Just add a diced ripe plantain to pancake batter and cook on the griddle for a heartier, exotic spin on this traditional American breakfast.

If you're looking for sweet-flavored plantains, they need to be thoroughly ripe, as in totally blackened, before frying. See Chapter 1 for more information on this great, thick-skinned cooking banana.

Seared Chard

This recipe could change the way you think about cooking and eating your greens (see photo in the color insert). After you master this quick searing technique, you'll be able to use it to whip up your favorite leafy greens on a moment's notice — without relying on a recipe.

Chard is a dark green, leafy vegetable with a thick white stem. Vitamin- and mineral-rich spinach, mustard, kale, escarole, dandelion, and turnip greens all taste fabulous cooked this simple, lowfat way. Serve alongside Grilled Turkey Escabeche (Chapter 13).

Preparation time: *10 minutes*

Cooking time: *5 minutes*

Yield: *4 servings*

2 bunches green chard

2 tablespoons butter

2 tablespoons olive oil

½ teaspoon salt

Pepper to taste

1 Trim and discard the stems of the chard and wash and dry the leaves, including the triangular core between the leaves. Stack the leaves, roll lengthwise into cylinders, and cut across the rolls into 1-inch strips.

2 Melt 1 tablespoon each of the butter and olive oil in a large skillet over medium-high heat until bubbly. Sauté half of the chard with the salt and pepper, stirring and tossing, for less than a minute, until limp. If the chard begins to brown before it wilts, sprinkle in a few drops of water for steam. Transfer to a covered platter and repeat with the remaining chard. (If your skillet is smaller, just cook in several batches.) Serve immediately.

 Don't throw out those leftover seared greens! They are delicious the next day dressed with vinegar or lime juice and a touch of olive oil. Eat the greens as a salad or use them as a layer, in place of lettuce, in a grilled chicken, fish, or fried egg sandwich.

Try combining two or three greens, such as escarole, endive, kale, mustard, or spinach, for an interesting layering of flavors.

Spicy Grilled Corn

Here is a refined version of a popular Mexican street snack. Just one bite will leave you wondering how you'll ever go back to plain old buttered corn.

Special tool: *Pastry or barbecue brush*

Preparation time: *15 minutes, plus 10 minutes soaking*

Cooking time: *15 minutes*

Yield: *6 servings*

6 ears fresh sweet corn, in the husk

4 tablespoons butter, softened

Salt and pepper to taste

2 arbol chiles, seeded, stemmed, and coarsely chopped

2 tablespoons chopped fresh cilantro

1 tablespoon freshly squeezed lime juice

1 Preheat the grill to medium-hot.

2 Carefully remove the corn silks, leaving the husks attached. Soak the ears of corn in their husks in a large bowl or sink of cold water for 10 minutes.

3 In a small bowl, mix together the softened butter, salt and pepper, chiles, cilantro, and lime juice until smooth. Set aside.

4 Drain the corn well and place each husk-enclosed ear on the hot grill. Cook for about 12 minutes, turning frequently. The corn is steamed when it loses its raw crunch. Remove each cob from the grill and, when cool enough to handle, strip off and discard the husks.

5 Brush each cob with the seasoned butter mixture and return to the grill for a minute or two just to heat. Serve immediately.

Chapter 11

Best Braises, Stews, and Moles

In This Chapter

▶ Stewing and braising basics

▶ Making magnificent moles

▶ Cooking traditional Mexican stews

▶ Getting innovative with some twists on old favorites

As chefs who have cooked plenty of la-dee-dah sauces in our professional lives, nothing pleases us more than to sit down to a lovingly pre-pared bowl of succulent meat stewed in its own juices. To us, a homemade stew or chili shows off the talents and confidence of the home cook more than any fancy restaurant creation ever could. Besides, the kind of richness that develops when all the flavors of a dish slowly mingle in one pot can never be duplicated in sepa-rate pans.

Traditional Mexican stewed meats are wonderful for home entertaining. Your centerpiece dish — the stew — can be bubbling away on the stove a day or two before the party, giving you a chance to set the table, prepare a side dish or two, mix up a pitcher of margaritas, and then just kick back and enjoy the conversation when guests arrive. For conjuring up memories of mom's cooking and satisfying hearty winter appetites, few foods get the juices flowing like a well-turned-out stew — even if menudo meant a Mexican rock group to mom.

Stewing, the Technique

Stewing and braising are similar techniques. In both methods, meats are sea-soned and browned, covered with liquid, and then cooked gently and slowly until the meat is tender and the cooking juices are rich and flavorful. Large cuts of meat like pot roast are usually braised, and smaller, cut-up pieces are stewed.

To get the most from your stews, follow these tips:

✔ Always sauté seasonings and spices in the fat first to release their flavors. Do not toss raw spices into the liquid.

✔ Gently simmer stews at the lowest boil. Rapidly boiling toughens the meat's fibers.

✔ If your stew contains wine, always add it *after* the meat has been browned. Wine should be simmered until reduced by half.

✔ Always cook the food for a longer — rather than shorter — time, using the suggested cooking times as your guide. It can take a long time for all the goodness from silver skin (the thin slivery membrane covering muscle), connective tissue, ligaments, and tendon to dissolve into the broth. The good stew maker is patient.

✔ Coating the stewing meat first with flour helps thicken the sauce. Don't be too concerned with dusting off excess flour — more is fine.

✔ Pieces of meat should always be seared, or browned, in fat before the liquid is added. Searing caramelizes the surfaces for added flavor.

✔ Use a big, heavy, deep pot with a lid for even, gentle cooking for stewing and braising. A sturdy soup pot is fine, as is a large Dutch oven or heavy casserole.

✔ Whatever meat you choose, do not start with the puny 1-inch cubes prewrapped and sold in the market as stewing meat. Ask the butcher to trim your meat into 2-inch cubes or buy larger cuts and trim the meat yourself. Because meat shrinks with cooking, you need to start big if you want to end with the kind of stew meat that guests can sink their teeth into. And don't be compulsive about removing all the fat. Stew tastes better if some fat remains.

Meats for stewing

The best meats for long, slow cooking are also the least expensive. They derive from the most exercised parts of the animal, parts that have developed more muscle. Look for the following cuts:

✔ Pork butt and shoulder

✔ Lamb shank, shoulder, leg, and riblets

✔ Beef pot roast, chuck, shank, and short ribs

The Traditional Stews

Though it takes time to cook a mole or menudo from scratch, nothing captures the feeling of the traditional Mexican kitchen as well, and the time investment is well worth it. Earthy, spicy, tried-and-true stews such as these are what first convinced us that cooking and eating don't always have to be French to be sophisticated.

Menudo

Menudo, the spicy stew of tripe, chiles, and hominy, is traditionally eaten as a hangover cure on New Year's Day in Mexico. (See the sidebar "What is this thing called tripe?" in this chapter for more information on tripe.) With its big, gamey flavor, chewy texture, and bracing broth, it's guaranteed to open the eyes and revive the soul of even the most weak-in-the-knees reveler.

You don't need to take your vitamin B when menudo is on the menu. Tripe is exceptionally high in the vitamin that aids the digestion of carbohydrates, fats, and protein. No wonder it's good for hangovers!

We prefer our menudo colored red from ancho chiles and served piping hot, with a nice stack of warm tortillas for dipping in the broth.

Special tool: *Blender*

Preparation time: *20 minutes*

Cooking time: *2 hours and 40 minutes, plus 10 minutes soaking*

Yield: *6 servings*

1½ pounds precleaned tripe

1 tablespoon plus 2 teaspoons salt

1 tablespoon white vinegar

12 cups cold water

2 teaspoons dried oregano

2 ancho chiles, stemmed and seeded (see Chapter 3 for more information on working with chiles)

2 tablespoons olive oil

1 medium yellow onion, diced

4 cloves garlic, peeled and minced

2 cups canned white hominy, drained

2 poblano chiles, roasted, peeled, seeded, and cut into strips

Garnishes: 1 bunch scallions, sliced thinly at an angle; lime quarters; chopped cilantro; dried oregano; and cayenne

12 warm 6-inch tortillas for serving

(continued)

1 Trim excess fat from the tripe and wash well in cold water. Cut into ½-inch strips and place in a large pot with cold water to cover. Add 1 tablespoon of salt and the white vinegar. Bring to a boil and continue boiling for 5 minutes. Drain in a colander and rinse well with warm water.

2 Transfer the tripe to a large, heavy soup pot with 12 cups water, oregano, and 2 teaspoons salt. Bring to a boil, reduce to a simmer, and cook, uncovered, about 2 hours. Check the pot occasionally, skimming off the foam and adding more water as necessary to cover the tripe.

3 Toast the ancho chiles in a dry medium skillet over low heat for less than a minute, just to soften. Transfer to the blender jar, pour in 1 cup of the tripe cooking liquid, and let soak for 10 minutes. Then puree until smooth.

4 Heat the olive oil in a large skillet over medium heat. Sauté the onion until translucent, but not brown, about 5 minutes. Add the garlic and cook for 1 additional minute. Pour in the pureed chile mixture and cook over high heat for 5 minutes. Transfer the chile mixture to the tripe pot along with the hominy and poblanos. Bring to a boil, reduce to a simmer, and cook, uncovered, for 20 minutes. Serve in deep bowls with the scallions, limes, cilantro, oregano, and cayenne and lots of warm tortillas.

A calf's foot added to the menudo pot, along with the tripe, results in an even richer, more gelatinous broth. It's a very traditional Mexican version of this dish. You can purchase a foot from your supermarket butcher or from a Mexican meat market.

If you're the only tripe eater in the house, treat yourself well and cook up a pot of menudo. Leftovers can be chilled, divided into individual servings, stowed in plastic bags, and stored in the freezer for future cravings.

What is this thing called tripe?

Tripe is the stomach of any animal used for food. In America, most tripe comes from the lining of a cow's second stomach. Honeycomb tripe is the most tender and delicately flavored kind of tripe.

Most of the tripe available in the supermarket has been partially cooked by the packing house to start the tenderizing process. Look for a pale, off-white color when shopping for tripe and plan on cooking it the same day.

Mexican Rice with Stewed Chicken

After learning the technique of toasting noodles, we found ourselves adding toasted noodles to lots of dishes for that addictive, dark brown, burnished wheat flavor. Arroz con pollo, as this dish is known in Mexico, is as much a celebration of rice and noodles as it is of chicken.

Special tool: *Blender*

Preparation time: *20 minutes*

Cooking time: *1 hour*

Yield: *4 to 6 servings*

2½- to 3-pound chicken, cut into 6 or 8 serving pieces with bone

Salt and pepper to taste

1 tablespoon vegetable oil

3 tablespoons butter

4 ounces fine noodles, such as fideo or capellini, broken into 1-inch lengths

1½ cups short-grain white rice, rinsed and drained well

1 cup canned crushed tomatoes

1 large yellow onion, chopped

1 large clove garlic, peeled and chopped

5 cups boiling water

Salt and pepper to taste

1 cup fresh or frozen baby peas

½ bunch parsley leaves, coarsely chopped

1 Rinse the chicken and pat dry. Generously season with salt and pepper.

2 Heat the oil in a large, heavy ovenproof casserole or pan over medium-high heat. Add the chicken and fry until brown all over. Transfer to a platter and set aside.

3 Drain the fat from the pan and add the butter. Place over medium heat and toss in the noodles. Sauté, stirring constantly, until well-browned, about 5 minutes. Reduce the heat to low and add the rice. Cook, stirring occasionally, about 5 minutes longer, until lightly browned.

4 Meanwhile, combine the tomatoes, onion, and garlic in a blender. Puree until smooth and pour into the rice mixture in the pan. Continue cooking, stirring frequently, for 2 minutes.

5 Return the chicken to the pan. Add the boiling water and salt and pepper. Bring to a boil over high heat. Reduce to a simmer and cook very gently, covered, about 30 minutes, until the chicken is almost done. Stir in the peas and cook, covered, 5 minutes longer. The rice should have absorbed all the liquid, but if any remains, cook a few minutes longer. Stir in the parsley, cover again, and let stand 5 minutes before serving.

(continued)

If you're a rice lover as I am, this casserole will become part of your everyday repertoire. By cooking the rice with such a rich array of ingredients — browned chicken, toasted noodles, onion, and garlic — it becomes the most flavorful pilaf you'll ever taste.

Pork Chile Verde

Tart, green tomatillos are perfect for cutting the richness of pork — our favorite stewing meat and a popular meat in Mexico. What makes this dish typically Mexican is its focus on chiles rather than beans. To round out the meal, serve with warm tortillas and Red Rice (see Chapter 10), which provides a delightful contrast.

Preparation time: *20 minutes*

Cooking time: *2 hours and 30 minutes plus 50 minutes for Red Rice*

Yield: *6 to 8 servings*

2½ pounds boneless pork butt or shoulder, trimmed of fat and cut into 2-inch cubes

Salt and pepper to taste

Flour for dredging

¼ cup vegetable oil

2 small yellow onions, cut into 1-inch chunks

3 poblano chiles, cut into 1-inch chunks

4 jalapeño peppers, seeded and finely chopped

3 cloves garlic, minced

1½ pounds tomatillos, roasted, peeled, and chopped (see Chapter 3 for tips on roasting)

2 teaspoons dried oregano

1 teaspoon ground cumin

1 bunch cilantro leaves, chopped (½ cup)

3 cups chicken stock (see Chapter 8)

1 Generously season the pork with salt and pepper. Lightly coat with the flour. Heat the oil in a large, heavy skillet over medium-high heat. Fry the pork in small batches until well browned on all sides. With a slotted spoon or tongs, transfer the pork to a wide, heavy soup pot.

2 Drain the fat from the pan. Place the onions in the same skillet and cook over moderate heat, stirring occasionally, until limp, about 5 minutes. Add the poblano chiles and jalapeños and cook for 4 minutes longer. Stir in the garlic and cook for about 2 minutes longer.

3 Transfer the onion-chile mixture to the pot with the pork. Add the tomatillos, oregano, cumin, and cilantro. Pour in the chicken stock and bring to a boil. Reduce to a simmer and cook, uncovered, for 2 hours, or until the pork is fork tender. Adjust the seasonings with salt and pepper.

To turn our green chile red, substitute 2 red bell peppers for the poblanos, 1½ pounds tomatoes for the tomatillos, and 3 tablespoons ground red chile for the jalapeños and eliminate the cilantro.

Dark Mole with Turkey

The trick to tackling a *mole,* the saucy chile, seed, and nut-based stew from Mexico, is to assemble and measure all the ingredients beforehand because there's an awful lot of stuff to keep track of. The cooking itself is simple — just toasting, pureeing, and simmering — but the results are as complex as any finicky French sauce.

Whenever you're faced with a long ingredient list like the one for mole, get a grip before turning the page in horror. If you take a relaxed attitude toward the list, cooking complicated foods won't seem so daunting. In the ingredient list for mole, for example, almost any dried fruit can be substituted for the raisins (apricots, prunes, and apples are fine), almonds or walnuts can stand in for the peanuts, the chocolate can be left out entirely, no one will miss the ground cloves, and one type of chile can be used instead of two if both are not available. Think of the recipe list as an idealized template that you can adjust according to what is available and what you prefer. You'll increase your fun in the kitchen that way.

A hidden bonus of cooking mole is that it freezes so well. We recommend making a double batch and keeping one in the freezer for a second special dinner, or for enchiladas, tamales, or other Mexican treats.

Serve mole with plenty of White Rice (see Chapter 10) and a vinegary garnish like pickled, sliced jalapeño peppers or Pickled Onions (see Chapter 14) to cut the sauce's richness.

Special tool: *Blender*

Preparation time: *40 minutes, plus 20 minutes for cooling plus 45 minutes for White Rice*

Cooking time: *1 hour and 30 minutes*

Yield: *6 servings*

2 turkey legs and thighs, cut into 8 pieces with bone and skin

Salt and pepper to taste

4 dry pasilla chiles

4 dry ancho chiles

(continued)

5 cups boiling water

¼ cup vegetable oil

1 medium yellow onion, diced

2 cloves garlic, peeled and minced

½ teaspoon ground cinnamon

¼ teaspoon ground coriander

⅛ teaspoon ground cloves

1 teaspoon pepper

2 tablespoons skinless raw peanuts

2 tablespoons golden raisins

4 Roma tomatoes, peeled, cored, and chopped

1 6-inch corn tortilla, lightly toasted over an open flame and broken into small pieces

½ cup sesame seeds

1½ cups chicken stock (see Chapter 8)

1 ounce bittersweet chocolate, coarsely chopped

1½ teaspoons salt

6 cups White Rice (see Chapter 10)

Garnish: 4 limes, cut in wedges

1 Season the turkey all over with salt and pepper.

2 Core, seed, and devein the pasilla and ancho chiles. Toast the chiles, a few at a time, in a dry, heavy skillet over medium heat until the skins begin to blister and the aromas are released, about 2 minutes. (See Chapter 3 for additional chile handling techniques.) Transfer to a bowl. Pour on the boiling water and set aside to cool. When cool, transfer the chiles with their liquid to a blender. Puree until smooth and set aside. (You don't need to wash the blender jar yet.)

3 Heat the oil in a large, heavy-bottomed casserole or Dutch oven over moderate heat. Fry the turkey until brown all over and set aside.

4 In the same casserole, add the onion and sauté until golden. Add the garlic and sauté for 1 minute longer. Stir in the cinnamon, coriander, cloves, and pepper and cook 2 minutes longer. Add the peanuts and raisins and cook for 1 more minute. Then add the tomatoes and tortilla and cook for 5 minutes longer, until the tortillas soften.

5 In a small, dry sauté pan over medium heat, toast the sesame seeds until golden, shaking the pan occasionally. Transfer half of the seeds to the blender or food processor and reserve half for garnish. Transfer the onion mixture to the blender with the seeds and pour in the stock. Puree until smooth.

6 Pour the reserved pureed chiles into the same casserole, leaving any fat in the bottom of the pan. Cook over low heat for 10 minutes, stirring frequently. Add the blended seed mixture, chocolate, 1½ teaspoons salt, and browned turkey. Cook, covered, at a low simmer for 45 minutes or until the turkey is fork tender. (The finished mole should be the consistency of barbecue sauce or ketchup. If your sauce is too thick, thin it with chicken stock or water to taste.) Serve the hot turkey over white rice. Spoon on plenty of sauce, sprinkle with the reserved toasted sesame seeds, and top with lime wedges for squeezing.

TOQUE TIP

Use a heavy cleaver to cut the turkey into parts. The trick is to choose a spot between the joints or where the bone is thin, hold the cleaver high, and bring it down with a forceful chop or two.

Mole is not a fudge sauce

Moles are cooked throughout Mexico, although the region most known for the complexity of its moles is the southern state of Oaxaca. There, in the land of the seven moles, luscious moles range from the thick, green, herb-based *mole verde* to the deep reddish-brown *colorado,* the brighter *coloradito,* and the exotic black mole derived from the local chile chichilo.

What all moles have in common is that they are stews featuring an abundant quantity of sauce thickened with toasted chiles, nuts, and seeds. Each region has its own version, and local markets sell preground mole pastes for time-pressed cooks.

If Mexico does have a national mole, it's Mole Poblano from the city of Puebla in central Mexico. Legend has it that the original chocolate-tinged sauce was created by a nun of the Santa Rosa convent for a dinner honoring a visiting archbishop. Her goal was to blend Indian and Spanish ingredients in one glorious dish celebrating Mexican culture, and she did.

The role of chocolate in mole has been overemphasized outside of Mexico. Chocolate goes back to ancient times in Mexico and was traditionally considered a savory — not a sweet — ingredient. Cacao beans are spicy and bitter before sugar is added. The pat or two of chocolate stirred in at the end of a mole adds a slight underpinning of yet another, mysterious, slightly sweet ingredient. Guests shouldn't taste the chocolate, and if the chocolate is omitted, it should not be too noticeable.

Green Pumpkin-Seed Mole

This fresh, green, buttery mole includes rich pepitas (which are pumpkin seeds), herbs, and vegetables. In Mexico, pepitas have a more distinctive squash flavor, and they are traditionally ground with the shells on for even more flavor and texture.

Special tools: *Blender or food processor, cast-iron skillet, 13-x-10-inch flameproof baking dish*

Preparation time: *20 minutes plus 45 minutes for White Rice*

Cooking time: *45 minutes*

Yield: *6 servings*

(continued)

¾ cup raw pumpkin seeds, or pepitas

1 teaspoon cumin seeds

½ teaspoon black pepper

10 tomatillos, husked and quartered

2 serrano chiles

2 cloves garlic, peeled

2 romaine lettuce leaves

⅛ teaspoon ground cinnamon

1 bunch cilantro, including stems and leaves (½ cup)

Green tops from 2 radishes

1 small yellow onion, quartered

Salt and pepper to taste

2 tablespoons olive oil

2 cups chicken stock (see Chapter 8)

3 large skinless, boneless chicken breasts, split in half

6 cups cooked White Rice (see Chapter 10)

Garnishes: 1 bunch radishes, thinly sliced, and 3 limes, cut in wedges

1 Place a dry cast-iron skillet over low heat. Toast the pumpkin seeds or pepitas, cumin seeds, and pepper, shaking the pan occasionally, until their aromas are released, about 5 minutes. Do not brown. Set aside to cool and then grind to a powder in a blender or food processor.

2 Combine the tomatillos, serranos, garlic, lettuce, cinnamon, cilantro, radish tops, onion, and salt in a food processor or blender. Puree until smooth.

3 Preheat the oven to 350°.

4 Heat the olive oil in a large saucepan over high heat. Standing back to avoid splatters, pour in the pureed tomatillo mixture and sizzle for 30 seconds. Stir in the stock, reduce the heat, and simmer for 10 minutes. Turn up the heat to high and bring to a boil. Stir in the ground nut mixture and remove from heat. Puree in a blender or food processor, in batches if necessary. Transfer to a 13-x-10-inch flameproof baking dish.

5 Season the chicken all over with salt and pepper. Place the chicken breasts in the sauce and bring to a boil over moderate heat. Cover with foil, transfer to the oven, and bake for 20 minutes. Serve the chicken and its sauce over a bed of White Rice. Sprinkle the radish slices over the top and serve with lime wedges.

The Innovations

In the less-traditional preparations in this section, we take a method or an ingredient from the Mexican kitchen and translate it in a way that resonates with American palates. All three dishes deliver big, impressive flavors without demanding complicated techniques in the kitchen, and all are great for parties.

Chile Braised Lamb Shanks

We like to cook and serve our lamb shanks whole so that a big, knobby bone is sticking up out of the bowl, Flintstone-style, just begging to be gnawed on (see photo in the color insert). (You may need to ask your butcher for a shank or front leg bone that's not already cut into smaller osso-bucco-style slices.) In general, lamb shanks are a great cut to use for rich-tasting broths because they contain such gelatinous goodness.

In Mexico, young goats, or *cabritos,* are as prized as lamb in a dish like the Chile Braised Lamb Shanks.

Special tool: Dutch oven

Preparation time: 20 minutes

Cooking time: 1 hour and 40 minutes

Yield: 6 servings

6 lamb shanks, trimmed of excess fat

Salt and pepper to taste

2 teaspoons cayenne

2 teaspoons paprika

2 teaspoons ground cumin

2 cups flour for coating

½ cup vegetable oil

2 medium yellow onions, sliced

6 cloves garlic, peeled and minced

2 teaspoons dried oregano

12 cups chicken stock, water, or combination of both (see Chapter 8 for the chicken stock recipe)

2 tomatoes, seeded and diced

3 poblano chiles, roasted, peeled, seeded, and diced (see Chapter 3 for more information on working with chiles)

6 cups cooked White Rice (see Chapter 10)

1 cup (4 ounces) grated añejo cheese

1 Generously sprinkle the shanks with the salt and pepper, cayenne, paprika, and cumin. Dip in the flour to lightly coat. Heat the oil in a large Dutch oven over high heat. Brown the shanks on all sides, transfer to a platter, and reserve.

2 Reduce heat to medium and cook the onions in the same pan, stirring occasionally, until golden brown. Add the garlic and oregano and cook for 1 minute to release aromas. Return the shanks to the pan and pour in the stock or water. (If the shanks are not completely covered by liquid, add enough water to cover.)

(continued)

3 Bring to a boil, reduce to a simmer, and cook, covered, about 45 minutes, occasionally skimming foam and fat from the top. Stir in the tomatoes and chiles and cook for an additional 40 minutes, or until tender. To test for doneness, pierce with a fork. If the shank easily slides off fork, the meat is tender. Remove from heat.

4 To serve, arrange each shank over a bed of rice in each serving bowl. Top with plenty of broth and vegetables. Garnish with the cheese and serve immediately.

Caldo de Pescado

A rustic fish stew such as this caldo is a great healthful choice for entertaining (see photo in the color insert). You can make the fish stock and broth ahead and toss in the fresh fish at the last moment. All it takes is a few crusty baguettes and a fresh green salad for everyone to feel well fed.

Special tool: *Blender*

Preparation time: *20 minutes*

Cooking time: *30 minutes*

Yield: *4 servings*

3 Roma tomatoes, cored

5 cloves garlic, peeled

1 tablespoon olive oil

1 medium yellow onion, thinly sliced

1 teaspoon salt

½ teaspoon pepper

⅔ cup dry white wine

4 cups fish stock (see following recipe) or clam juice

2 carrots, peeled, halved lengthwise, and cut into ⅛-inch slices

3 small boiling potatoes, peeled, halved lengthwise, and cut into ⅛-inch slices

1½ pounds assorted fish fillets, such as flounder, sea bass, and snapper, cut into 2-inch chunks

Garnishes: ½ cup chopped cilantro leaves, lime wedges, and sliced serrano chiles

1 Preheat the broiler. Place the tomatoes and garlic on a baking tray and broil until the tomatoes are charred all over and the garlic is golden. (Tuck the garlic under the tomatoes to prevent burning.) Transfer to a blender and puree.

2 Heat the olive oil in a heavy soup pot over moderate heat. Cook the onions with the salt and pepper until translucent. Pour in the wine, turn the heat up to high, and reduce the liquid by half. Pour in the fish stock or clam juice and bring back to a boil. Add the carrots, potatoes, and garlic tomato puree and cook for about 5 minutes. Stir in the fish. Cook for about 7 minutes, until the fish is just done. Sprinkle in the cilantro and serve immediately with the lime wedges, squeezed and tossed in the bowl, and chiles.

TOQUE TIP If you don't have time to make fish stock, substitute all clam juice or half bottled clam juice and half water; however, you will miss out on the authentic flavor that fish stock provides. Remember that you can make fish stock days in advance of serving!

Fish Stock

Ask your local fish store to sell you heads and bones for soup making.

Special tool: *Strainer*

Preparation time: *10 minutes*

Cooking time: *1 hour and 15 minutes*

Yield: *4 cups*

2 tablespoons olive oil	*7 cups water*
1 carrot, peeled and chopped	*1 cup dry white wine*
1 stalk celery, chopped	*Bay leaves to taste*
1 medium yellow onion, chopped	*Black peppercorns to taste*
2 cloves garlic, peeled and chopped	*Parsley to taste*
2 pounds fish heads and bones (avoid fatty fish like salmon but any white fish is fine)	*Dried thyme to taste*
	Tarragon to taste

Heat the olive oil in a large stockpot over medium-high heat. Sauté the carrot, celery, onion, and garlic until golden. Add the fish bones and heads and sauté for 5 minutes longer. Add the water, wine, bay leaves, black peppercorns, parsley, thyme, and tarragon. Bring to a boil, reduce to a simmer, and cook, uncovered, for about 1 hour, skimming the foam occasionally. Strain, discarding the solids, and set aside to cool. Store in the refrigerator as long as 4 days or freeze up to 3 months. Remove the fat from the top before using.

Chipotle Black Bean Turkey Chili

This updated, reduced-fat chili features three of our favorite ingredients: smoky chipotle chiles, creamy beans, and rich, meaty turkey. A chili this satisfying doesn't need a lot of garnishes — a dab of sour cream and a moist square of corn bread are all it takes to round out the meal. For advanced chili making, toss out the bottled chili powder and blend your own spice mix as outlined in the following recipe for Chili Powder Mix.

(continued)

Preparation time: *10 minutes*

Cooking time: *2 hours*

Yield: *4 servings*

2 cups dry black beans	*2 green bell peppers, stemmed, seeded, and diced*
8 cups water	*1 tablespoon chili powder (or see the following recipe for a homemade chili powder mix)*
2 arbol chiles	
3 bay leaves	
2 tablespoons vegetable oil	*1 tablespoon ground cumin*
1 pound coarsely ground turkey, dark meat	*4 canned chipotle chiles, stemmed and minced*
1 large yellow onion, diced	*2½ cups chicken stock (see Chapter 8)*
1½ teaspoons salt	
½ teaspoon pepper	*Garnish: Sour cream*
3 cloves garlic, peeled and minced	

1 Place the beans in a large pot with 8 cups water, arbol chiles, and bay leaves. Bring to a boil, reduce to a simmer, and cover. Cook until tender, about 1 hour. Remove the chiles and bay leaves and discard. Do not drain the beans.

2 Heat the vegetable oil in a large heavy pot over medium-high heat. Fry the turkey, stirring often and breaking up with a spoon, until evenly browned. Add the onion, salt, and pepper and sauté over moderate heat, stirring occasionally, until lightly golden, about 10 minutes. Stir in the garlic, green peppers, chili powder, cumin, and chipotles. Cook, stirring frequently, for 3 minutes, or until aromas are released.

3 Stir in the black beans, their liquid, and the chicken stock and cook, uncovered, for 40 minutes or until the flavors have blended and the chili has thickened. Serve in bowls with a dollop of sour cream on top.

Like all good chilis, Chipotle Black Bean Turkey Chili is a great dish to make ahead and freeze for a party. You can store it in the refrigerator a few days or freeze as long as 4 weeks.

Chili Powder Mix

If you love chili as we do, mix up your own blend of chili spices instead of settling for the uninspired blend at the supermarket. Just the right combination of cumin, oregano, coriander, and red chile powder lifts a pot of ground meat and beans into the galaxy of the truly great chilis. Just store any remaining spice mix in a jar on your spice shelf and use it to season meats, chicken, and turkey, as well as any chili, stew, or soup that needs spicing up.

Preparation time: 5 minutes

Yield: *⅓ cup*

3 tablespoons ancho chile powder

1 tablespoon ground cumin

2 teaspoons dried oregano

1 teaspoon ground coriander

1 teaspoon pepper

1 teaspoon coarse salt

Mix the ingredients together and store in a sealed jar.

As far as I'm concerned, our custom chili mix can always use a bit more cumin. Feel free to pump it up, as long as Mary Sue's not watching! Just be careful that the cumin doesn't overpower all the other flavors.

Cold facts about chili

Chili is one of those dishes that stirs up unreasonable passions — especially among Texans. Although chiliheads may not agree on much, here are a few points that most people won't dispute:

- Chili with meat and beans did not originate in Mexico.

- Chili was born in Texas and then took a few twists and turns west to Arizona and California and east to the Atlantic seaboard. Along the way, it has been garnished with everything from cheddar cheese to oyster crackers and chopped onions, enriched with beer, and stretched with various beans and vegetables. The meat has even been eliminated for vegetarian chili, but to a Texan, if it contains beans, it's not chili — it's blasphemy.

- The premier chili contest in America is the Annual World Championship Chili Cookoff sponsored by the Chili Appreciation Society in Terlingua, Texas. Frank X. Tolbert started the contest in 1966 to promote his book, *A Bowl of Red,* written with Hallie Stillwell and published by Texas A&M Univeristy Press.

Chapter 12

Fish and Seafood Stars

· ·

· ·

With Mexico's 6,000 miles of coastline along the Pacific Ocean, Gulf of Mexico, Sea of Cortez, and the Caribbean, it's not surprising that fresh fish plays such an important part in the Mexican diet. It's eaten in sparkling ceviches (see Chapter 5), rustic seafood stews, impressive whole fish entrées, and quick tacos and enchiladas (Chapter 6).

Tasting the Fruit of the Sea

In this section, we focus on two popular types of seafood that we know people love to order in restaurants but we suspect people may be uncomfortable cooking at home — squid and shrimp. Once you understand their characteristics better — both benefit from quick exposure to heat — you'll be ready to dazzle your guests with your (Mexican) seafood prowess.

Sampling squid

Of all the cephalopods — conical-headed sea creatures having eight to ten tentacles — squid has gained the greatest acceptance in the American market. Not as large, scary, and chewy as its cousin, the octopus, squid is a good, cheap source of protein that's easy to prepare. Because many of us have been turned off by tough squid, you'll be amazed by how tender squid can be when properly prepared.

Squid can be purchased precleaned and frozen at fish markets. It should smell clean and sweet, and the color should be white to light purple.

Unlike other seafood, freezing does not diminish squid's quality too much. After you clean the squid and remove the beaks, you can eat both the body and tentacles.

Our general rule for squid cookery is to cook it quickly, no more than a minute or two, over high heat to avoid toughening the meat. When sautéing a food like squid, which releases lots of water, always avoid overcrowding the pan so that the ingredient doesn't boil or steam in its juices rather than sauté. For a quick sauté such as Garlicky Squid Sauté, your pan should be so hot that the oil is smoking and you can hear the oil sizzle when the squid hits the pan.

Garlicky Squid Sauté

If you're a fried calamari fan, chances are you'll love this quick squid sauté (see photo in the color insert). Without the usual breaded crust, you can really taste the mild meaty flavor of squid, our favorite cephalopod.

Special tool: *Blender*

Preparation time: *15 minutes*

Cooking time: *10 minutes*

Yield: *4 servings as an entrée, 6 servings as an appetizer*

1½ pounds squid, cleaned	*2 large tomatoes, seeded and diced*
15 cloves garlic, peeled	*1 large bunch oregano leaves, chopped (½ cup)*
½ cup olive oil	
1 teaspoon salt	*Any rice from Chapter 10*
½ teaspoon pepper	*Any beans from Chapter 10*

1 Cut the squid into ¼-inch rings. Wash, pat dry, and place in a mixing bowl.

2 Puree the garlic with ¼ cup of the olive oil in a blender until smooth. Pour over the squid. Add the salt and pepper, tossing well to combine.

3 Heat a dry medium skillet over high heat. Then add a generous tablespoon of the remaining ¼ cup olive oil and heat until almost smoking. Pour in one-third of the squid with its marinade and sauté for about 30 seconds. Stir in one-third each of the tomatoes and oregano and cook for about 2 minutes longer, just until the tomatoes dissolve and the garlic colors slightly. Transfer to a platter in a 200° oven and wipe out the skillet. Repeat twice, until all the squid is done. Serve hot with rice and beans as an entrée, or with flour tortillas as an appetizer.

Showing off with shrimp

Since discovering rock shrimp a few years ago, we've started using it a lot. It's less expensive than shell-on shrimp, the texture is good, and the taste is consistently sweet, almost like lobster meat. These tiny crustaceans, caught in the Gulf of Mexico and off the Atlantic seaboard's southern states, are sold peeled and frozen in vacuum-sealed packs. Because they're already cleaned, they are exceptionally handy for quick ceviches (see Chapter 5), breading and frying, or any shrimp dish that doesn't feature the taste of a large whole shrimp.

Shrimp in a Garlic Bath

In this traditional dish, called *al mojo de ajo* in Mexico, a quick, rustic sauce of garlic and dried chile slivers is cooked in the same pan as juicy rock shrimp. Serve with Seared Chard finished with fresh lime juice (Chapter 10) and plenty of White Rice (Chapter 10) for contrast and balance.

A simple hot garlic and chile oil like the one in Shrimp in a Garlic Bath is also delicious drizzled over broiled or grilled fish.

Preparation time: *10 minutes*

Cooking time: *20 minutes*

Yield: *2 servings*

¼ cup olive oil

10 cloves garlic, peeled and thinly sliced

¾ pound rock or medium shrimp, peeled, deveined, washed, and dried

Salt and pepper to taste

1 large ancho chile, wiped clean, stemmed, seeded, and finely julienned (see Chapter 3 for more information on working with chiles)

3 tablespoons chicken stock or clam juice (see Chapter 8 for the chicken stock recipe)

1 tablespoon freshly squeezed lime juice

2 tablespoons chopped fresh Italian parsley

2 cups cooked White Rice (see Chapter 10)

(continued)

1 Heat the olive oil in a large skillet over medium-low heat. Cook the garlic slices until tender but not brown, 2 to 3 minutes. Transfer with a slotted spoon to paper towels and reserve.

2 Turn the heat under the pan up to high. Quickly toss the shrimp with the salt and pepper in a bowl. When the oil is nearly smoking, add the shrimp. Sauté, stirring and shaking the pan to prevent sticking, 3 to 4 minutes or just until the shrimp are still slightly undercooked. Remove from the heat. With a slotted spoon, transfer the shrimp to a platter, leaving as much liquid as possible in the pan.

3 Return the pan to the burner and reduce the heat to medium. Add the garlic slices and chile and sauté, stirring frequently, until the oil begins to turn orange from the chile. Stir in the chicken stock or clam juice, along with the shrimp and any juice that has collected on the platter. Add the lime juice and parsley, bring to a boil, and remove from the heat. Serve immediately over the White Rice.

Whatever you do, do not reduce the quantity of garlic called for in this recipe. What's the point of a mild-mannered garlic bath? The trick is to cook the garlic slowly and carefully, without browning, for a delicious sauce that doesn't overpower the fish.

South of the Border Fish Dishes

We approve of the unfussy Mexican approach to cooking fish. Each of the dishes is this section captures the fun and excitement of real Mexican food, while also highlighting the ease of cooking with fish. In fact, we promise to get you out of the kitchen in 30 minutes or less. Promise.

Shopping for fresh fish

Fish that is not fresh is no fun to eat. In fact, part of the reason that fish has a bad rap in this country is because often the fish available at the supermarket has an overpowering, fishy smell.

Purchase fish from a specialty market whose reputation is staked on the quality of its fish. Look for the following when you're fish shopping:

✔ Spotlessly clean display cases and counters.

✔ Salespeople who really know their product.

- Clams, oysters, and mussels that are sealed shut and feel heavy in the hand, but not too heavy. If one is much heavier than the rest, it may be filled with sand and should be discarded.

- Whole fish with moist skin and bright red blood. Cloudiness or clarity of a fish's eyes is not a trustworthy measure.

- Filets that are translucent and glistening, not opaque or transparent.

- Fish that smells clean and fresh, not at all "fishy." The surface of the flesh or skin should never be sticky or slimy.

Fish tastes best when you cook it the same day that you purchase it. If you must store the fish, wrap it in plastic wrap, place it on a rack in a small roasting pan, and then cover the fish with ice and refrigerate. Do not store fish longer than a day or two.

Cooking fish to perfection

The trickiest part about cooking fish properly is judging when it's done. An additional minute or two of high heat can make a big difference with such tender flesh.

We are big believers in slightly undercooking fish because it continues to cook even after you remove it from the heat. If you cook fish all the way through, it will probably taste dry by the time it's served. At our restaurants, we cook our fillets until opaque on either side but still slightly translucent in the middle.

To judge doneness, trust your senses rather than the clock because too many variables come into play when you're cooking delicate fish. Toss out those old-fashioned cooking charts and use the tip of a knife to pull aside the flesh and peek at the center to judge for yourself.

Fresh garlic

As lovers of big, bold flavors, we are hopelessly addicted to garlic. At the market, look for firm, heavy heads with no green sprouts or hollow patches and don't buy more than a supply for a week or two. Garlic changes flavor and grows stronger as it ages.

At home, store your garlic in a dark, well-ventilated place — those ceramic countertop crocks with air holes work quite well. As for garlic breath, forget about it!

Salmon Baked in Salsa Verde

By roasting the fish in its sauce, sweet salmon, tart tomatillos, and spicy chiles all blend into one flavorful dish. And you have only two things to clean up afterwards — the roasting pan and the blender jar!

Special tool: *Blender or food processor*

Preparation time: *10 minutes, plus 10 minutes for the Green Tomatillo Salsa*

Cooking time: *10 minutes*

Yield: *6 servings*

6 salmon, halibut, or sea bass fillets, 4 ounces each	*1 poblano chile, roasted, seeded, and chopped*
Oil for greasing baking dish	*2 teaspoons dried oregano*
Salt and pepper to taste	*2 tablespoons olive oil*
2 cloves garlic, peeled	*Salt and pepper to taste*
1½ cups Green Tomatillo Salsa (see Chapter 5)	*Garnish: 6 scallions, thinly sliced at an angle*

1 Preheat the oven to 400°. Season the fish all over with salt and pepper and place it in a single layer in an oiled ovenproof baking dish.

2 To make the salsa verde, combine the garlic cloves, salsa, chile, oregano, olive oil, and salt and pepper in a blender or food processor and puree.

3 Pour the salsa mixture over the fish in the pan and bake, covered, for 10 minutes, until the thickest part of the fish is done. Serve hot with sliced scallions.

Grilled Swordfish with Fresh Tomato and Herb Salsa

Our favorite fish preparations are often the simplest, and things don't get much simpler than this (see photo in the color insert). A fresh tomato and herb salsa supplies just enough bright acidity, color, and texture to highlight the fish, without overpowering it the way a cooked sauce might.

Preparation time: *15 minutes plus 15 minutes chilling time*

Cooking time: *15 minutes*

Yield: *6 servings*

½ cup extra-virgin olive oil

1 teaspoon salt

½ teaspoon pepper

6 ripe tomatoes, seeded and diced

½ bunch oregano leaves, chopped (¼ cup)

½ bunch cilantro leaves, chopped (¼ cup)

½ bunch Italian parsley leaves, chopped (¼ cup)

3 tablespoons capers, chopped with juice

3 scallions, light green and white parts, thinly sliced

6 skinless swordfish fillets, 6 ounces each

Sea salt and black pepper to taste

1 To make the salsa, combine the olive oil, salt, pepper, tomatoes, oregano, cilantro, parsley, capers, and scallions in a bowl. Reserve in the refrigerator.

2 Season the fish all over with the sea salt and pepper. Cook on a very hot, clean grill, about 3 minutes per side. The inside should be bright pink. Transfer to a platter and chill 15 minutes.

3 To serve, arrange the fillets on individual plates. Spoon the salsa over the fish and serve cold.

Sure, oregano, cilantro, and parsley are good choices for the Fresh Tomato and Herb Salsa. But a fresh salsa such as this one is no time to be fussy. Substitute other herbs, such as tarragon, chervil, basil, or chives, as the spirit (or the marketplace) moves you.

Pan-Seared Bass with Chile Lime Broth

Popular sea bass is a great choice for home entertaining. It's not easily overcooked, and it holds its own with assertive flavors like olives, garlic, chiles, and lime. For a complete meal, serve with wedges of roasted potatoes and seared greens.

Special tool: *Draining rack*

Preparation time: *15 minutes*

Cooking time: *20 minutes*

Yield: *4 servings*

(continued)

1½ pounds skinless, boneless filets of sea bass, or other firm-fleshed fish, cut in 4 portions

Salt and pepper to taste

3 tablespoons olive oil

1 small yellow onion, thinly sliced

4 cloves garlic, peeled and minced

2 serrano chiles, stemmed and sliced in ¼-inch disks

1 lime, cut in 8 wedges

1 tomato, cored, seeded, and cut in strips

½ bunch fresh oregano leaves, coarsely chopped (¼ cup)

½ cup Spanish green olives, sliced

½ cup white wine

¾ cup fish stock (see Chapter 11) or clam juice

1 Season the fish fillets evenly with salt and pepper. Heat one very large skillet or two medium skillets over medium-high heat for a minute and then coat the pans with the olive oil. Add the fillets and turn the heat to very high. Sear until golden brown, about 2 minutes, then flip to sear the other side, about 1 minute. Transfer the fillets to a rack over a plate to catch the juices, and reserve.

2 Return the pan (or pans) to high heat. Add the onion slices and sauté, stirring frequently, for 1 minute or until they start to brown. Add the garlic, chile slices, lime wedges, tomatoes, oregano, and olives and sauté briskly for 1 minute. Add the wine and boil until reduced by half.

3 Pour in the fish stock or clam juice, bring to a boil, and then reduce to a simmer. Return the fish fillets, along with their juices, to the pan. Cover and cook gently for 2 minutes or longer, depending on the thickness of fillets. Taste the broth and adjust the seasoning with salt and pepper. Serve immediately in soup plates with a generous puddle of broth and garnish of vegetables.

TOQUE TIP If you've ever considered preparing fish for a crowd but ruled it out as too scary, this light, healthful, one-skillet dish is a great choice. We've prepared it for 500 guests at a time without a hitch. To serve a large group, just pan-sear all the fish, transfer to a casserole, cover with foil, and reserve. Then, when it's time to serve, cook the sauce in a few pans, pour over the fish, and finish cooking in a 350° oven for about 5 minutes. What a great party dish!

Chapter 13

Four Chickens and a Turkey

- -

In This Chapter

▶ Marinating chicken for maximum effect

▶ Trimming the bones from chicken

▶ Cooking Mexico's native bird, the turkey

- -

1f you've been stuck in the same old lemon, parsley, and garlic rut with your poultry, take a walk on the wild side and try cooking your next chicken or turkey Mexican style. It's bound to give you a tangier, spicier perspective on meats that we don't often look to for new taste sensations.

Chicken + Chiles = Incredible Flavor

One of our fondest memories of Mexico is wandering the streets of Cabo San Lucas, in Baja, not really expecting anything wonderful to happen foodwise, and coming across a man selling rotisserie chicken in his front yard. Thanks to his exuberant use of chiles, citrus, and spices, that front-yard chicken sang with so much flavor that it made most of our American preparations pale by comparison. We hope that you are as pleasantly surprised by the chicken recipes in this section!

Selecting chicken

Although we don't plan on launching an investigation, we have a sneaking suspicion that all is not as it seems in the world of the new, improved free-range chicken. Unlike produce, standards for what is labeled free-range or organic in the poultry world are not closely regulated by a government agency. Here are the definitions as we understand them:

- **Free-range chickens** must be kept in coops with open doors so that the birds can eat their feed outside. We've heard that these chickens are not exactly roaming around free as a bird but leave the coops only at feeding time and that they are not much different from conventional chickens.

- **Organic birds** must be fed only organic grain and raised on land that has not been treated chemically for three years.

The fact is, these more expensive birds normally do have more flavor and better texture than mass-produced birds, so they are hard to resist. We also recommend purchasing kosher chickens. They are available at the supermarket, hormone- and additive-free, and their flavor is as good or better than free-range.

If you've ever been disappointed after spending lots of time preparing a great-sounding chicken dish only to find that the meat has dried out when the dish is served, try switching to chicken legs and thighs, rather than breasts, for home entertaining. Dark meat stays moist much longer. And gnawing on a chicken bone is the passionate eater's inalienable right.

Trimming out the bone

Because you probably won't find boneless chicken legs and thighs at the supermarket, you may have to remove the bone the old-fashioned way, with a knife. Here's how:

1. **Place the still connected leg and thigh, skin side down, on a work counter.**

2. **With a heavy knife or cleaver, chop off the knobby part at the end of the drumstick.**

3. **Using the tip of a sharp, thin-bladed knife, carve along both edges of the leg and thigh bone and then underneath until the bone, with ball joint intact, can be lifted out.**

   Don't worry about neatness. Nicks in the meat won't matter after it is cooked. Also, in case you were wondering, the leg and thigh will remain attached because the skin still holds them together. Remember to freeze the bones for stock making!

It's all about the marinade

Because modern chickens are often depressingly bland, we depend on a marinade to add juiciness and character. Think of marinades as exaggerated salad dressings. Like a dressing, a marinade is a mixture of oil and acid — vinegar, citrus juice, or a combination — plus spices, herbs, and other flavorings like Tabasco or honey. Just remember that every component, including the oil, is there for the flavor, and you should always lean towards more rather than less spice when blending your own marinade.

Here are some guidelines for making your own marinade:

✔ If you have only a short time — less than 2 hours — to marinate, make a strongly flavored marinade. Remember that a cold marinade combined with raw meat needs strong flavors to make a difference. For longer marinating times, more than 8 hours, flavors can be toned down. Reduce the proportion of acid for longer marinades as well.

✔ Eight hours is a good length of time for marination — long enough for the flavors to be absorbed without doing any damage to the meat's fibers. Mary Sue suggests mixing a marinade in the morning before going to work. Then just place the chicken with its marinade in a resealable plastic bag and store in the refrigerator until evening. When you come home at night, the chicken will be ready to face the flames and your appetite.

✔ Yes, there is such a thing as marinating too long. If you've ever tasted beef that sat in red wine too long, you know what we're talking about. Because acid breaks down fibers, you never want to marinate poultry longer than a day or it may develop an unpleasant mushy, mealy texture on the surface. Delicate fish should never sit longer than a half hour in an acidy marinade.

Spicy, citrusy chicken

Any of the following chicken recipes will have people begging to come eat at your house.

Citrus Chicken with Orange Cilantro Salsa

As flavor mavens, we've developed a special method for cooking chicken breast, one of the least flavorful cuts of meat. First we boost flavor with a strong marinade and then we moisten the grilled meat some more with a sprightly salsa. The natural sugar in the orange juice caramelizes and adds the perfect sweetness. This is a great choice for your summer barbecues.

Special tool: *Blender*

Preparation time: *15 minutes, plus 35 minutes for Red Roasted Tomato Salsa, plus 6 hours marination*

(continued)

Cooking time: 25 minutes

Yield: 6 servings

½ cup freshly squeezed orange juice	*2 tablespoons vegetable oil*
2 tablespoons freshly squeezed lime juice	*½ teaspoon salt*
1 morita chile or 3 arbol chiles or 1 chipotle	*6 whole chicken breasts, boneless with skin on*
¾ cup Red Roasted Tomato Salsa (see Chapter 5)	*Orange Cilantro Salsa (see the following recipe)*

1 To make the marinade, combine the orange juice, lime juice, and chile in a small saucepan and bring to a boil. Reduce to a simmer and cook, uncovered, until the chile is plump, about 5 minutes. Set aside to cool and pour into a blender. Add the Red Roasted Tomato Salsa, oil, and salt and puree until smooth.

2 Wash the chicken breasts and place them in a large stainless steel or plastic container. Pour on the marinade, cover, and refrigerate for at least 6 hours.

3 Preheat the grill or broiler until medium-hot.

4 Grill the chicken breasts, skin side down on the grill, or skin side up in the broiler, about 3 minutes. Then turn and cook the other side, moving away from direct heat. Keep turning the chicken every minute or two to prevent it from blackening or sticking. Total cooking time is about 12 minutes for small breasts and about 20 minutes for larger breasts. If checking meat with a thermometer, the internal temperature should be 175°. Let sit off heat about 5 minutes. Serve over Red Rice and Refried Black Beans (see Chapter 10) and top with the Orange Cilantro Salsa.

Grilling chicken breasts calls for careful technique. With any citrus marinade, you need to be watchful not to burn the meat, because the sugars in the juice will caramelize quickly on the grill. The trick is to stay nearby and keep turning the chicken frequently, never blackening the skin or meat. We always keep the skin on for flavor, moisture, and a little insurance against charring. If guests prefer skinless chicken, we just remove it before serving.

Leftover Citrus Chicken is delicious served at room temperature the next day. For a quick main-course salad, slice the chicken and serve over mixed bitter greens, using the salsa as part of the dressing.

Orange Cilantro Salsa

A refreshing fruit and herb salsa such as this one is also great over grilled salmon. Make the salsa no more than a day ahead to really enjoy the freshness.

Preparation time: 10 minutes

Yield: 1½ to 2 cups

4 oranges or other citrus fruit, peeled and sectioned

1 bunch cilantro, leaves and stems, coarsely chopped (½ cup)

2 serrano chiles, stemmed and thinly sliced

1 small red onion, freshly julienned

¼ cup olive oil

¼ cup red wine vinegar

1 teaspoon salt

½ teaspoon cracked black pepper.

Combine the oranges, cilantro, chiles, onion, olive oil, vinegar, salt, and pepper. Mix well and set aside or chill until serving time.

Chipotle Glazed Chicken

When roasting chicken, all anyone seems to know is the Italian method — a combination of lemon, olive oil, and herbs. It's delicious, but why not break out and try roasting a Mexican-style chicken for a change? Smoky, brown chipotles add a unique, complex touch to the sweet and sour glaze.

Special tool: *Sieve*

Preparation time: *15 minutes, plus 1 hour marination*

Cooking time: *1 hour and 15 minutes*

Yield: *4 servings*

3-pound roasting chicken

3 cloves garlic, peeled and finely chopped

Salt and pepper to taste

2 tablespoons paprika

3 tablespoons red wine vinegar

3 tablespoons olive oil

1 cup freshly squeezed orange juice

½ cup honey

⅔ cup red wine vinegar

3 canned chipotle chiles

Garnish: ½ bunch parsley leaves, coarsely chopped (¼ cup)

1 Rinse the chicken, remove any excess fat, and pat dry with paper towels. In a small bowl, mix together the garlic, salt and pepper, paprika, 3 tablespoons vinegar, and olive oil. Rub the vinegar mixture all over the chicken, including the cavity. Cover with plastic wrap and marinate, at room temperature, for 1 hour.

2 Preheat the oven to 450°.

(continued)

3 To make the glaze, combine the orange juice, honey, ⅔ cup vinegar, and chiles in a small saucepan. Cook over medium heat until the liquid is reduced by half. Strain, pushing the chiles through a sieve, and reserve.

4 Unwrap the chicken and place in a roasting pan. Roast for 15 minutes. Then reduce the heat to 375° and continue roasting for another 45 minutes. Begin brushing glaze generously all over the chicken, every 5 minutes until done, about another 20 minutes. When a leg can be loosely twisted, the chicken is done. Sprinkle with parsley, let rest 10 minutes, and serve.

Ancho Chile Sauced Chicken

If you like the complexity of chiles but not the heat, this saucy chicken dish made with earthy anchos should become a favorite. We use more flavorful dark meat for this, our most traditional chicken entrée. This chile sauce also goes well with roasted lamb or pork.

Special tool: *Blender*

Preparation time: *15 minutes*

Cooking time: *50 minutes*

Yield: *4 servings*

4 ancho chiles, wiped clean, stemmed, and seeded

1 cup freshly squeezed orange juice

2 cups chicken stock (see Chapter 8)

3 tablespoons vegetable oil

1 large yellow onion, diced

Salt and pepper to taste

6 almonds, with skins

4 seeded prunes

Pinch of ground cinnamon

Pinch of ground cloves

½ teaspoon dried oregano

4 boneless chicken legs and thighs, attached, with skin on

Salt and pepper

Garnishes: 1 bunch cilantro leaves (½ cup) and ½ cup freshly chopped red onion

1 Lightly toast the chiles over an open flame. (See Chapter 3 for chile toasting techniques.) Transfer to a blender with the orange juice and chicken stock.

2 Heat 1 tablespoon of the oil in a medium skillet over medium-low heat. Cook the onion with the salt and pepper until golden, about 10 minutes. Add the almonds, prunes, cinnamon, cloves, and oregano, and cook for 10 minutes, stirring often, until the aromas are released. Transfer to the blender with the chiles and puree until smooth.

3 Pour the pureed mixture back into the skillet and bring to a boil. Reduce to a simmer and cook for 10 minutes. Remove from heat and reserve. (If the sauce is too thick, thin it with a bit more stock or water.)

4 Preheat the oven to 350°.

5 Heat the remaining 2 tablespoons of vegetable oil in an ovenproof skillet over medium-high heat. Season the chicken all over with salt and pepper. Sauté, skin side down, for about 4 minutes, shaking the pan frequently to prevent sticking. Then turn and sauté the second side for 4 minutes. Pour on the reserved chile sauce, transfer to the oven, and bake for 20 minutes. Serve hot, preferably over White Rice (see Chapter 10). Garnish generously with the cilantro leaves and chopped onion.

Roasted Achiote Chicken

Achiote (ah-chee-OH-teh) paste, the blend of ground annatto seeds, garlic, black pepper, spices, and vinegar from the Yucatán, gives this chicken its distinctive orange hue and spicy aroma. Always be careful when handling the paste so that you don't get it on your clothes or let it linger on cooking equipment because it tends to dye whatever it touches.

Special tool: *Blender or food processor*

Preparation time: *20 minutes, plus 1 hour marination*

Cooking time: *1 hour and 30 minutes*

Yield: *4 servings*

½ cup freshly squeezed orange juice

¼ cup achiote paste

3 serrano chiles, stemmed, seeded if desired

7 garlic cloves, peeled

1 tablespoon pepper

1 tablespoon salt

1 bunch cilantro, stems and leaves (½ cup)

3 tablespoons red wine vinegar

3-pound roasting chicken, rinsed and patted dry

1 medium yellow onion, peeled

1 head garlic

1 orange

2 medium yellow onions, cut into 3 slices each

3 Roma tomatoes, cut into 4 slices each

(continued)

1 To make the marinade, combine the orange juice, achiote paste, serranos, garlic cloves, pepper, and salt in a blender or food processor. Puree until smooth. Add the cilantro and vinegar and puree until smooth.

2 Rub the marinade all over the chicken, inside and out. Place in a bowl, cover, and refrigerate for at least 1 hour or as long as overnight.

3 Preheat the oven to 400°.

4 Lift the chicken from the marinade and place it on a work surface. Cut the onion, head of garlic, and orange in half and stuff inside the chicken's cavity. Tie the legs together and place them on a rack in a roasting pan, breast side down. Roast for 20 minutes. Reduce the heat to 350° and roast for 20 minutes longer.

5 Meanwhile, heat a dry cast-iron skillet over high heat. Char the onion slices until blackened on both sides. Then char the tomato slices on both sides. Reserve.

6 Turn the chicken, breast side up, and bake for about 45 minutes longer, basting occasionally with the pan juices. Add the charred onion and tomato slices to the roasting pan for the last 20 minutes. The chicken is done when a drumstick feels loose when jiggled and the skin is golden brown. Remove from the oven and let sit for 10 minutes before serving. Serve warm with the charred onions and tomatoes, rice, and beans. (Turn to Chapter 10 for some rice and bean recipes.)

Cooking a whole chicken

A surprising misconception of home cooks is that cooking a whole chicken, rather than one already cut in parts, is somehow more difficult. It doesn't make any sense at all. Why give up all those special parts, like the dark knobs of meat on a chicken's back, not to mention the carcass and a crackling crisp skin, just because you have to stick your hand inside a wet chicken? Trust us. Washing a chicken and cooking it whole is a cinch. In fact, after it's in the oven, the bird needs very little attention.

We prefer high heat when roasting a bird at home. A standing roasting frame, if you have one, is lovely. By standing the bird upright, the skin browns evenly with no soggy parts. The trickiest part to roasting a whole bird is judging when it's done. We use two tests: A leg should move freely when wiggled, and the interior juices should run clear. As with any roasted meat, let the bird rest for about 10 minutes before carving for the juices to settle into the meat.

As expert chicken eaters, we follow this game plan for eating the bird:

✔ Day one: Eat all the bony parts, such as the back, wings, and drumsticks.

✔ Day two: Cut up leftover breast meat for tacos, enchiladas, and tortas.

✔ Day three: Although it's highly unlikely that you'll have any meat remaining by now, if you do, make a chicken salad with the thighs.

Garnishing the Mexican way

In Mexico, garnishes are used to add contrasting flavor and texture to a finished dish. They rarely exist just for their good looks. This differs from the European style, where garnishes are often added to give the plate more eye appeal, like a dollop of puree in a bowl of soup, or a scattering of fresh herbs over a finished dish.

Typical Mexican garnishes, such as lime wedges; chopped raw onion, tomatoes, and cilantro; mashed avocado or guacamole; and sour cream or crema, are considered an integral part of the dish, not an afterthought. Though we believe in a loose interpretation where garnishing is concerned (see Chapter 8), the true Mexican style is to go for the garnish.

Turkey, the Native Mexican Bird

The Aztecs of central Mexico were the first to domesticate turkeys as a food source, beating out the Pilgrims by a couple centuries. In modern Mexico, a turkey pecking for food in a backyard is not an unusual sight.

The Mexican turkey is smaller and gamier than the American bird, with a flatter breast. Its meat is traditionally used for preparing the festive mole poblano, as well as everyday enchiladas, tortas, and tamales. Our first turkey sighting in Mexico was at a restaurant in the Yucatán.

Turkey breast contains very little fat, so it's easy to overcook and dry it out. Thin breast slices need no more than a minute per side to cook.

Grilled Turkey Escabeche

The tradition of spicy sauces or marinades called *escabeches* (es-keh-BEHSH-es), goes back to the Spanish. To get the full flavor from this quick translation, make sure that you caramelize the onion or even add a pinch of sugar if your onions are on the old side. To save even more time, purchase frozen, presliced turkey scallops at the market — they take about 5 minutes to thaw!

Preparation time: *15 minutes*

Cooking time: *25 minutes*

Yield: *4 servings*

(continued)

Pinch of ground allspice

Pinch of ground cloves

½ teaspoon ground cumin

½ teaspoon dried oregano

1½ pounds skinless, boneless turkey breast, cut into thin slices

Salt and pepper to taste

6 tablespoons cold butter

1 large red onion, diced

1½ teaspoons salt

⅔ cup white vinegar

1½ cups turkey or chicken stock (see Chapter 8) or canned broth

1 tablespoon cracked black pepper

1 To prepare the seasoning mixture, mix together the allspice, cloves, cumin, and oregano in a bowl.

2 Cover the turkey slices with plastic wrap and pound to flatten. Sprinkle all over with salt and pepper and the seasoning mixture, and reserve.

3 Preheat the grill or broiler to hot.

4 Melt 3 tablespoons of the butter in a medium skillet over low heat. Cook the onion with 1½ teaspoons salt, stirring and shaking the pan frequently, until golden, about 15 minutes. Pour in the vinegar, turn the heat to high, and simmer until the liquid is reduced by half. Then pour in the turkey or chicken stock and boil until the liquid is reduced again by half.

5 Thinly slice the remaining cold butter. Reduce the heat to low and whisk the butter into the sauce a little at a time. Remove from the heat and stir in the cracked pepper.

6 Grill or broil the turkey slices less than a minute per side. Serve over a bed of Seared Chard (see Chapter 10) with the sauce over both the turkey and the chard.

Skinless, boneless chicken breasts, sliced and pounded, are also delicious prepared the Turkey Escabeche way. To save time, you can sear the chicken or turkey breasts in a tablespoon or so of vegetable oil in a skillet over high heat instead of grilling them.

Chapter 14

Main Course Meats

- -

In This Chapter

▶ Traditional pork main dishes

▶ Beautiful beef treats

▶ Luscious lamb main courses

- -

Although beef and pork are beloved in Mexico, they are not often featured as a meal's center-piece. In traditional foods like posole or mole, a small amount of meat is eaten along with a healthful array of fresh vegetables and spices so that the focus is on the artfulness of the whole dish rather than on the quality of a lone slice of beef. And although Mexicans greatly enjoy beef and pork, they do not eat those meats every day, but a few times a week, as one small part of a larger meal.

Mexican cooks are legendary for cooking inexpensive cuts of beef and pork to perfection. Nothing goes to waste. Stomachs, intestines, hooves, ears, tongues, and butts are slowly cooked with just the right amount of lime and chiles to enhance their natural flavors without overwhelming their essential meatiness.

In the recipes that follow, we try to balance Mexican authenticity with American appetites. We include recipes for pork butt braised in banana leaves and simmered in lard for those who are ready for an authentic cooking and eating adventure. And for those who love big flavors but need to get out of the kitchen fast, we offer steaks and chops that dazzle the taste buds without demanding a large commitment of time and energy in the kitchen.

Experiencing the Richness of Pork

These very traditional main courses all highlight the rich meatiness that only comes from good, fresh pork. We love it slow-roasted in banana leaves in Cochinita Pibil, simmered in its own fat in classic Carnitas Nortenas, and marinated and barbecued to perfection in Baby Back Ribs Adobado.

When shopping for pork, look for light pink flesh. The freshest tasting pork is always pale, not blood red.

Cochinita Pibil

In this traditional dish from the Yucatán, meat from baby pigs, or *cochinitas,* is marinated in a blend of achiote paste, citrus juices, and spices, wrapped in fragrant banana leaves, and then buried underground for a long, slow bake. The resulting meat is tender, fragrant, earthy, and unlike anything you've ever tasted — even when roasted in an oven, as ours is here.

Special tool: *Large baking dish*

Preparation time: *15 minutes, plus 4 hours marination*

Cooking time: *3 hours and 10 minutes*

Yield: *8 to 10 servings*

½ cup achiote paste or ⅓ cup annatto seeds (see Chapter 2)

8 cloves garlic, peeled and chopped

½ cup freshly squeezed orange juice

¼ cup freshly squeezed grapefruit juice

⅓ cup freshly squeezed lime juice

8 dried bay leaves

2 teaspoons cumin seeds

½ teaspoon ground cinnamon

1 teaspoon dried oregano

1 teaspoon salt

2 teaspoons pepper

4 pounds pork butt, cut in 3-inch cubes

2 medium white onions, sliced ½-inch thick

5 Roma tomatoes, sliced ½-inch thick

1 pound banana leaves, softened over a low flame, or collard greens, stems trimmed and blanched (see Chapter 2)

4 Anaheim chiles, roasted, peeled, and sliced into strips (see Chapter 3 for more information on roasting chiles)

Pickled Onions for garnish (see following recipe)

1 In a medium bowl, mash together the achiote paste, garlic, orange juice, grapefruit juice, lime juice, bay leaves, cumin seeds, cinnamon, oregano, salt, and pepper with a fork. Add the pork, toss to evenly coat, and marinate in the refrigerator for at least 4 hours.

2 Preheat the oven to 300°.

3 Heat a dry cast-iron skillet over high heat. Char the onion slices until blackened on both sides. Then char the tomato slices on both sides. Reserve.

4 Line a large baking dish with one layer of the banana leaves or collards. Arrange the pork in an even layer and top with the charred onions, tomatoes, chiles, and all the marinade. Cover with banana leaves and wrap the dish tightly in foil.

5 Bake for about 3 hours or until the pork is tender and moist. Remove from the oven and let sit 10 minutes. Unwrap and serve with Pickled Onions, Fried Plantains, and White Rice (the two latter recipes are in Chapter 10).

Chicken or lamb, cut in big chunks with the bone in, are both delicious when slow-roasted in the same manner as Cochinita Pibil. Slow roasting chicken or lamb in this way will certainly spark up your family's perception of these meats!

Pickled Onions

These pungent purple onion rings are the natural accompaniment to achiote-seasoned foods from the Yucatán. They're also a good condiment for turkey, barbecued beef, or Pork Torta (see Chapter 6).

1 red onion, sliced into thin rings

1 teaspoon salt

½ teaspoon dried oregano

1 habañero chile, seeded and sliced

½ cup freshly squeezed orange juice

¼ cup freshly squeezed lime juice

Place the onion rings in a bowl and pour on enough boiling water to cover them. Let sit for 2 minutes. Drain, add the salt, oregano, chile, orange juice, and lime juice, and store in the refrigerator for 4 hours or as long as 2 days.

Baby Back Ribs Adobado

Ribs need special attention to cook up tender, juicy, and falling off the bone. We like to first give ours a strong spice rub for flavor, followed by a steamy bake for tenderness, and then a quick turn on the grill or in a high oven for a crisp edge and some smoke.

Because undercooked ribs are so awful, steaming a little longer can never hurt.

(continued)

Preparation time: 20 minutes, plus 2 hours refrigeration, plus 1 hour and 25 minutes to make the Adobado

Cooking time: 1 hour and 35 minutes

Yield: 4 servings

¼ cup paprika	2 tablespoons salt
¼ cup ground ancho chiles or chili powder	4½ pounds pork baby back ribs
¼ cup cumin	3 cups Adobado (see following recipe)

1 Combine the paprika, chiles, cumin, and salt in a small bowl. Pat the spice mixture all over the ribs. Place in a pan, cover with plastic wrap, and refrigerate for at least 2 hours or overnight.

2 Preheat the oven to 350°.

3 Place the ribs in a single layer in a baking pan and pour in water to a depth of about ¾ inch. Bake, uncovered, for 45 minutes. Cover with foil and return to the oven for an additional 30 minutes.

4 Meanwhile, make the Adobado.

5 Turn up the oven heat to 450° or heat the grill to medium-high.

6 If finishing the ribs in the oven, brush generously with the Adobado and bake for another 10 minutes per side, basting every 5 minutes To grill, generously glaze the ribs and grill for 5 minutes per side, frequently brushing with additional Adobado sauce. Cut the ribs apart and serve hot.

Inexpensive country-style ribs, available at the supermarket, are a meaty, tasty alternative to baby back ribs. After applying the spice rub, steam in a sealed heavy-duty plastic bag in the top of a double boiler over simmering water for 45 minutes. Then finish in a hot oven as described in Step 6.

Adobado

Adobado is a very traditional, sweet, tart Mexican barbecue sauce. It's great to have on hand for heating up with leftover bits of chicken, pork, or lamb and serving on rolls for delicious barbecue sandwiches.

Special tool: Blender or food processor

Preparation time: 20 minutes

Cooking time: 65 minutes

Yield: 3 cups

6 ancho chiles, wiped clean

¼ cup white vinegar

1 cup water

2 tablespoons olive oil

1 medium yellow onion, thinly sliced

3 garlic cloves, peeled and sliced

½ tablespoon ground cumin

2 cups chicken stock (see Chapter 8)

1 tablespoon brown sugar

2 tablespoons freshly squeezed orange juice

2 tablespoons freshly squeezed lemon juice

1 tablespoon tomato paste

½ tablespoon salt

⅛ teaspoon pepper

1 Briefly toast the chiles directly over a medium gas flame or in a cast-iron skillet until soft and brown, turning frequently to avoid scorching. (See Chapter 3.) Transfer the toasted chiles to a saucepan and add the vinegar and water. Bring to a boil, reduce to a simmer, and cook for 10 minutes to soften.

2 Transfer the chiles and liquid to a blender or food processor. Puree until a smooth paste the consistency of barbecue sauce or ketchup is formed, adding 1 or 2 tablespoons of water if necessary to thin. Set aside.

3 Heat the olive oil in a medium saucepan over medium-high heat. Sauté the onion until golden brown, about 10 minutes. Stir in the garlic and cook briefly just to release the aroma. Then stir in the cumin and cook for another minute. Add the chicken stock and reserved chile paste. Bring to a boil, reduce to a simmer, and cook for 20 minutes.

4 Meanwhile, mix together the brown sugar, orange juice, lemon juice, tomato paste, salt, and pepper to form a paste. Add to the simmering stock mixture and cook for 15 minutes longer. Adobado can be stored in the refrigerator for 1 week or frozen indefinitely.

Carnitas Norteñas

Pork chunks slowly simmered in fat develop a heightened pork flavor and silky, smooth texture. Carnitas are delicious in tacos or burritos, with spicy salsa and the Pickled Onions described earlier in this chapter to offset their essential richness.

Preparation time: *10 minutes*

Cooking time: *1 hour and 40 minutes*

Yield: *6 servings*

(continued)

2 pounds pork shoulder or butt, cut into
2-inch cubes

Salt and pepper to taste

1½ pounds lard or pork fat or shortening

1 medium red onion, freshly diced

1 bunch cilantro, chopped (½ cup)

5 serrano chiles, chopped

Mashed avocado

Warm Corn Tortillas (see Chapter 10)

Green Tomatillo Salsa (see Chapter 5)

1 Generously season the pork all over with salt and pepper.

2 Melt the lard in a large, deep saucepan or Dutch oven over moderate heat. Add the well-seasoned meat and simmer, uncovered, over medium-low heat for 1 hour and 15 minutes, until fork tender. Remove the pork with a slotted spoon and transfer to a cutting board. The fat can be refrigerated for future use.

3 Preheat oven to 400°.

4 When cool enough to handle, shred the pork by hand or with the tines of two forks. In a mixing bowl, toss the pork with the onion, cilantro, and chiles to combine. Transfer to a casserole, cover tightly, and bake, until heated through, about 15 minutes. Serve hot with the mashed avocado, corn tortillas, and Green Tomatillo Salsa.

Pibil-style cooking from the Yucatán

A hidden benefit of being television chefs is that every once in a while we get to leave the studio to do field work under the guise of filming a television special. When we visited the Yucatán, the southern state on Mexico's Caribbean coast, a local caterer let us tag along to an area outside of Merida. There we watched him prepare Cochinita Pibil the old-fashioned way — in an earthen pit.

First a sizeable hole was dug, about 2 feet deep. After the pit was lined with stones, a wood fire was lit, and we waited until it had burnt long enough to create strong heat. Then a large

metal roasting pan lined with banana leaves was filled with large chunks of achiote-marinated meat and lowered into the pit. The pan was covered with more banana leaves and aromatic avocado branches to seal in moisture and flavor. And then came the ultimate pot cover. A corrugated metal sheet was placed over the pan, and dirt was shoveled on top until the ground was flat again and the pit was sealed. Several hours — and a couple of *cervezas* — later, we were delighted to taste some of the most fragrant, juicy chunks of pork we've ever unearthed.

Pork popularity in Mexico

Mexicans are wild about their pigs, and we don't blame them. Pork in Mexico has a richer, more definitive flavor than American pork, where flavor and texture often play second fiddle to the demand for less fat.

Pork is most popular in the southern states of Mexico, where every part of the animal is enjoyed. In Oaxaca, we ate a terrific lunch at an all-pork taco stand one day. Metal drums, about 5 feet wide, were bubbling away with pig's ears, feet, stomachs, butts, and shoulders, all smoldering in their juices and waiting to be tucked into a warm taco, doused with salsa, and happily consumed.

Beefing Up Your Meals

There's nothing like a properly grilled, well-marbled piece of beef for pleasing guests at a summer barbecue. In Los Angeles, the fragrance of Mexican spices and beef wafting from barbecues is as familiar as the scent of hot dogs at a baseball game.

Tough cuts of beef, like skirt and flank, should always be thinly sliced, across the grain, so that no one bite contains too much chewy muscle.

Cumin and Chile Marinated Skirt Steak

This marinated skirt steak is so flavorful that all it needs is some rice and beans (see Chapter 10 for some ideas) and maybe the Corn and Pepper Compote in Chapter 9 for contrast.

Special tool: *Blender*

Preparation time: *20 minutes, plus 4 hours marination*

Cooking time: *15 minutes*

Yield: *6 servings*

⅓ cup cumin seeds

6 serrano chiles, stemmed, cut in half, and seeded, if desired

6 cloves garlic, peeled

½ cup freshly squeezed lime juice

2 bunches cilantro, including stems and leaves (1 cup)

½ cup olive oil

(continued)

Salt and pepper to taste   *3 pounds skirt steak, trimmed of excess fat and cut into 6 serving pieces*

1 Lightly toast the cumin seeds in a dry medium skillet over low heat just until their aroma is released, about 5 minutes. Transfer the seeds to a blender.

2 Add the serranos, garlic, and lime juice and puree until the cumin seeds are finely ground. Then add the cilantro, olive oil, and salt and pepper and puree until smooth.

3 Generously sprinkle the steak all over with salt and pepper. Generously brush all over with the cumin seed marinade and roll each piece up into a cylinder. Arrange the rolled steaks in a shallow pan and pour on the remaining marinade. Cover and marinate in the refrigerator for at least 4 hours or as long as a day.

4 About 30 minutes before cooking, remove the meat from the refrigerator. Unroll the steaks and place on a platter.

5 Preheat the grill or broiler to very hot.

6 Cook the steaks just until seared on both sides, about 4 minutes per side for medium rare. (Or pan-fry in a hot cast-iron skillet lightly coated with oil.) Transfer to a cutting board and slice across the grain into diagonal strips. Serve hot with warm flour tortillas.

Don't skirt this steak

Thin, chewy skirt steak, cut from the diaphragm muscle of the cow, tastes like essence of cow, and if you like your steak beefy-tasting, inexpensive, and quickly cooked, it is well worth seeking out.

Skirt steak is prized in Korean, Japanese, French, and Mexican cultures. In America, it falls into a category of less-expensive cuts like flank and hanger, referred to as butcher cuts because, in the past, the butcher would take them home and cook them himself. And what self-respecting butcher would take home anything but the best? Now that skirt steak is being rediscovered, its price is on the rise.

These days, skirt is available, pretrimmed and packaged at the supermarket. If any silver skin remains on the outside, remove it with a thin sharp blade. If you have a choice, go for thicker pieces, cut from the outside edge.

Some markets may label skirt steak "Steak for carne asada."

Chile and Garlic Stuffed Rib Eye Steaks

A big, fat, juicy rib eye stands up to strong flavors like chile and garlic. In this easy, spicy steak, those flavors permeate the meat so distinctively that a salsa is not necessary.

Preparation time: *15 minutes*

Cooking time: *20 minutes*

Yield: *4 servings*

¼ cup olive oil

10 jalapeño chiles, stemmed, halved lengthwise, and seeded

20 cloves garlic, peeled

4 rib eye steaks, 10 to 12 ounces each and at least 1-inch thick

Salt and pepper to taste

Garnish: Lime wedges

1 If grilling, preheat the grill to medium-high.

2 Heat the olive oil in a small saucepan over moderate heat. Add the chiles and cook until the skins start to blacken and the chiles soften, about 2 minutes. Remove with a slotted spoon and drain on paper towels. Reduce the heat to low. Add the garlic and cook until soft and lightly browned, about 5 minutes. Transfer to paper towels and let cool.

3 With a paring knife, make 7 to 10 1-inch horizontal slits along the edge of each steak. Stuff each slit with either a garlic clove or chile half. Generously season all over with salt and pepper.

4 Grill the steaks or sauté them in a lightly oiled cast-iron pan over high heat, about 4 minutes per side for medium rare. Serve with lime wedges.

VARIATION

For those who prefer their garlic and chiles on the subtle side, simply remove them before serving. The meat will still have the flavor of heat and spice without any large bites of chili or garlic to upset sensitive palates. And for garlic lovers who are not chile fans, just eliminate the chiles for a wonderfully easy garlic steak.

Why rib eye?

Rib eyes, cut from the front rib section of the cow, are always our first choice for a special steak dinner. Rib eye, also known as a spencer or Delmonico steak, is the ultimate well-marbled cut. As a steak cooks, the fat melts into the flesh, giving it that unmistakable rich flavor we sometimes crave. When cooking rib eye, it's important to cook all the fat, including any along the edges.

On the Lamb

Though Americans tend to think of lamb as a special occasion meat, in Mexico it is eaten frequently, along with similar-tasting goat.

Cumin Pepper Lamb Chops with Sweet and Sour Salsa

Thick lamb chops are coated with a crunchy peppercorn and cumin seed crust, similar to the French steak au poivre, and then served with a smooth, tangy salsa. We like a side of potatoes or rice with such an assertive entrée, but for a lighter summer menu, serve these chops over a dressed green salad.

Special tools: *Potato masher, strainer, large cast-iron skillet, large baking dish*

Preparation time: *20 minutes*

Cooking time: *60 minutes*

Yield: *4 servings*

8 ounces tamarind pods, peeled	*½ teaspoon cayenne pepper*
1 tablespoon butter	*1½ tablespoons honey*
3 large garlic cloves, peeled and minced	*¼ cup cracked black pepper*
1 teaspoon salt plus salt to taste	*½ cup cumin seeds*
½ teaspoon ground pepper	*Salt to taste*
½ cup chicken stock (see Chapter 8)	*8 lamb chops, 4 ounces each*
1 tablespoon Worcestershire sauce	*¾ cup vegetable oil*

1 To make the salsa, place the tamarind in a large saucepan and pour in enough water to cover by 1 inch. Cook over medium-low heat, covered, until soft, about 30 minutes. Mash with a potato masher and then push through a strainer, discarding the seeds and strings. Reserve the pulp.

2 Melt the butter in a saucepan over medium-high heat. Sauté the garlic with the salt and pepper until golden brown. Add the mashed tamarind and chicken stock. Bring to a boil, reduce to a simmer, and cook for 10 minutes. Stir in the Worcestershire sauce, cayenne, and honey. Remove from heat and keep warm.

3 Preheat the oven to 350°.

4 Mix together the cracked pepper and cumin seeds in a small shallow bowl. Season the chops all over with salt. Firmly press each into the seed mixture to coat all over. Set aside.

5 In a large skillet, preferably cast-iron, that comfortably holds all 8 chops, heat the oil to very hot, but not smoking. Cook the chops in the bubbling oil until the seeds are golden, about 2 minutes per side. (Do not worry about a few seeds slipping off the chops.) Transfer to a baking dish and bake for 2 minutes for medium rare.

6 To serve, coat 4 plates with the salsa. Top each with 2 lamb chops and serve.

To eliminate the unpleasant taste of uncooked lamb fat when cooking chops, use your tongs to stand the meat upright and sear the fat along the edges in the hot pan.

If you can't find tamarind, substitute a puree of 2 peeled Granny Smith apples and ½ cup seedless prunes and follow the same cooking times. The result will be a slightly sweeter salsa than with the tamarind.

Worcestershire sauce and its medicinal connections

In case you had any doubt, Lea & Perrins brand is the original and genuine Worcestershire sauce, as it says on the label. This top-secret family recipe dates back to the early 1800s when an English military man returning from a tour in Bengal brought the salty brown condiment to his local pharmacists and asked them to duplicate it. The pharmacists were Mr. Lea and Mr. Perrins. The formula that they developed from a blend of tamarind, dried anchovies, molasses, soy, garlic, chiles, peppercorns, and onions continues to support a small company in New Jersey. No small feat when you consider that most families purchase only one bottle a year.

Chapter 15

Sweets for Spice Lovers

*J*ust as Mexicans prefer extremes at the spicy end of the spectrum, they also like their sweets extra sugary. Sticky, gooey candies are sold on the street and stacked in candy stores to be nibbled throughout the day, and hardly a meal ends without its requisite flan, rice pudding, or some more elaborate dessert.

Our own tastes, on the other hand, veer toward simplicity — an ice cold mango with a wedge of lime or a refreshing fruity ice cream sounds just fine at the end of a long, satisfying meal. And though we do offer a spectacular chocolate cake at the restaurant, we can't resist sneaking in something sour, like a topping of crème fraiche, to take the edge off all that sweetness.

The selections that follow reflect our respect for what's traditional in Mexico, our own acid-craving appetites, and the American hunger for a deliciously sweet reward for finishing dinner.

Old-Fashioned Endings

These unfussy puddings, the most traditional Mexican desserts, are offered at restaurants all over Mexico. They're easy to prepare, taste just as good after a day in the refrigerator, and offer tummy-coating comfort after the excitement of a spicy Mexican meal.

Mexican Bread Pudding

More like a soft and crunchy bread casserole than an eggy pudding, this sweet and savory dessert, known as *capirotada* (kah-pee-ROH-tah-thah) in Mexico, is bound to appeal to those who don't usually like custards. It doesn't contain any eggs or milk.

Special tools: *13-by-9 inch glass casserole or lasagna pan, baking sheet*

Preparation time: *25 minutes*

Cooking time: *20 minutes*

Yield: *8 to 10 servings*

8 tablespoons (1 stick) butter	*½ cup golden raisins*
½ loaf crusty Italian or French bread, crust on, cut into small cubes (about 6 cups)	*1 large Granny Smith apple, peeled, cored and chopped*
1½ cups brown sugar	*½ cup walnuts, chopped*
1½ cups water	*½ pound crumbled añejo cheese*
1½ teaspoons ground cinnamon	*Garnish: 1 cup Crema (see following recipe), heavy cream, or créme fraiche*

1 Preheat the oven to 350°. Butter the glass casserole or lasagna pan.

2 Melt the butter in a medium saucepan, add the bread cubes, and stir them to coat evenly. Spread the cubes on a baking sheet and bake for 15 minutes, stirring one time, or until lightly brown and crisp. Remove the bread and turn up the oven temperature to 400°.

3 Combine the sugar and water in a small saucepan and bring to a boil. Remove the syrup from the heat. Stir in the cinnamon and the raisins and set aside.

4 In a large mixing bowl, combine the chopped apples, walnuts, cheese, and toasted bread cubes. Drizzle with the reserved sugar syrup and mix ingredients to evenly distribute the syrup. Transfer the mixture to the prepared pan.

5 Bake, uncovered, stirring occasionally, for 15 minutes. Then bake an additional 5 minutes, without stirring, until the top is golden brown and crusty and the liquid is absorbed. Serve the bread pudding warm in bowls, with pitchers of Crema or heavy cream for adding at the table.

This is my absolute favorite. I'm not normally a bread pudding fan, but trust me, this is the best!

Crema de la Crema

Mexican crema, French-style créme fraiche, and American sour cream are all versions of sour milk. We prefer Mexican crema, with its higher salt content, for garnishing savory dishes like tacos and tostadas. Créme fraiche, with its lighter, purer milk flavor is better for garnishing sweets and making pastries, and sour cream can be substituted whenever you want its thicker consistency and super sour flavor. (We love it on potatoes.)

For topping desserts, if you don't feel like making our homemade salt-free Crema, substitute créme fraiche.

Crema

A drizzle of Crema adds that sour tang we crave with our sweets.

Preparation time: *5 minutes, plus 8 hours setting*

Yield: *2 cups*

2 cups heavy cream   ¼ cup buttermilk

Whisk the cream and buttermilk together in a bowl. Cover and set the bowl in a warm place (a gas oven with just the heat from the pilot light is fine) for 8 hours until thick as custard. Store in the refrigerator for as long as a week. You don't need to stir before serving.

Flan

One thing you can count on in most Spanish or Mexican restaurants is this classic caramel-flavored, sweet and silky vanilla custard. The perfect make-in-advance dessert, flan is a soothing, light finale to spicy foods, and, as an added bonus, it keeps for a few days in the refrigerator without losing freshness or flavor.

See the Caramel and Homemade Condensed Milk recipes, as well as flan variations for intriguing riffs on plain vanilla, later in this chapter.

Special tools: *9-inch round cake pan, strainer, large roasting pan*

Preparation time: *25 minutes, plus 4 hours refrigeration, plus 20 minutes for Caramel*

Cooking time: *1 hour and 15 minutes*

Yield: *8 to 10 servings*

(continued)

1 recipe Caramel (see the following recipe)   *2 teaspoons vanilla extract*

6 large eggs   *2 cups milk*

6 large egg yolks   *2 cups half-and-half*

1 14-ounce can sweetened condensed milk   *1 vanilla bean*

1 Prepare the Caramel and coat a 9-inch round cake pan.

2 Preheat the oven to 325°.

3 In a large mixing bowl, gently whisk together the eggs, yolks, sweetened condensed milk, and vanilla extract. (Avoid incorporating air as happens when you whisk more briskly.)

4 Pour the milk and half-and-half into a medium saucepan. Split the vanilla bean lengthwise and, using the tip of a pairing knife, scrape the black seeds into the milk. Add the bean also and bring the milk to a boil. Remove the saucepan from the heat.

5 Gradually pour the hot milk into the egg mixture, whisking constantly. Pass the milk and egg mixture through a strainer into the caramel-coated cake pan. Place the cake pan inside a large roasting pan and carefully pour hot tap water in the larger pan until it reaches halfway up the sides of the flan pan.

6 Bake for 1 hour and 10 minutes, until the center just feels firm when pressed with a finger. Set aside to cool in the pan of water. Then remove from the water bath, cover with plastic wrap, and refrigerate at least 4 hours or overnight.

7 To serve, run a knife along the inside edge of the pan and gently press the center of the bottom to loosen. Cover the pan with a platter, invert, and lift the pan off the flan. Cut the flan in wedges and serve topped with cold Caramel.

Vanilla beans, the long, thin, dried, brown pods sold in the supermarket spice section, are the fermented pods of a Mexican or Tahitian yellow orchid. Look for pliability when purchasing. A good vanilla pod should be as flexible as a dried apricot. To release the bean's essential oils and flavor, always split it lengthwise with the tip of a paring knife, and scrape the small brown seeds into whatever you're infusing. Those tiny dark seeds are the speckles in "pure" vanilla ice cream. Their perfume is unmistakable — some even say it's an aphrodisiac.

Caramel

A truly great flan should have a luxuriously silky consistency and a rich caramel flavor that lingers on the tongue. To make the caramel, you want to cook the sugar slowly, a longer time than you suspect, and watch it carefully. The color should turn from light caramel to dark coffee, and the fragrance should be rich and very caramelly. Leftover sauce can be stored in the refrigerator and thinned with some hot water the next day.

Special tools: *9-inch round cake pan, pastry brush*

Cooking time: *20 minutes plus 1 hour chilling time*

Yield: *Enough for 1 9-inch flan*

2 cups sugar   *1¼ cups water*

1 Have ready a 9-inch round cake pan. Combine the sugar and ½ cup of the water in a medium saucepan. Cook over moderate heat, swirling the pan occasionally, until the color is dark brown and the mixture has a distinctive fragrance of caramel, about 15 minutes. Use a pastry brush dipped in cold water to wash down any sugar granules from the pot's sides. Pour enough of the hot caramel into a 9-inch round cake pan to coat the bottom and sides. Swirl to coat evenly.

2 Slowly and carefully add the remaining ¾ cup water to the caramel in the saucepan. Bring to a boil and cook over moderate heat until the caramel dissolves, about 5 minutes. Occasionally stir and brush down the sides with the pastry brush dipped in cold water to prevent crystallization. Set this caramel sauce aside to cool and then chill until serving time.

TOQUE TIP

The flan plan

As major custard lovers, we have devoted years to refining our flan technique. Here are the details to keep an eye on when baking any pudding:

✔ Always cook at a low temperature — adjust your oven accordingly if you know it runs high.

✔ Err on the side of under rather than overcooking. To test for doneness, gently press the custard in the center. The center should jiggle slightly, while the edges remain firm. Even if the flan falls apart a bit when leaving the pan, the texture and taste will be superb.

✔ Tiny air bubbles in the finished product are a sign of overcooking. Other signs of too much time spent in the oven are: graininess, chewiness, and a watery texture.

The purpose of a water bath, or the French *bain marie,* is to cook delicate egg-based custards, flans, and mousses as gently as possible. By placing the flan in a larger pan filled with water, you insulate it and prevent uneven cooking and browning on the bottom and sides.

To avoid spills, place your larger roasting pan as close as possible to the oven. Place the flan pan inside, pour hot water into the larger pan, halfway up the sides of the flan pan, and carefully transfer to the oven. Be cautious removing the roasting pan from the oven so that the hot water doesn't splash you or the flan.

The many faces of flan

For Coconut Flan: Substitute 1 (14-ounce) can unsweetened coconut milk plus enough milk to make 2 cups for the 2 cups milk. (Make sure that you purchase unsweetened canned coconut milk. It's available in the ethnic section of the market near the Thai ingredients. Do not buy the canned coconut milk in the beverage section, because it is probably sweetened for cocktails like piña coladas and smoothies.) Sprinkle 1 cup of grated unsweetened coconut over the uncooked flan in the pan. When the flan is served, the coconut will be scattered on the bottom.

For Chocolate Flan: Use 5 rather than 6 whole eggs and stir 3 ounces chopped bittersweet chocolate into the milk mixture just before it boils.

For Red Yam Flan: In a large bowl, combine all of the ingredients in the plain flan list with 1 cup cooked pureed yams, sweet potato, or pumpkin, 2 teaspoons ground cinnamon, 1½ teaspoons ground allspice, 1½ teaspoons ground clove, and 3 tablespoons dark rum. Mix well, strain into the caramel-coated pan, and bake.

Homemade Condensed Milk

For a less sugary, purer tasting condensed milk, try making your own with this simple recipe. To use for the flan, substitute 3 cups Homemade Condensed Milk for the milk and the sweetened condensed milk. You also need another ½ cup sugar in the whisked egg mixture. If you love flan, you owe it to yourself to give this outstanding recipe a try.

Special tool: *Strainer*

Cooking time: *1 hour*

Yield: *3 cups*

6 cups nonfat milk	*5 tablespoons sugar*

Pour the milk into a medium heavy saucepan and bring to a boil. Reduce the temperature to a simmer and cook, uncovered, for 45 minutes, stirring occasionally. Stir in the sugar and continue simmering about 12 minutes or until the mixture is reduced to 3 cups. Strain. Homemade condensed milk can be refrigerated up to a week.

Rice Pudding

Mexicans love their rice pudding and who can blame them? It's studded with rum-soaked raisins and laced with just enough cinnamon.

Cook this traditional pudding to a loose consistency and serve in glass bowls for the best effect. This is a terrific use for leftover rice!

Preparation time: *5 minutes*

Cooking time: *30 minutes*

Yield: *4 to 6 servings*

3½ cups milk	1 vanilla bean, seeds scraped
2 cups cooked white rice	¼ cup dark rum
⅔ cup granulated sugar	½ cup golden raisins
1 cinnamon stick	3 egg yolks

1 In a large, heavy saucepan, bring the milk to a boil. Add rice, sugar, cinnamon stick, and vanilla bean. Reduce heat to low and cook, uncovered, stirring frequently, until mixture begins to thicken, about 25 minutes.

2 Meanwhile, in a small saucepan, heat the rum and raisins until simmering. Set aside to let the raisins plump for 10 minutes.

(continued)

All about cajeta

Cajeta (kah-HEH-tah) is the light-brown, milky, Mexican caramel sauce traditionally served with crepes and fruit after a meal. It's much easier to make than European-style caramel. All it takes is time.

To make cajeta, place an unopened can of sweetened condensed milk (the label does not have to be removed) in a heavy saucepan and completely cover with water. Cook at the barest simmer for 3 hours, adding more water as necessary to keep the can submerged. Using tongs or an oven mitt, turn the can over and cook an additional 2½ hours. Cool to room temperature and chill for 1 hour.

To serve, open the cold can, stir the contents with a fork until smooth, and pour over crepes or a sundae of ice cream, salted, roasted peanuts or almonds, and sliced bananas. If your cajeta cooks up too thick, cook it over low heat with a little heavy cream a few minutes until loose and runny.

3 Beat the egg yolks in a bowl until runny. Ladle a small amount of the hot milk and rice mixture into the eggs and stir. Then spoon the egg mixture back into the milk mixture in the pan. Continue cooking over low heat, stirring frequently, until as thick as pancake batter, about 2 more minutes.

4 Stir in the raisins and remove the cinnamon stick and vanilla bean. Serve warm, at room temperature, or chilled, according to your preference.

New Border Sweets

For these personal favorites, we've taken ingredients that ring true to Mexico — chocolate, coconut, lime, cinnamon, pecans, and coffee — and given them an American spin. Two luscious cream pies, a few of our favorite cookies, and a refreshing tequila ice will end any get-together, Mexican or not, on an upbeat, sugar-induced note. As an added bonus, each of these little gems is easy to prepare.

Creamy Lemon Lime Pie

Here is a delicious unbaked version of Key Lime Pie that you can simplify even more by substituting a baked graham cracker crust. It's one of our best-sellers at the Border Grill.

Special tools: Food processor, 9- or 10-inch pie plate, pie weights or raw rice or beans, parchment paper

Preparation time: 25 minutes baking, plus 1 hour chilling for dough

Mixing time: 10 minutes, plus 4 hours chilling for filling

Yield: 6 to 8 servings

1 recipe Empanada Dough (see Chapter 7)

½ cup freshly squeezed lime juice

⅓ cup freshly squeezed lemon juice

1 pound cream cheese

1 14-ounce can sweetened condensed milk

Zest of 1 lime, finely grated, without any bitter white pith

1 cup heavy cream, cold

2 tablespoons powdered sugar

Garnishes: ½ lime and ½ lemon

1 Preheat the oven to 350°.

2 On a floured board, roll out the dough into a ¼-inch thick, 12-inch circle. Place in a 9-inch or 10-inch glass pie plate. Trim the edges with a paring knife, leaving a ½- to ¾-inch overhang. Tuck under and crimp the edges. Chill 1 hour. Prick the dough all over with a fork. Line the pie shell with parchment paper or foil, fill with raw beans, rice, or weights, and bake about 25 minutes or until very lightly browned. Remove from the oven, immediately remove the weights, and thoroughly cool on a rack.

3 Combine the lime and lemon juices, cream cheese, and sweetened condensed milk in the bowl of a food processor with a metal blade and mix until smooth, scraping down the sides often. Add the lime zest and mix thoroughly. Pour into the chilled pie shell and return to the refrigerator.

4 Meanwhile, whisk the cream and powdered sugar in a bowl until soft peaks form. Spread over the top of the pie. Slice 8 thin circles each of lime and lemon from the center of each fruit and cut each disk once from the center to the edge to make twists. Stand these twists upright, evenly spaced, along the edge of the pie and chill at least 4 hours or overnight. Serve cold.

In recipes that call for citrus zest and juice, make sure that you grate the zest first, and then juice the fruit. If your recipe calls for more zest than juice, store the leftover fruit, in its white pith, in the refrigerator.

Margarita Sorbet

Delicious, fresh fruit ices play such an important role in the Mexican diet that we offered handmade, miniature popsicles at our first Mexican restaurant. The ingredients for this sparkling, tart, lime and tequila sorbet should be on the shelf of any well-stocked Mexican-style pantry.

Special tool: *Ice cream maker*

Preparation time: *10 minutes, plus ½ hour chilling time for syrup and 1 hour for tequila mixture*

Yield: *4 servings*

1½ cups tequila	*½ cup light corn syrup*
1 cup freshly squeezed lime juice	*2 cups Simple Syrup (see following recipe)*
½ cup Triple Sec	*½ cup water*

(continued)

1 Pour the tequila into a small saucepan and bring to a boil. Cook until the tequila is reduced by half (most of the alcohol boils off). Pour into a bowl and stir in all of the remaining ingredients. Refrigerate until cold.

2 Pour the chilled mixture into an ice cream maker and process according to the manufacturer's instructions for sorbet. Store in the freezer.

Simple Syrup

Cooking time: *5 minutes*

Yield: *2 cups*

1¼ cups sugar	*1¼ cups water*

Combine the sugar and water in a saucepan and bring to a boil, stirring until the sugar dissolves. Let cool. The syrup can be stored in the refrigerator.

Quick and Easy Buñuelo Sticks

Our inspiration for these sweetened, baked tortilla strips was the typical cinnamon sugar cookies our moms used to bake with leftover scraps of pie dough (see photo in the color insert). Buñuelo sticks make a great last-minute treat when you want to serve something homemade for dessert but don't have the time to fuss.

Special tool: *Baking or cookie sheet*

Preparation time: *10 minutes*

Cooking time: *12 minutes*

Yield: *36 pieces*

9 8-inch flour tortillas	*1 cup granulated sugar plus 1 tablespoon ground cinnamon, mixed*
¾ cup melted butter	*⅓ cup sliced almonds*
1 egg, beaten	*⅓ cup chopped pecans*
⅓ cup shredded coconut	

1 Preheat the oven to 350°.

2 Lay 3 tortillas on the counter and brush with butter. Transfer the tortillas, butter-side-down, to a cookie sheet and brush the second side with beaten egg. Sprinkle with the coconut and about ⅓ of the cinnamon sugar and then slice into 1½-inch wide strips.

3 Repeat Step 2 with the next 3 tortillas, sprinkling with the almonds instead of coconut, and do the same with the remaining 3 tortillas, sprinkling with the pecans.

4 Bake for 12 minutes or until golden and crisp and cool on rack. Eat with coffee or tea.

TOQUE TIP

Many cooks are unnecessarily cautious when it comes to using cinnamon, or *canela,* which is very popular in Mexico. We like a strong dose of its spicy, sweet flavor and recommend you try upping the ante in your other recipes.

Hahas

Similar in consistency to macaroons, these sweet and chewy coconut haystacks are great for the inexperienced baker (see photo in the color insert). Just mix them up by hand and pop them in the oven for a wonderful, moist-keeping cookie guaranteed to spread joy to all those who take a bite.

Special tools: *Cookie sheets, parchment paper*

Preparation time: *20 minutes*

Cooking time: *30 minutes*

Yield: *20 to 24 cookies*

¾ cup pecan halves	*¾ cup chopped golden raisins*
1 tablespoon butter, melted	*7 ounces sweetened condensed milk*
2½ cups sweetened shredded coconut	*½ cup chopped semisweet chocolate or chocolate morsels*

1 Preheat the oven to 325°. Line a cookie sheet with parchment paper or use a nonstick baking sheet.

2 In a bowl, toss the pecans with the melted butter to coat evenly. Spread on another baking sheet and bake about 15 minutes, stirring occasionally, until the pecans are golden and aromatic. Cool and coarsely chop.

3 Combine the chopped pecans and remaining ingredients, except the chocolate, in a bowl and mix with a wooden spoon until evenly moistened. Drop about 2 tablespoons of batter for each cookie onto the lined cookie sheet and gently flatten with your finger-tips or a fork to 2¼-inch circles. (These cookies do not spread.)

4 Bake for 10 minutes, until the coconut turns pale golden, being careful not to over-brown. Cool completely on racks.

(continued)

5 Melt the chocolate in a bowl over simmering water or in the microwave for 1 minute at high power. Dip the tines of a fork in the hot chocolate and drizzle over cooled cookies for a freeform pattern. Let set until hardened.

Any dried fruit can be substituted for the raisins in Hahas: Apricots, sour cherries, and strawberries make excellent substitutions. Just chop larger fruit into chunks about the size of raisins.

Mocha Crackles

Chocolate and espresso is an unbeatable combination — especially when baked into a tender, thin, dark chocolate wafer like this one (see photo in the color insert). Mocha Crackles are sure to knock the socks off any experienced chocolate lover.

Special tools: *Electric mixer, cookie sheets, parchment paper*

Preparation time: *15 minutes*

Cooking time: *25 minutes*

Yield: *26 cookies*

2 ounces unsweetened chocolate, coarsely chopped	*2 eggs*
	¾ cup sugar
4 ounces bittersweet chocolate, coarsely chopped	*1 teaspoon vanilla extract*
3 tablespoons butter	*2 tablespoons coffee liqueur, such as Kahlua*
¼ cup plus 1 tablespoon flour	*2 tablespoons finely ground espresso beans*
¼ teaspoon baking powder	*⅔ cup semisweet chocolate chips*
¼ teaspoon salt	*About ¾ cup powdered sugar*

1 Preheat the oven to 350°. Line the cookie sheets with parchment paper.

2 Combine the chocolates with the butter in a heavy saucepan and place over low heat, stirring occasionally, until melted and smooth. Set aside to cool.

3 In a bowl, stir together the flour, baking powder, and salt with a fork.

4 In another large bowl, slowly beat the eggs and sugar with an electric mixer until pale and thick, about 5 minutes. Beat in the vanilla, coffee liqueur, and ground espresso beans. Pour in the melted chocolate and fold to combine. Add the flour mixture and fold until the flour disappears. Stir in the chocolate chips. The dough will be quite loose.

5 Drop about a tablespoon of batter for each cookie, about 1½ inches apart, onto the lined cookie sheets. Sprinkle each generously with powdered sugar through a sieve until evenly coated and thoroughly white. Bake 8 to 10 minutes, until the tops are cracked and the cookies are slightly puffed. Let them cool on the cookie sheet about 10 minutes, then transfer the cookies to racks to completely cool.

When baking delicate Mocha Crackles, it's important to let the finished cookies set on the cookie sheets the full 10 minutes, or longer. These cookies are so soft that they may droop miserably and possibly break apart if lifted too soon.

For a deeper, darker flavor in your chocolate recipes, substitute unsweetened chocolate for part of the bittersweet or semisweet quantity. Combining two chocolates adds a depth of flavor sometimes lacking in less-expensive bittersweet chocolates. As a general rule, we like 1 part unsweetened to 4 parts bittersweet chocolate. This tip does not apply to first-rate bittersweet chocolates such as Valhrona or Sharfenberger.

Part IV
Menus for Every Occasion

The 5th Wave   By Rich Tennant

©RICHTENNANT

"Now THIS is authentic Mexican cooking. The beans in this dish came from a fresh pair of maracas I picked up this afternoon."

In this part . . .

Party and brunch planning becomes a snap (and fun!) thanks to the two chapters in this part. We tell you how to pull off all sorts of gatherings with grace and style, including tamale and taco parties, Cinco de Mayo celebrations, and breakfasts.

Chapter 16

Fiestas and Theme Parties

. . . .

In This Chapter

▶ Throwing a tamale party

▶ Surviving the Day of the Dead with style

▶ Hosting a Mexican beach barbecue

▶ Planning a taco party for Cinco de Mayo

. . . .

Recipes in This Chapter

↻ Spinach Salad with Lime Pepitas and Pickled Onions

↻ Mexican Spiced Popcorn

▶ Chicken Chilaquiles

↻ Pan de Yema

▶ Grilled Red Snapper Tikin-Chik

*I*nvite friends over for French food, and they're bound to be on their best behavior. Make the menu Italian, and they just may feel pressured to discuss Italian red wines and the proper temperature at which to serve them. But announce that the party is Mexican, and the guests breathe a sigh of relief and put on their dancing shoes.

We're not sure why, but Mexican food helps people relax, switch into party mode, and get a little crazy. We even have statistics to prove it! The number of parties booked at our Border Grill restaurants far exceeds the number held at our other restaurants.

To help you get in on this fun phenomenon, we give you this chapter full of party ideas and tips. We organize our suggestions around seasonal themes, but don't feel limited by our menus. Feel free to pick the ideas that inspire you, turn to Chapter 18 for easy pointers on setting the scene with music, flowers, and other decorations, and get ready for a walk on the wild side. Mexican food is meant for sharing!

The Winter Holiday Tamale Party

If the prospect of spending an entire day with your family waiting for the turkey to be done is a little scary, instead try throwing an interactive tamale party during the winter holidays. You'll be amazed how much more relaxed people are after you give them a fun job to do and the entire focus isn't on making conversation. If you plan it right, everyone will be too busy stuffing corn husks and sipping sangria to ask you why little Timmy has pierced his tongue.

In Los Angeles, where winter temperatures have been known to dip into the not-quite-frigid 50s, warm, spicy tamales are a common sight in homes and restaurants at holiday time. (See the sidebar "Christmas foods in Mexico" in this chapter to read about specialty foods served in Mexico during the holidays.) The idea of a meal that comes wrapped in a package seems just right during gift-giving time, and tamales offer that taste of rich indulgence we all crave during winter holidays.

You can also throw a tamale party at other times of the year to spice up more mundane events. Consider fragrant, earthy corn tamales in place of a proper afternoon tea for your next bridal or wedding shower or gals' get-together. Who says women want to sip tea with their pinkies extended?

Because guests love to leave with leftovers, especially around the holidays when time is precious, sending them home with a little care package is a nice touch. We keep a stack of Chinese restaurant takeout containers in the kitchen so that departing guests can carry home tomorrow's lunch in style.

All a great tamale party really needs (besides the tamales) is rice and beans, with sour cream, a spicy salsa, Fresh Salsa on the side, and a big green salad like our Spinach Salad with Lime Pepitas and Pickled Onions that follows.

Here's the menu to help you get organized:

- Any rice from Chapter 10
- The beans of your choice, refried or not, from Chapter 10
- Any tamale from Chapter 7
- Fresh Salsa from Chapter 5
- Green Tomatillo Salsa or Smoked Chile Salsa from Chapter 5
- Sour cream or Crema from Chapter 15
- Spinach Salad with Lime Pepitas and Pickled Onions

Spinach Salad with Lime Pepitas and Pickled Onions

A bright, refreshing salad such as this provides tart contrast and also holds up exceptionally well on a long-standing buffet.

Preparation time: *15 minutes plus 5 minutes for onions*

Cooking time: *5 minutes*

Yield: *12 servings*

1 cup pepitas or pumpkin seeds

¼ cup lime juice mixed with 1 teaspoon salt

1 large jícama, peeled

1½ pounds baby spinach, washed

2 onions, pickled (See Chapter 14)

1½ teaspoons salt

1 teaspoon pepper

⅓ cup red wine vinegar

⅔ cup extra-virgin olive oil

1 cup (4 ounces) grated añejo cheese

1 In a small, dry frying pan over medium heat, toast the pepitas until golden brown. Remove from heat, add the lime juice mixed with 1 teaspoon salt, and shake vigorously. Cook, shaking often, until the pan is dry and cool.

2 Slice the jícama into ⅛-inch slices and then julienne as thinly as possible. Transfer to a very large salad bowl, along with the spinach and well-drained onions. Whisk the 1½ teaspoon salt, pepper, vinegar, and olive oil together in a small bowl and drizzle over the salad. Add the pepitas and grated cheese and toss well. Serve immediately.

The setup

To set the mood for your holiday tamale party, look for Spanish language Christmas carols in music stores and don't be afraid to play them loudly. This is supposed to be a party, isn't it?

Any of the decorative suggestions in Chapter 18 will work wonders during this tamale party, as well as large bowls of chips, salsa, and guacamole strategically placed around the rooms where guests will be congregating. (Chapter 5 contains mouthwatering recipes for salsas and guacamole, as well as suggestions for chips.)

Christmas foods in Mexico

Christianity is so pervasive in Mexico that everyone, it seems, celebrates Christmas. At family holiday gatherings, the most popular foods are traditional ones like menudo (Chapter 11), posole (Chapter 8), tamales (Chapter 7), and mole (Chapter 11).

And there is no shortage of sweets to satisfy the seemingly universal yearning for something sweet at holiday time. Specially sweetened tamales made with sweet corn, sugar, raisins and cinnamon, buñuelos (Chapter 15), or platters of bite-sized candied yellow and orange squashes are enjoyed throughout the day, just as you might share a platter of cookies when guests drop in during the holidays.

A typical holiday drink is hot fruit punch spiked with tequila, or *atole* (ah-TOH-leh) the traditional unsweetened masa-thickened drink.

For an inexpensive natural-fiber tablecloth, try setting out tamales and their accompaniments buffet-style on a large table lined with layered, bright green banana leaves. Just heap the steamed tamales directly onto the leaf-lined table and, when the party is over, toss the tablecloth directly into the compost heap.

The game plan

Check these items off as you complete them!

The day before

The morning before your tamale party, you'll need to do the following things:

- ✔ Make the savory fillings for the tamales and put them in the refrigerator to chill.
- ✔ Make the rice and beans.
- ✔ Prepare any do-ahead salsas like Red Roasted Tomato, Smoked Chile, Roasted Ancho, or Roasted Green Chile Salsa.

The morning of the party

Here's a quick list of your preparations for the morning of the party:

- ✔ Prepare the masa.
- ✔ Mix the drinks and chill.
- ✔ Prepare Fresh Salsa.
- ✔ Soak the corn husks to soften them (see Chapter 2).
- ✔ Toast banana leaves to soften (see Chapter 2).
- ✔ Cover the kitchen table or counter to be used for wrapping tamales with newspaper. The papers can be lifted and tossed in the trash for easy cleanup.

Beverages for party lovers

Big pitchers of Sparkling Fruit Punch or Sangria set on the kitchen counter inspire excellent tamale-making and improve any of the parties we tell you about in this chapter. (See Chapter 4 for the recipes.) With their bright colors and slices of fresh fruit, both beverages look festive, and their alcohol content is low enough for guests to sip throughout the day without anyone expressing regret the next day.

For a really special ending, have a pitcher of Rompope (also in Chapter 4), the spiced Mexican eggnog, stashed in the fridge for after-dinner drinks.

Extreme tamale parties

Ever have trouble sleeping and wonder what to do with all that excess energy? How about throwing an extreme tamale party, with several courses of fabulous Mexican food complementing your luscious, light-as-a-feather and lovingly made homemade tamales? A party organized around any of these menus is guaranteed to solidify your position in the community as an extremely generous party-giver and expert on Mexican cooking.

Mole Tamales Party

- Basic Red Snapper Ceviche (Chapter 5)
- Basic Masa Tamale with Chicken Mole Filling (Chapter 7)
- Watercress and Radish Salad (Chapter 9)
- Fried Plantains (Chapter 17)
- Any rice or bean recipe (Chapter 10)
- Creamy Lemon Lime Pie (Chapter 15)

Roasted Chicken Tamales Party

- Down 'n' Dirty Bean Nachos (Chapter 5)
- Basic Masa Tamale with Roasted Tomato Chicken Filling (Chapter 7)
- Bread Salad (Chapter 9)
- Seared Chard (Chapter 10) or other greens
- Flan (Chapter 15)

Vegetarian Tamales Party

- Queso Fundido (Chapter 5)
- Green Corn Tamales (Chapter 7)
- Fiesta Bean Salad (Chapter 9)
- Red Rice (Chapter 10)
- Mocha Crackles (Chapter 15)

The Day of the Dead Celebration

Looking for a new twist for an adult Halloween party? Try gathering friends and family together on November 1 for a Mexican-style Day of the Dead celebration. (See the sidebar "Celebrating Day of the Dead in Mexico" for more information about this holiday.) Death may not exactly be a traditional American party theme, but after you get past the cultural taboos, you'll find that making light of a somber subject helps everyone relax and get silly.

Your menu for the Day of the Dead Celebration includes the following:

- Mexican Spiced Popcorn (recipe follows)
- Jamaica (Chapter 4)
- Pan de Yema (recipe follows)
- Smoked Mussel Ceviche Tostadas (Chapter 5)
- Chicken Chilaquiles (recipe follows)

- ✔ Refried Pinto Beans (Chapter 10)
- ✔ Watercress and Radish Salad (Chapter 9)
- ✔ Flan (Chapter 15)

Mexican Spiced Popcorn

This popcorn with Mexican spices always comes in handy for gatherings where you want to set out easy nibbles before the serious eating gets under way. Although corn has so many uses in the Mexican diet, surprisingly we don't know of any tradition of popped corn south of the border.

Preparation time: *5 minutes*

Cooking time: *5 minutes*

Yield: *12 cups, about 6 servings*

½ teaspoon cayenne	*1 teaspoon salt*
½ teaspoon ground cumin	*¼ cup vegetable oil*
1 teaspoon freshly ground black pepper	*½ cup popcorn kernels*

1 Combine the cayenne, cumin, pepper, and salt on a plate and place near the stove.

2 Combine the oil and one popcorn kernel in a large pot. Place on a burner, turn the heat to high, cover, and cook until the kernel pops. Then add the remaining popcorn and cover again. When the corn starts popping, quickly add the spices. Cover and cook, shaking *constantly,* until the popping stops. Transfer to bowls to serve.

Be careful not to inhale the spiced fumes because they can burn your throat. Just don't hold your face directly over the open pot and you should be safe from the fumes. Keep a tortilla on hand, just in case.

Chicken Chilaquiles

If you like the ease of lasagna for serving a crowd — or your family for a couple of week-night dinners — you owe it to yourself to try this popular Mexican casserole. It's as easy and satisfying as lasagna, but with its layers of crumbling tomatillo-drenched tortillas, soothing cheese, and familiar chicken, its taste is entirely unique. This homey dish is one of the most popular dishes at our restaurants.

Special tools: *Strainer, large colander, 4-quart casserole or 6 individual casseroles*

Preparation time: 30 minutes, plus 35 minutes to make the Red Roasted Tomato Salsa, plus 2 hours and 10 minutes for chicken stock

Cooking time: 50 minutes

Yield: 6 to 8 servings

2 whole chicken breasts, split

Salt and pepper to taste

2 cups chicken stock (see Chapter 8)

3 cups Red Roasted Tomato Salsa (see Chapter 5)

½ cup heavy cream

1 teaspoon salt

½ teaspoon pepper

1 medium yellow onion, sliced paper-thin

12 large tomatillos, husked, cored, and thinly sliced

½ cup vegetable oil

12 day-old 6-inch corn tortillas, 18 if individual casseroles are being made (see Chapter 10)

Butter for greasing casserole

1 cup (4 ounces) grated Mexican manchego cheese

1 cup (4 ounces) grated panela cheese

½ cup (2 ounces) grated añejo cheese

1 Season the chicken all over with salt and pepper. Bring the chicken stock to a boil in a large saucepan. Place the breasts in the stock, reduce the heat to low, cover, and cook until the meat is tender, about 15 minutes. Set aside to cool in the stock. When cool, remove and discard the skin and bones and shred the meat into bite-sized pieces. Strain and reserve the stock for another use.

2 In a large mixing bowl, combine the salsa, cream, salt, pepper, onion, tomatillos, and shredded chicken pieces.

3 Heat the vegetable oil in a medium skillet over medium-low heat. Cook the tortillas just about 5 seconds per side to soften, and then transfer to a large colander to drain.

4 Preheat the oven to 350°. Butter a 4-quart casserole or 6 to 8 individual casseroles (at our restaurants, we use small soup bowls).

5 Combine the manchego, panela, and añejo cheeses in a mixing bowl.

6 To assemble the chilaquiles, spread a thin layer of the cheese mixture over the bottom of the baking dish. Push the solids in the bowl of chicken and salsa to the side so that the liquids form in a pool on one side. Dip all the softened tortillas in the pool to moisten. Layer one third of the moist tortillas over the cheese and top with half of the chicken mixture with its sauce. Sprinkle half of the remaining cheese over the chicken. Repeat the layers, ending with a layer of tortillas on top. Cover tightly with aluminum foil.

7 Bake for 30 minutes or until the edges are slightly brown. Let sit for 10 minutes before slicing or unmolding from individual casseroles.

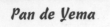

Pan de Yema

Dress up your Day of the Dead celebration with this rich, sugar-coated egg bread, delicious enough to be pulled apart and eaten like pastry (see Figure 16-1).

Special tools: *Electric mixer, damp towel, coated baking sheet, pastry brush, cooling rack*

Preparation time: *½ hour plus 2½ hours for rising*

Cooking time: *30 minutes*

Yield: *2 loaves*

2 packages dry yeast (2 tablespoons)

½ cup warm water

⅔ cup sugar

3 eggs beaten with 3 yolks

¾ teaspoon salt

1½ tablespoons aniseed, steeped in ¼ cup water for 10 minutes

½ teaspoon ground nutmeg

1 stick melted butter

4½ cups flour plus flour for dusting work surface

Vegetable oil for coating bowl

1 egg beaten with 1 tablespoon water for wash

⅓ cup sugar for sprinkling

1 In a large mixing bowl, stir together the yeast, warm water, and 1 tablespoon of the ⅔ cup sugar. Let sit until foamy, 10 minutes.

2 Add the beaten eggs and yolks, salt, the remaining sugar, aniseed with water, nutmeg, and melted butter. Stir well until evenly combined. By hand or with the beater of an electric mixer, mix in 4½ cups of the flour and transfer to a lightly floured board or counter. Knead the dough for 10 minutes, until the dough is smooth and slightly sticky.

3 Place the dough in a large oil-coated bowl. Cover with a lightly moistened tea towel and let rise in a warm place until doubled, about 1½ hours.

4 Punch the dough down and turn out onto a floured counter. Pinch off about 2 cups of dough and set aside for decoration. Divide the remaining dough into 2 pieces. Shape each into a round loaf, about 1-inch thick, and place on a greased baking sheet.

5 Divide the reserved dough into 8 pieces. Knead each piece into a ball, reserving 2 for center "skulls." Pull and shape the other 6 pieces into long bones, the diameter of the loaves, with knobs on either end. With your fist, make a deep indentation in the center of each loaf and criss-cross three bones over each like the spokes of a wheel. Then poke 2 eyes in each remaining dough ball with your fingers. Place a "skull" in the center of each loaf. Cover the assembled dough with a damp towel and set aside to rise until the loaves hold a fingerprint when pressed, about 50 minutes.

6 Meanwhile, preheat the oven to 375°. Brush the risen loaves with egg wash and sprinkle with remaining ⅓ cup sugar. Bake until golden, 25 to 30 minutes. Cool on a rack.

pan de yema

The setup

Here's your chance to decorate the house with skeletons and skulls, light all
the candles you've received as gifts throughout the year, burn some incense,
and dress as outrageously as you want. Best of all, the theme will be so weird
and destabilizing that inhibitions are sure to melt away. A California friend of
ours gives her yearly Day of the Dead celebration a boost by choosing a
beloved icon from the past — one year it was Lucille Ball — for the group to
come together and pay tribute to.

At our restaurants, we set the tone by building an altar, as Mexican families
might at home. We prop up a papier-mâché skeleton at a big, wooden communal
table called the *mesa* and offer tags to hang from the skeleton for those who wish
to remember the names of dead friends and relatives. For added ambience and
to encourage offerings, we arrange tequila and other treats nearby, as well as the
traditional egg bread *pan de yema*. Bright orange marigolds, burning incense,
and flickering candles, all considered traditional in Mexico, complete the scene.

The game plan

Start the party early by inviting a few close friends over to help you with
the following preparations.

A day or two before

We love a party menu that allows for most of the food to be prepared a day or
two in advance. It's so much more fun than having an audience around you in
the kitchen.

- ✔ Make the Red Roasted Tomato Salsa for the Chicken Chilaquiles.
- ✔ Make the Chicken Chilaquiles.
- ✔ Make the Jamaica.
- ✔ Make the Flan.

> ✔ Make the Refried Pinto Beans.
> ✔ Build an altar.
> ✔ Make the Pan de Yema.

The morning of the party

You won't have too much to do before your guests arrive the day of the party. Just do these few things the morning of the big day, and you'll be all set for all sorts of visitors, spirits or otherwise:

Celebrating Day of the Dead in Mexico

Day of the Dead is celebrated by the Indians of central and southern Mexico starting at midnight on October 31. To prepare for the holiday, when celebrants believe that the gates of heaven open so that the spirits of deceased family members can return for a visit, the family builds and decorates an elaborate altar at home to welcome the spirits back in style. People believe that happy, well-fed spirits will provide protection and good luck for the rest of the year. The ritual of building a special, expensive holiday altar is similar to the American Christmas tree concept.

In addition to festive foods like mole (Chapter 14) and pan de yema for the visiting spirits, stacks of tortillas, fruits, nuts, sodas, mezcal, toys, playing cards, cigarettes, and bingo cards are arranged on an altar already overflowing with buckets of flowers, incense, folk art skeletons, and decorative sugar skulls.

In Mexican folk art, skeletons and skulls are common subjects in dioramas, sculptures, toys, and paintings. During Day of the Dead, delicate white sugar skulls decorated with brilliant frostings, pieces of bright foil, colored sugars, and the name of the person being memorialized are common decorations. (Sugar skulls and other Day of the Dead materials can be ordered by mail from Reign Trading Company, 818-788-7717, or on the Internet at www.reigntrading.com.)

On the afternoon of November 1, after the tolling of church bells, villagers leave their homes to finish the party at local graveyards, where often a local band is playing. Favorite foods and drinks are brought along, as well as some of the flowers from home, and the family gathers around for one last reminiscence and a final toast before the spirits return to heaven, and life returns to its normal rhythm.

> ✔ Make the Smoked Mussel Ceviche Tostadas and the Watercress and Radish Salad.
>
> ✔ Make the Mexican Popcorn.
>
> ✔ Decorate the house.

A Mexican Beach Barbecue

Some of our most memorable meals in Mexico were eaten at the tiny, palm-thatched huts called *palapas* that dot the coastline. Bright sunshine and Mexican food go together — and when you factor in the informality of eating with your hands, in a seminude state, with your toes buried in the sand, it's hard to imagine anything going seriously wrong.

Beaches often feature built-in barbecues, but we included directions for building your own just in case. You always have the option of bringing along a portable grill, or hibachi, or preparing this delicious menu in your own backyard as well.

Wherever you choose to serve it, this light, refreshing menu is sure to be an exciting alternative to the usual burgers and steak:

> ✔ Guacamole and Chips (Chapter 5)
>
> ✔ Grilled Vegetables (see the sidebar "Vegetables on the grill" in this chapter)
>
> ✔ Grilled Red Snapper Tikin-Chik (recipe follows)
>
> ✔ Corn and Pepper Compote (Chapter 10)
>
> ✔ Corn Tortillas (Chapter 10)
>
> ✔ Cold beer (see Chapter 4 for some suggestions)

Grilled Red Snapper Tikin-Chik

The idea for this juicy whole grilled fish came from an outing we took in the Yucatán with a local fisherman who operated his own tiny beachfront restaurant. We always love the added flavor and drama of whole fish grilled on the bone.

Special tools: *Fish grilling basket (see Figure 16-2) or screen, grill, paper towel or brush*

Preparation time: *10 minutes, plus 35 minutes for Corn Tortillas*

Cooking time: *15 minutes*

Yield: *4 servings*

(continued)

Olive oil for coating the fish basket and brushing the fish

½ cup achiote paste

½ cup orange juice

½ cup lime juice

½ cup olive oil plus oil for brushing

Salt and pepper to taste

2 whole snappers, salmon or groupers, 2 pounds each, scaled and cleaned

Coarse salt and pepper to taste

Lime wedges and 12 Corn Tortillas for serving (see Chapter 10)

1 Preheat the grill to medium-high. With a paper towel or brush, coat a fish grilling basket or screen with olive oil.

2 In a small pot, combine the achiote paste, orange and lime juices, olive oil, and salt and pepper. Cook over moderate heat until slightly thickened, about 5 minutes.

3 Rinse the fish and pat dry. With a sharp knife make three long slashes down to the spine, at an angle parallel to the gills, on both sides of the fish. Generously season with the coarse salt and the pepper, brush with olive oil, and place the fish inside the grill basket.

4 Place the basket over medium-high hot spot to grill. Cook for about 3 minutes per side, turning when the skin is golden and crispy. Brush the fish all over with the sauce, and cook for 1 to 2 minutes longer per side, depending on the thickness of the fish. Remove from the basket and transfer the whole fish to a platter. Serve with plenty of lime wedges and fresh Corn Tortillas.

The trick to turning fish on the grill is judging just the right moment to turn without pulling the delicate skin and flesh apart. The best way to turn a whole fish is with two spatulas, one on either end. Slide the spatulas under and quickly flip by just flicking your wrists. Do not lift the fish in the air and then drop it down. If the fish resists the flip, it needs to cook a bit longer. Wait a few minutes for the skin to crisp and then try again.

Vegetables on the grill

Some of our favorite vegetables to bring along for a summer barbecue include small red potatoes, beets, zucchini, peppers, scallions, and asparagus.

For minimal sand in your teeth, prepare the vegetables the night before and chill. Wash and trim the vegetables, cutting peppers and large squash into 4 by ½-inch strips or chunks. Toss in a bowl with olive oil, seasoned with salt, pepper, and oregano to coat. Then make double-thick aluminum foil packets (unless you're using heavy weight foil), about 8 inches square, and wrap and seal each vegetable separately. Cook the vegetable packets over a medium-high fire for about 30 minutes for root vegetables and 15 minutes for other vegetables, turning often. Flavorful, smoky grilled and roasted vegetables can be served hot or at room temperature.

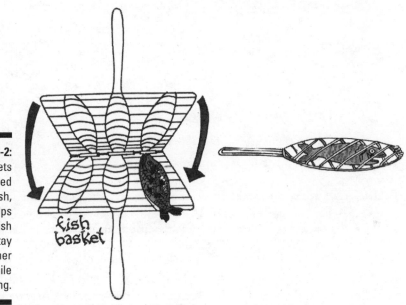

Figure 16-2:
Fish baskets are shaped like a fish, which helps the fish meat stay together while grilling.

The setup

Because this party is scheduled to take place outside, you won't have to do too much to prepare except hope for good weather. We do have some tips to help you entertain away from home.

Improvising a pit barbecue

If you plan on building a pit at the beach, be sure to bring along the grate from your home barbecue or keep an extra one in the car. To build the pit, follow these instructions (and refer to Figure 16-3):

1. **Scooping out the sand with your hands (unless you've packed a pail and shovel), dig a shallow hole — about 6 to 8 inches deep and as large around as the grate.**

2. **Place large (10 to 12-inch) stones all around the circumference, where the rack will be positioned.**

3. **Build a fire in the center of the sand.**

4. **Brush the grate with oil and rest it on top of the stones.**

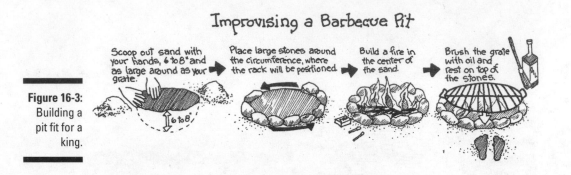

Improvising a Barbecue Pit

Scoop out sand with your hands, 6 to 8" and as large around as your grate.

Place large stones around the circumference, where the rack will be positioned.

Build a fire in the center of the sand.

Brush the grate with oil and rest on top of the stones.

Figure 16-3: Building a pit fit for a king.

Taking your show on the road

Traveling with a cooler in the trunk of the car for food emergencies is always wise. An ice chest eliminates any concerns about spoilage in the heat of the summer. For this easy summer beach barbecue, we recommend packing two coolers: one for the beer and the other for the cleaned, wrapped fish and pre-made vegetable packets. And don't forget the tongs and spatulas for turning hot foods on a grill.

You can skip the plastic spoons and forks. Hands and tortillas are the most authentic utensils. But don't forget to pack these items:

- Lemon or lime wedges for seasoning the food and the beers
- Miniature salt, pepper, and Tabasco containers for seasoning
- A squeeze bottle or small container of olive oil
- Bottled water for sprinkling and drinking
- Beer and soft drinks
- Garbage bags for cleanup, resealable plastic bags for leftovers, and napkins and paper towels for tidying up

The game plan

The beauty of this menu lies in its simplicity: just a great piece of fish and fragrant grilled vegetables served with warm tortillas and salsa.

The day before

Of course, it's always a good idea to purchase the beer, tortillas, and chips in advance so you don't have to stop at the store on your way to someplace beautiful. The day or evening before you can also:

> ✔ Cut up and marinate the vegetables.
>
> ✔ Prepare the Corn and Pepper Compote, except for the avocado that should be added the next day.
>
> ✔ Mix the achiote and citrus flavoring rub and store in a plastic resealable bag in the refrigerator.

The same day

Maximum freshness will make a great deal of difference in the quality of some of the foods. Wait until the day of the party to do the following:

> ✔ Purchase the fish.
>
> ✔ Make the guacamole.

The grilling order

Once the grill is hot, arrange the vegetable packets over indirect heat, saving the hot spots for the fish. After the veggies have cooked about 10 minutes, you can start the fish. If you're heating the tortillas, they can be wrapped in foil and tossed on, away from direct heat, for 10 minutes.

The day after

Wondering what to eat the day after the perfect beach barbecue? Leftover whole fish, reheated or cold according to taste, can be flaked to make the Fish Tacos in Chapter 6 — terrific with the Cucumber Salsa in the same chapter.

And as for those heavenly (and healthful) grilled veggies you carefully tucked into a resealable plastic bag before leaving the beach, bring them to room temperature, cut into bite-sized pieces, and toss with greens and dressing for a deliciously smoky salad. Or if you feel up to turning on the oven, cut the vegetables into strips and stuff a memorable quesadilla (see Chapter 6).

A Cinco de Mayo Taco Party

Just in case you need an excuse to party in early May, try inviting your friends over for a totally informal, mix-and-match Cinco de Mayo taco party.

Because tacos are vehicles for tasty fillings of all kinds, this easy party can be built around takeout foods. You purchase a few of your favorite fillings, as we've suggested below, and a few packages of good quality corn tortillas. Then you whip up one or two of your favorite salsas from Chapter 5, some guacamole and chips, big pots of rice and beans the day before, and Corn and Pepper Compote from Chapter 10 if you're feeling really energetic. As long as there are plenty of beers on ice and a pitcher of margaritas in the fridge, a make-it-yourself taco party designed around takeout fillings is a surefire low-stress theme party.

The typical condiments to serve in addition to salsas are:

- ✔ Lime wedges
- ✔ Chopped cilantro
- ✔ Diced fresh onions
- ✔ Thinly sliced radish and peppers

Five easy fillings

Almost any meat that can be chopped small and wrapped in a tortilla can be used for making tacos. Here are some likely candidates that can be purchased from takeout sources and matched with a salsa from Chapter 5:

- ✔ Roasted or barbecued chicken from your favorite source with Roasted Ancho Salsa
- ✔ Flaked, cleaned crabmeat from a fresh fish market with Cucumber Salsa from Fish Tacos (Chapter 6)
- ✔ Barbecued duck or pork from a Chinese market with Smoked Chile Salsa
- ✔ Brisket from deli counter or barbecue stand with Smoked Chile Salsa
- ✔ Grilled vegetables from the supermarket or deli with Fresh Salsa or Green Tomatillo Salsa

The setup

The idea for this easy taco party is that everyone makes his or her taco according to taste. Just cover a big table with a bright tablecloth or serape (red, white, and green are the Mexican colors) and place a bucket of fresh flowers (paper or fresh) in the center. Complete your preparations by arranging everything around the table at the same time: warmed chopped or shredded fillings, rice and beans, salsas and other garnishes, and plenty of warmed tortillas — wrapped in a tea towel and nestled in a basket. Your guests can then circulate around the table and build their tacos using their favorite ingredients.

The game plan

Preparing for this party will be almost as much fun as having it!

The day before

We bet that your total preparation time the day before will be less than 2 hours — tops:

- ✔ Prepare at least two fresh salsas.
- ✔ Make the rice and beans and transfer them to ovenproof casseroles for reheating and bringing to the table.
- ✔ Purchase takeout fillings.

The day of the party

Besides these few simple steps, don't forget to dig out your copy of the Spanish-language song "Cinco de Mayo" on the day of the party:

- ✔ Mix or chill the drinks in the morning.
- ✔ Gently reheat fillings to be served warm.
- ✔ Chop up the fresh garnishes just before the party for maximum crunch.

Chapter 17

Breakfast Specials

• •

In This Chapter

▶ Spicing up your ordinary eggs

▶ Adding a sweet touch to your morning meal

▶ Starting your day with a sandwich

• •

*W*e tend to do our home entertaining on holidays and Sundays. After we work late at our restaurants all week, the idea of having people over for a meal before noon on the weekend is scary. We understand, however, that weekend brunch is an informal way for those who don't work nights to entertain on the weekend, minus all the pressure associated with Saturday night.

The Mexican kitchen is brimming with excellent ideas for brunch. Mexicans like to eat big, soul-satisfying, spicy foods for breakfast just like they do at other meals. Their breakfast choices include some world-class egg dishes and foods like meat-filled tacos that we don't normally associate with the morning. All our recommendations for brunch centerpieces are easy, unfussy dishes that would be equally delicious for a cozy supper.

Eggs Worth Waking Up For

Buckle your seat belts. If you love huevos rancheros, but that's all you're familiar with from the Mexican breakfast menu, you're in for a treat. Mexican cooks have a wide range of lesser-known egg dishes that are equally delicious and spicy. All these traditional dishes are easy to prepare and are guaranteed to start your day with a shout rather than a whisper.

Chile Poached Eggs

What could be more comforting than a nice hot bowl of spicy tomato broth enriched with a poached egg and cheese for breakfast? Make it really easy by preparing the broth two days ahead and poaching the eggs the night before.

Special tools: *Strainer, blender, slotted spoon, 6 soup bowls*

Preparation time: *15 minutes, plus 2 hours and 10 minutes for Chicken Stock, plus 55 minutes for Flour Tortillas*

Cooking time: *30 minutes*

Yield: *6 servings*

2 medium tomatoes, roasted (see Chapter 3)

2 jalapeño peppers, roasted

4 cups chicken stock (see Chapter 8)

2 tablespoons olive oil

1 medium yellow onion, julienned

1½ teaspoons salt

1½ teaspoons pepper

2 cloves garlic, peeled and minced

2 red bell peppers, roasted, seeded, peeled, and julienned

6 eggs

Garnishes: ½ cup (2 ounces) grated añejo cheese and ½ cup sour cream

12 to 18 warm Flour Tortillas, for serving (see Chapter 6)

1 Place the unpeeled roasted tomatoes and jalapeños in a blender with 1 cup of the chicken stock. Puree until smooth, strain, and reserve.

2 Heat the olive oil in a large skillet over medium-high heat. Sauté the onion with the salt and pepper until golden brown, about 12 minutes. Add the garlic and cook for 1 minute longer. Add the red peppers, roasted tomato puree, and the remaining 3 cups of chicken stock. Bring to a boil, reduce to a simmer, and cook for 5 minutes.

3 To poach the eggs, crack one at a time into a coffee cup and, holding the cup's edge at the surface of the broth, gently slide each into the simmering broth. Cook for about 5 minutes or until done to taste, occasionally spooning hot broth over the tops.

4 With a slotted spoon, gently lift out the eggs and place one in each soup bowl. Divide the broth and ladle over the eggs. Garnish with the cheese and a dollop of sour cream. Serve immediately with warm flour tortillas.

TOQUE TIP

To poach eggs in advance, bring 2 inches of water to a boil in a shallow, wide skillet. Have ready a shallow pan of iced water and paper towels. Season the boiling water with a tablespoon of plain white vinegar and reduce to a simmer. Carefully crack the egg shells and lower the cracked eggs, one at a time, into a small bowl, slide them into the water, and cook until just set. Lift the eggs out with a slotted spoon and immediately plunge them into iced water to stop the cooking. Lift out with a slotted spoon, transfer to paper towels to drain, and then transfer to a platter. Cover tightly with plastic wrap and refrigerate. To reheat, bring the broth to a boil and add the eggs. Cook briefly, just to warm.

Scrambled Eggs with Chorizo

Chorizo, the strongly spiced Mexican pork sausage, is a typical enrichment for scrambled eggs. To use as a breakfast burrito filling, simply spread the tortilla with mashed avocado and top the eggs with a dollop or two of Fresh Salsa from Chapter 5. (Also see the sidebar "Burrito folding basics" in this chapter.)

Preparation time: *10 minutes*

Cooking time: *15 minutes*

Yield: *4 servings*

½ pound bulk or chopped chorizo	*½ bunch cilantro leaves, chopped (¼ cup)*
1 medium yellow onion, chopped	*3 scallions, trimmed and sliced for garnish*
Salt and pepper to taste	*6 (10-inch) flour or 8 to 12 (6-inch) corn tortillas warmed for serving*
2 jalapeños, thinly sliced, seeds optional	
10 eggs	

1 Fry the chorizo in a large nonstick skillet over medium-high heat until browned, about 10 minutes. Drain off any excess oil. Add the onion and salt and pepper, and fry for about 5 minutes longer. Stir in the jalapeños and fry for 2 minutes longer.

2 Beat the eggs until frothy, season with salt and pepper, and pour into the pan. Reduce the heat to medium-low. Stir with a fork to scramble until soft, not browned. Stir in the cilantro and scallions a few seconds before the eggs are set and remove from heat. Serve immediately with warm tortillas.

We highly recommend going for the full burn with the jalapeños in this dish. Chorizo is such a rich sausage that it really needs the heat of as many chiles (and seeds) as you can handle.

Burrito folding basics

The following method will keep your burrito filling piping hot and inside the tortilla (rather than down your shirt front).

Huevos Rancheros

This classic Mexican breakfast for two tastes much better when prepared on Sunday morning by your loved one while you catch up on some extra rest.

Preparation time: *10 minutes, plus 2 hours 10 minutes for Refried Pinto Beans, plus 35 minutes for Red Roasted Tomato Salsa*

Cooking time: *5 minutes*

Yield: *2 servings*

⅔ cup refried beans (see Chapter 10)

Water or chicken stock (see Chapter 8) to taste

1 tablespoon butter

4 eggs

Salt and pepper to taste

4 crispy corn fried tortillas, whole (see Chapter 10)

¼ cup (1 ounce) grated añejo cheese

1 cup Red Roasted Tomato Salsa, warmed (see Chapter 5)

½ bunch cilantro leaves, coarsely chopped (¼ cup)

1 Reheat the refried beans in a small skillet over low heat, adding water or chicken broth until the beans are the consistency of applesauce. Keep warm.

2 Heat a large nonstick or cast-iron skillet over medium heat and add the butter. Carefully break the eggs into the skillet and season with salt and pepper. Cover and cook for 1 minute or until done to taste. Remove from heat.

3 Place 2 tortillas on each plate and coat with a thin layer of warm refried beans. Sprinkle each with half the cheese. Top each tortilla with an egg and ladle on warmed salsa. Sprinkle on the remaining cheese and cilantro. Serve immediately.

Fried Eggs on Chilaquiles

Chilaquiles (chee-lah-KEE-lehs) are a casual dish of leftover corn tortillas (or their chips) and salsa that is interpreted many different ways by inventive Mexican cooks. It can be made with red or green salsa, with an added dose of protein from leftover chicken or beef, layered in a casserole like a lasagna, or served in a soup bowl like the version below. Anyway you cook it, it's always delicious!

It may not be pretty, but this dish of soggy tortilla chips in spiced-up creamy tomato salsa is a great dish for the morning after a big night out, like New Year's. The fat and spice in this rich dish are guaranteed to connect a few dots in the addled brains of your guests, and best of all, everything but the fried egg can be made a day in advance.

Preparation time: *10 minutes, plus 35 minutes to make the Red Roasted Tomato Salsa, plus 10 minutes for Fried Tortilla Chips, plus 2 hours and 10 minutes for Chicken Stock*

Cooking time: *25 minutes*

Yield: *4 servings*

1 cup Red Roasted Tomato Salsa (see Chapter 5)

½ cup heavy cream

½ cup chicken stock (see Chapter 8)

3 cups Fried Tortilla Chips (see Chapter 10) or bagged chips

½ cup (2 ounces) grated cheeses (añejo, manchego, or a mix)

1 tablespoon butter

4 eggs

2 tablespoons chopped red onion

2 serrano chiles, thinly sliced

2 tablespoons chopped fresh cilantro

1 Combine the salsa, cream, and stock in a medium saucepan and bring to a boil. Add the corn chips, reduce the heat to a simmer, and cook, stirring frequently, until the chips break up and soften, about 15 minutes. Stir in the cheese and remove from heat.

(continued)

2 Melt the butter in a large nonstick skillet. Fry the eggs, sunny-side up, just until set. Ladle the corn chip mixture onto 4 plates and sprinkle each with fresh onion, chile, and cilantro. Top each with a fried egg. Serve immediately.

If making in advance, be prepared to thin the tortilla mixture the next day with some additional broth until it's the consistency of oatmeal because the tortillas will have absorbed lots of liquid.

These easy chilaquiles make a nice side dish the second day. Just reheat and omit the fried egg. Substitute the Green Tomatillo Salsa from Chapter 5 for a green variation.

Sweet Beginnings

If it takes a little sugar in the morning to get your mojo working, you came to the right place. Here's our version of an intensified French toast, a classic Mexican breakfast pastry, and fried bananas over rice — all guaranteed to get your day headed in the right direction.

What to serve with brunch?

Because our tastes run toward the easy and undemanding for early morning entertaining, we won't burden you with precise menus for brunch. We would like to recommend some of our favorite accompaniments to a Mexican brunch, if you feel like jazzing things up a little:

✔ Add a green salad or simple seared greens for that unusual morning wake-up call.

Seared Chard from Chapter 10 or the Spinach Salad from Chapter 16 would both be wonderful.

✔ Serve homemade beverages, such as Mexican Spiced Coffee (Chapter 4), and a selection of fresh juices, especially orange, watermelon, and carrot juice.

Banana Stuffed Mexican Toast with Coconut Syrup

For unabashed morning sweet lovers, here's our twist on an old favorite — French toast. By stuffing the bread with mashed bananas and flavoring it with cinnamon and homemade coconut syrup, it has a Mexican twist.

Preparation time: *30 minutes, plus 25 minutes for Coconut Syrup*

Cooking time: *10 minutes*

Yield: *2 servings*

2 double-thick (about 1-inch) pieces crusty white bread

1 large or 2 small ripe bananas

2 eggs

⅔ cup milk

½ teaspoon salt

1 teaspoon sugar

¼ teaspoon ground cinnamon

1 tablespoon butter

Coconut Syrup (see following recipe)

1 Using a sharp, serrated knife, cut a horizontal pocket in each bread slice, coming close to the edges but leaving the crusts intact. Be careful not to cut holes in the dough.

2 In a small bowl, mash the banana with a fork. Using a spoon, stuff each piece of bread with mashed bananas, as full as possible.

3 In a shallow bowl, lightly beat the eggs with the milk, salt, sugar, and cinnamon. Dip the stuffed bread in the egg mixture and let soak about 15 minutes, turning occasionally, until all the egg mixture is absorbed.

4 Melt the butter in a large cast-iron or nonstick skillet over medium heat. Fry the toast in the hot skillet until cooked through, about 3 minutes per side. Serve with warm Coconut Syrup.

Coconut Syrup

Special tool: *Blender*

Preparation time: *5 minutes*

Cooking time: *20 minutes*

Yield: *2 cups*

1 (4½-ounce) can unsweetened coconut milk

1 cup sweetened shredded coconut

¾ cup packed brown sugar

(continued)

1 Combine the coconut milk, coconut, and brown sugar in a small heavy saucepan. Bring to a boil, reduce to a simmer, and cook, uncovered, for 20 minutes, stirring occasionally.

2 Transfer to a blender and puree until smooth. Serve immediately. The Coconut Syrup can be stored in the refrigerator for 2 weeks and reheated.

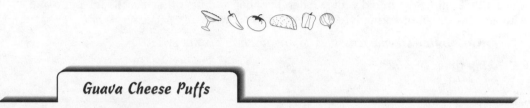

Guava Cheese Puffs

One of the delights of the Mexican kitchen is the interplay between sweet and salty, as displayed in this delicious fruit- and cheese-filled tart. A special breakfast pastry such as this is always a big hit served with coffee throughout the day.

Guava paste can be found in the jam and jelly section or the ethnic section of the supermarket. This concentrated jam, thick enough to slice with a knife, is often served in Spanish-speaking countries, along with an aged salty cheese, for a light dessert. Pastes made of quince or pear may be eaten in the same way.

Special tools: *Baking sheet, parchment paper, pastry brush, cooling rack*

Preparation time: *30 minutes, plus 2½ hours chilling*

Cooking time: *50 minutes*

Yield: *8 servings*

8 ounces cream cheese, softened

1 cup grated añejo cheese

2 pieces puff pastry, ½ pound each, each cut into a 12-inch circle

1 egg, lightly beaten

¾ cup guava paste mixed with ¼ cup freshly squeezed lime juice or ¾ cup other fruit jam or puree

1 tablespoon heavy cream

1 Combine the cream cheese and añejo cheese in a bowl and mix well with a spoon.

2 Line a baking sheet with parchment paper. Place 1 of the puff pastry circles on the baking sheet. Brush a 1-inch rim around the outside edge with the beaten egg. Pat the cheese mixture into an 8-inch circle in the center and spread the guava paste evenly over the top.

3 Fold the remaining piece of puff pastry in half and place over the first piece, edge-to-edge. Unfold the pastry to enclose the filling and chill for 30 minutes, or until thoroughly cold.

4 Remove from the refrigerator. Working about 1½ inches from the outside, firmly press the edges of pastry together with the tines of a fork to seal. Then trim the excess dough around the edge, leaving an even 1-inch border of crust around the filling. With a sharp paring knife, cut out and discard a ¾-inch circle of dough from the center, and press out any trapped air with your hands. Then, making shallow cuts, trace 6 to 8 circular lines in a spiral pattern from the center hole to the inside edge of the sealed crust, like the spokes of a wheel. (If the dough gets too warm to work with, just return it to the refrigerator for 30 minutes or so to harden.)

5 Mix the heavy cream with the remaining beaten egg and brush over the top of the tart. Cover with plastic wrap and chill for at least 2 hours or overnight.

6 To bake, preheat the oven to 450°.

7 Transfer the tart from the refrigerator to the oven and bake for 15 minutes or until puffed and golden brown on top. Reduce the oven temperature to 350°. Bake until the jelly is bubbling and the bottom crust, when lifted with a spatula, is browned, about 35 minutes. Set aside to cool on a rack for 10 to 15 minutes. Serve warm or at room temperature.

Make the pastry with quince jam in place of guava paste and Spanish blue cheese in place of the salty añejo cheese for a delicious Spanish twist that will make you jump out of bed in the morning for breakfast.

Fried Plantains and Rice

If your kids like a banana in their morning oatmeal, they stand a good chance of really enjoying this warm grain and fruit alternative. It's a great way to use up last night's rice and start the day with a sweet and salty spin.

Preparation time: *5 minutes plus 45 minutes for White Rice*

Cooking time: *15 minutes*

Yield: *4 servings*

3 cups cooked White Rice (see Chapter 10)

3 tablespoons butter

2 very ripe plantains, peeled and cut in ¼-inch diagonal slices

1 tablespoon sugar and ½ teaspoon ground cinnamon, mixed together

(continued)

1 Preheat the oven to 350°. Place the rice in a buttered ovenproof casserole and cover with a damp paper towel and foil. Bake for 10 minutes to reheat.

2 Melt the butter in a large skillet over medium-high heat. Fry the plantains 3 minutes per side, until deep golden brown.

3 Place the hot rice in serving bowls and sprinkle with the cinnamon sugar. Top with fried plantains and serve immediately.

A Quick Breakfast Sandwich

We love picking up a savory little sandwich like this one or a meaty taco for breakfast when we make the rounds of the morning food markets in Mexico.

Mollettes

This traditional dish of bread toasted with yesterday's refried beans reminds us of the little toasted baguettes called *tartines* that we used to have for breakfast in France as hungry young chefs. Serve mollettes (moh-LEH-tehs) with Chile Poached Eggs for an instant Mexican breakfast. Like so many great dishes in Mexico, this one makes excellent use of a few simple ingredients.

Preparation time: *5 minutes, plus 15 minutes to make the Fresh Salsa*

Cooking time: *10 minutes*

Yield: *2 servings*

2 crusty hard sandwich rolls

1½ tablespoons butter

¾ cup Refried Black Beans or Refried Pinto Beans, reheated (see Chapter 10)

1½ cups (6 ounces) grated manchego cheese

½ cup Fresh Salsa (see Chapter 5)

1 Preheat the broiler.

2 Split the rolls lengthwise and spread with butter. Place on a baking tray and put under the broiler until toasted. Spread each half with hot beans and sprinkle with cheese. Return to the broiler for about 3 minutes, until bubbly. Garnish with Fresh Salsa and serve hot.

Part V
The Part of Tens

The 5th Wave   By Rich Tennant

©RICHTENNANT.COM

"Well, if you're not drinking tequila with your breakfast burrito, then why is your cereal bowl rimmed in salt."

In this part . . .

We've assembled some of our favorite top ten lists in this part, including ten things to make out of tortillas and chips, ten ways to create the right atmosphere for your gatherings, ten very handy Spanish phrases for travelers, and ten Web sites that we want you to visit if you can pry yourself away from the kitchen.

Chapter 18

Ten Ways to Set the Scene

- -

- -

As chefs we may want the food to speak for itself, but as restaurateurs we know that great food is only one part of the equation. When people come to one of our restaurants, they are looking for a total experience. Setting the stage with lighting, music, and art, as well as friendly service, helps guests forget about their everyday problems and enjoy the moment — what mañana is all about.

Giving a party or entertaining at home is a little bit like playing restaurateur for a day (or night). By supporting the menu with the right flowers, music, tableware, and lighting, you give your party that extra boost that lifts it out of the ordinary. The incredible food you've cooked from this book, of course, will be the icing on the cake.

Playing Latin Music

In Mexican homes, music is almost always playing in the background. What more authentic accompaniment to spicy, earthy Mexican food could there be than hot, sensual Latin music?

Browse the World Music and Salsa sections at the music store for Latin-flavored sounds. Some of our favorite artists are Gloria Estefan, Tito Puente, Celia Cruz, Los Lobos, Flaco Jimenez, Los Reyes, and Lefty Perez. We also like recorded Mexican polka music, called *banda* and, best of all, live mariachis.

Because so many people ask us for music recommendations, we've put together a compilation CD of some of our favorite tunes. It's available at our Web site, www.bordergrill.com, or by phone at 310-451-1655.

In southern California, you can hire a group of three musicians for as little as $100 to add a few hours of spectacle and energy to the occasion. For big parties at our restaurants, we sometimes hire a pair of dancers to encourage those who are waiting for someone else to go first. Try calling the American Federation of Musicians for referrals in your area.

Adding Flowers and Plants

The fresh flowers that instantly say Mexico are sunflowers, calla lilies, marigolds, birds of paradise, and bougainvillea because they are so popular there. We like to place a few large buckets containing the same flower throughout the room.

If you prefer plants, a few large cactus can make a dramatic statement. And if you do much outdoor entertaining, you may want to plant a Mexican lime tree in the yard for easy seasoning on the grill.

If fresh flowers are too difficult or expensive, a terrific substitute that we use all the time in our restaurants is traditional, brightly colored, handmade crepe paper flowers from Mexico. You can order them from our source in Los Angeles, Los Olveritas, phone 213-972-9105, or fax 213-687-7234.

Setting the Table

The best advice we can give for setting a Mexican table is to keep it casual and colorful. The colors we use most often for tablecloths and napkins are bright red, orange, yellow, hot pink, and cobalt blue.

We like to use rustic serving pieces made of terra cotta or cast iron, and the rustic blue or green tumblers made from recycled bottles are terrific for beverages. Fresh tropical fruits, such as mangos, small watermelons, giant Mexican papayas, pineapples, and passion fruits, are just right for a centerpiece.

Serving Drinks

Bright, beautiful Mexican beverages (see Chapter 4 for recipes) look great in clear glass pitchers. If you don't have pitchers, giant glass jars, like the kind pickles come in, work just fine. Include a ladle to lift out the liquid.

Serving Tequila in Lime Halves

Because lime is the perfect accompaniment to tequila, what could be better than sipping your tequila out of a hollowed-out lime? For organic shot glasses, evenly slice off the ends of the lime, being careful not to puncture any holes in the skin, so that the bottoms can sit on a counter without tipping. Scoop out the pulp with a spoon and store the shells in the freezer until firm. Pour tequila shots straight into lime halves. A lime half should last for a few shots.

Dimming the Lights

A Mexican party is the perfect time to dim the lights and burn your candles. The tall, thick, colorful Latin prayer candles encased in glass and sold in the supermarket are great for setting a mood. Also nice are strings of party lights.

Placing Chips and Salsa in Strategic Locations

One reason that Mexican parties are so much fun is that the eating (and drinking) begins the moment guests open the door. With chips and salsa at the ready, the party doesn't take long to get rolling.

We like to fill big wooden bowls with chips and place them next to smaller ceramic bowls of salsas and guacamole at a few different stations to encourage guests to move around.

A *molcajete* (see Figure 18-1), a black grinding stone for spices and guacamole, is a terrific container for serving chips. Look for them at Latin markets.

Figure 18-1:
Try using a
molcajete
as an usual
serving dish
for chips.

Polishing up a Room with Decorative Accents

A whimsical piñata (preferably not a large purple dinosaur) strung up from a tree or the ceiling, some terra cotta pottery serving pieces, and bright hand-woven textiles as tablecloths or runners are perfect for creating Mexican ambience. Strings of colorful paper flags are also a nice accent.

Giving Guests a Dessert to Go

Miniature 2-piece gum containers make a great party favor for departing guests. We like to fill a bowl with the colorful paper packages for guests to grab a handful. People who've visited Mexico will remember seeing these gum containers sold on the street.

Chapter 19

Ten Delicious Treats to Make with Tortillas and Chips

In This Chapter

▶ Tantalizing guests and family members with tortilla treats

▶ Creating crunchy snacks with chips

*1*f you start cooking Mexican food frequently, an interesting question may arise: What do you do with all the leftover tortillas and chips after you get past the obvious dipping and chipping?

More so than bread, tortillas are amazingly versatile. They last quite a long time in the fridge, and in addition to being an integral ingredient in quesadillas, enchiladas, and chilaquiles, they can be used to garnish a soup, wrap a fish, or make a quick topping for ice cream. And good tortilla chips never die — they just go on crunching, as you'll see in the recipes in this chapter.

Crisped Tortilla Crackers

Flour tortillas, baked until crisp with different flavorings, make excellent low-cost hors d'oeuvres. Just follow these steps to create this quick and delicious snack:

1. **Brush one side of the tortillas with lime juice and sprinkle with ground Chili Powder Mix (Chapter 11). Or brush with beaten egg and sprinkle with assorted seeds like sesame, poppy, and flax.**

   Seeds are available at health food stores.

2. **Lay the tortillas, brushed side up, on baking sheets and bake in a 350° oven until crisp, about 8 minutes.**

3. **Serve in baskets while the crackers are still warm.**

For cylindrical crackers, trim ½-inch off each tortilla to create a straight edge. Wrap the tortillas around soda or soup cans and bake until crisp. Then remove the cans and stand the tortillas upright on the table for a dramatic effect.

Tortilla Buñuelos

Make instant *buñuelos,* or fried dough fritters, by deep-frying flour tortillas in oil. Dip the fried tortillas into cinnamon sugar to generously coat, and serve them hot and drizzled with honey for dessert.

Chapter 15 gives you another delicious and easy recipe for buñuelos.

The Instant Fish Wrapper

One of our favorite methods for imparting a Mexican flavor to fish fillets is to wrap and bake them in corn tortillas. The tortillas protect the fish and keep it moist while adding a layer of corn flavor.

This fish wrapper works with every sort of fish fillet except tuna or sword-fish. Just follow these steps:

1. **Marinate the fish fillets in orange and lime juices seasoned with salt, pepper, and oregano for about 1 hour.**

2. **Briefly saute the fillets until they are halfway cooked. Let cool.**

3. **Soften the tortillas by dipping them in hot oil, just as you do when making enchiladas (Chapter 6). Wrap each fillet in a tortilla or in a triangle made of three overlapping tortillas for larger pieces. Fold over to enclose and wrap in aluminum foil to seal.**

4. **Bake in a 350° oven until the fish is just done, about 10 minutes.**

Chips and Their Crunch

Crushed tortilla chips are a great way to add crunch to salads. Just crunch 'em and toss 'em. Chips can also stand in as crunchy toppings for casseroles.

Add a Mexican touch to your favorite fried or baked foods by using ground or crushed tortilla chips in place of bread crumbs as the coating medium.

Matzoh Brei Mexicana

How's this for cross-cultural chutzpah? Try the Mexican version of matzoh brei, which is the Jewish Passover dish of softened matzoh dipped in egg and scrambled in butter. Just follow these steps:

1. **Take 8 ounces of tortilla chips (about 3 large handfuls) and cover them with boiling water to soften. Drain.**

   In a traditional recipe for matzoh brei, this step would be done with matzoh.

2. **Beat the chips together with 3 eggs, salt, pepper, and a chopped serrano or jalapeño chile.**

3. **Scramble the egg mixture in lots of butter until the edges are brown. Serve hot with sliced scallions, salsa, and sour cream.**

Finger Food Wraps

You can use flour tortillas instead of lavosh (the Middle Eastern flat bread) to make pinwheel sandwiches for parties. Just follow these steps:

1. **Spread the tortillas with a generous layer of cream cheese.**

2. **Layer watercress, roasted red and green pepper strips, and thinly sliced salami onto the cream cheese.**

3. **Roll the tortillas into a cylinder and cut across the width into ½-inch slices. Arrange on platters, cut side up.**

Instant Soup Fixins

Crushed tortilla chips or homemade fried corn tortilla strips make excellent crunchy soup garnishes in place of crackers. Flip to Chapter 10 for the skinny on frying your own chips.

Tortilla Ice Cream Sundaes

You can make an instant ice cream topping with flour tortillas by following these steps:

1. Roll a few tortillas into a tight cylinder and thinly slice across the width.

2. Toss the tortillas with melted butter, sugar, and cinnamon and arrange on a baking sheet. Bake at 350° until golden brown.

3. Sprinkle the tortillas over your favorite ice cream — hot fudge sauce is optional.

   Roasted, salted peanuts or pecans, by the way, are also very Mexican ice cream toppers.

Healthful Tortilla Stock

You can use tortilla chips as a base for a soulful vegetarian stock for soups and chowders. Just follow these steps:

1. In a soup pot, sauté a coarsely chopped carrot, celery stalk, and onion in 1 tablespoon of oil. When soft, add 1½ quarts of crushed tortilla chips and briefly sauté.

2. Pour in 4 quarts of water, bring to a boil, reduce to a simmer, and cook, uncovered, about 45 minutes, until the flavor has developed.

3. Pass through a strainer, discarding the solids, and store in the refrigerator for 1 week or in the freezer as long as a month.

Chex Mex

Add a Mexican flair to a sweet and salty bar mix by following these steps:

1. Combine diced corn tortillas with peanuts, pepitas, golden raisins, and broken pretzel sticks.

2. Season with peanut oil, Worcestershire sauce, chile powder mix, cayenne, salt, pepper, and a pinch of sugar.

3. Spread on a baking sheet and bake in a 350° oven, stirring occasionally, until crisp, about 10 minutes. Cool before serving.

Chapter 20

Ten Spanish Phrases for Travelers

- -

In This Chapter

▶ Speaking the language when dining out

▶ Some phrases for shopping in Spanish-speaking countries

- -

Few things are more frustrating than wanting something in a restaurant or market and not having the words to ask for it. Although we're never too proud to point and act silly in order to get what we want, we've found it makes a big difference if we can at least speak a few words to let people know that we have respect for their culture and we're trying to learn. This way, when the waiter answers our kitchen Spanish in perfect English, we can grin sheepishly, say "Gracias," and humbly enjoy the meal.

Por favor

There's nothing like it. **Por fa-BOR** or "please" is definitely the magic word in any language when it comes to food service. Try to imagine taking orders all day long and never being addressed politely. Simply tack the phrase onto the end of your request and watch your waitperson smile (or at least bring you your food).

Muchas gracias

The partner to "por favor" is **GRAH-see-ahs** or "thank you." If you want to show extreme gratitude, you can add a **MOO-chahs** to the front of it for "thanks so much." You can never say this phrase too much, but do be careful not to mispronounce the gracias. "Grasa" means fat.

Lo quiero mas o menos picante

If you want to give the waitperson a better idea of your tastes, this little phrase should come in handy. **Loh kye-ER-oh mahs** means "I want it more" and **Loh key-ER-oh MEH-nohs** means "I want it less." **Pee-CAHN-teh** means "spicy." So if your heartburn is kicking in, go for option two and, if you're looking for a wilder ride, go for option one.

La cuenta, por favor

We know it's a bittersweet moment, but eventually we all want to get the check and hit the road. **La KWEN-TAH, por fa-BOR,** or "Bring me the bill please" should do the trick.

¿Dónde está el baño?

This is a handy little phrase to have when you're on the road sightseeing and drinking lots of water. **DON-deh es-TAH el BAH-nyo** simply means "Where is the bathroom?"

Quiero ordenar una comida tipica de la region, no la comida de los gringos

No question, this is a mouthful, but you can pick and choose the parts of it that work best for you. **Key-ER-oh or-deh-NAR una koh-MEE-thah TEE-pee-kah deh la re-hyon** means "I want to order a typical dish of the region," and **no la koh-MEE-thah deh los GREEN-gohs** means "not the food the gringos eat." This is the sentence to use if you've waited all your life to taste fried grasshoppers and the waiter is insisting that you'd be better off with a quesadilla. Set him straight and brace yourself for the real thing.

Sin hielo

A practical phrase you should commit to memory before stepping off the plane. **Seen YEH-loh** means without ice, the way you want your drinks in Mexico if you're concerned with traveler's diarrhea. Because it's bacteria in the water that causes the problem, you want to avoid iced drinks. However, some places with a lot of tourist traffic use purified water for ice. If you can string the words together, you can ask about the water in the ice.

Quiero agua purificada

Along with ordering your drinks without ice, another way to ensure you don't spend too much time in your hotel room is by saying **key-ER-oh AH-gwah pu-rih-fi-KAH-dah,** or "I want purified water."

¿Que platillo sugieres?

Keh plah-TEE-yoh suh-hye-RES is a phrase we use when we're not sure what we want to eat but we don't want to miss the specialties of the house. It means "What do you suggest?" or "What dish do you recommend?" and we generally hold the menu up for the waiter to kindly point to. Any waiter worth his or her salt should be happy to offer an opinion.

¿Cuánto cuesta?

We love tasting foods from markets or street vendors who may not have a printed menu. **KWAHN-toh KWEHS-tah**, or "How much is it?" is all you need to know to pay the tab. If you never got past 10 on *Sesame Street,* it's a good idea to carry a pad and pencil for salespeople to write down numbers.

Chapter 21

Ten Web Sites to Check Out

●●

In This Chapter

▶ Finding great recipes and supplies on the Web

▶ Getting cooking advice from world-class chefs online

●●

As chefs who have always been more interested in the future than the past, we're big believers in the Web. We use it to check out what's happening in the professional cooking community, research tidbits for our shows, or just browse the information highway for inspiring ideas.

The main thing to keep in mind if you're new to the Web is that the sites and information are constantly changing. So today's ten best cooking sites will not necessarily be tomorrow's best sites. Just get comfortable with the technology and you'll develop your own "nose" for what's good and useful on the Web.

As far as recognizing quality recipes or information, the same rules apply as to any publication in the marketplace. Chances are the big news organizations, like CNN, are checking their facts, retail sites have certain commercial interests, and homegrown individual sites will be as quirky as any human can be. If you cook from enough recipes, you'll learn to "taste" a good recipe with your mind.

As the geek of the group — I wanted to be the chef on the Starship Enterprise — our presence on the Web has been my pet project. I dragged Susan (and the Border Grill) on in 1994 with one of the first major restaurant sites. Our site still hasn't made any money, but even Susan has to admit I was right about getting on the Web. The jury may still be out on where it all will lead, but a Web presence is crucial in today's business world.

Yes, it's true. We even have matching laptops.

chefnet

If you're a food professional (or thinking about becoming one) chefnet will link you to all the heavy hitters. From www.chefnet.com you can surf up to two of our favorite organizations: Women Chefs and Restaurateurs and Chef's Collaborative 2000, a group that works to support small farmers and organic agriculture.

Under the site's Culinary Network banner, you can join discussion groups concerning pastry making, catering and professional training, as well as search for a job as a personal chef and trade gossip with colleagues from around the world.

FoodTV

At www.foodtv.com, the TV Food Network posts two weeks' worth of recipes from all its shows, as well as schedules for its programming and information on the chefs. This is a wonderful source of recipes for all sorts of cooking, including Mexican recipes.

Epicurious

One of the oldest and best-established food sites, Epicurious (www.epicurious.com) is so good that it has its own TV show on the Discovery Channel. We turn to this site to find quick tidbits for our own radio and TV shows.

At the site, you can search databases on the country's leading chefs and their restaurants; wines by type, region, and price; kitchen wisdom from leading food experts; food and wine terms and definitions; and a library of cookbooks that you can explore online. A special feature that we like is the "playing with your food" page. It instructs enthusiastic newcomers to the food scene on the proper way to handle intimidating products from artichokes to pomegranates. The site also has a weekly listing of farmers markets across the United States — great for printing out and taking on the road.

Slow Food

The International Slow Food Movement, started in Italy 10 years ago, champions the causes of small regional food producers, winemakers, and other aficionados who in an age of standardized tastes and microwave oatmeal refuse to gulp down lunch at their desks.

On its Web site, Slow Food (www.slowfood.com), this irreverent group posts its manifesto, information on cooking classes, upcoming symposia, and support for those interested in improving the length and quality of their time at the table.

Border Grill

Okay, we're prejudiced, but we do have one hot site. Come visit us at www.bordergrill.com and view photos of the restaurants, enter your name on our newsletter mailing list if you wish, peruse the menus of Border Grill and Ciudad (our latest Latin-flavored restaurant), drop us a personal note, check our schedules for when we might be visiting near you, shop in our gift store for our favorite pepper mills, or even print out a few recipes.

Digitalchef

Digitalchef (www.digitalchef.com) bills itself as the largest gourmet food and kitchenware retail site on the Internet. It offers brand-name appliances, pots and pans, specialty tools (including a tortilla press and a potato masher), and thousands of upscale gourmet foods. And the Culinary Institute of America, one of the country's top training schools for chefs, offers excellent cooking tips, recipes, and advice on choosing the best tool to do a specific job.

Melissas

If finding a cactus paddle at your supermarket is like searching for that proverbial needle in a haystack, come to Melissas (www.melissas.com). You can shop for hard-to-find imported exotica like cactus paddles, jamaica, tamarind, and chiles, as well as ingredients (fresh and dried) for other ethnic cuisines.

Chile Today — Hot Tamale

The place to shop for your favorite chile head online is Chile Today — Hot Tamale (www.chiletodayhottamale.com). You can purchase salsas and hot sauces, dried chiles and powders, highly seasoned snacks, and the kind of fun gifts bound to appeal to chile lovers.

Cibolo Junction

If you live in a part of the country where chiles are hard to find, Cibolo Junction (www.cibolojunction.com) offers you instant access to the whole world of chiles. From the chile page you can order ancho, cascabel, chipotle, arbol, and pasillas, among other chiles. And annatto seed can be found on the spice page!

CNN Food Central

Keeping up to date with the latest food news can be a full-time job. But CNN Food Central (www.cnn.com/food) puts it all together for you, every day. This is the place to check out the latest health and nutrition information, including nutritional analysis, chat with other food lovers, frankly critique your local restaurants, and get step-by-step instructions, with photos, for a new recipe each day.

Part VI
Appendixes

"The empanadas are coming out a little tough. Someone just requested a piñata bat to open hers with."

In this part . . .

We include two appendixes chock full of information that you can refer to for quick answers when you're looking for a substitution or equivalent for something listed in the book, and for when you come across a Spanish word that you don't understand or know how to pronounce.

Appendix A
Common Substitutions and Equivalents

Sometimes things just don't go as planned. You may read your recipe all the way through, make out a complete shopping list, purchase all the ingredients, and then at the moment of truth, you find that one or more of the required ingredients has mysteriously disappeared from the kitchen.

In most of our recipes, you can freely substitute some other ingredient to make up for the missing element; in fact, for many of the recipes throughout this book, we give you some hints on appropriate substitutions. However, when you need to get a little creative with your substitutions, you can turn to this appendix for some ideas. We also include two tables that will help you decipher ingredient lists when they seem a little less than clear.

Try these substitutions when you don't have time to go back to the store for a missing ingredient.

For thickening soups, stews, and sauces:

- ✔ 1 tablespoon (15 milliliters) cornstarch or potato starch = 2 tablespoons (30 milliliters) all-purpose flour

- ✔ 1 tablespoon (15 milliliters) arrowroot = 2^1/$_2$ tablespoons (37 milliliters) all-purpose flour

For leavening agents in baked goods:

- ✔ ^{1}/$_4$ teaspoon (1 milliliter) baking soda + ^{1}/$_2$ teaspoon (2 milliliters) cream of tartar = 1 teaspoon (5 milliliters) double-acting baking powder

- ✔ ^{1}/$_4$ teaspoon (1 milliliter) baking soda + ^{1}/$_2$ cup (125 milliliters) buttermilk or plain yogurt = 1 teaspoon (5 milliliters) double-acting baking powder in liquid mixtures only; reduce liquid in recipe by ^{1}/$_2$ cup (125 milliliters)

For dairy products:

- 1 cup (250 milliliters) whole milk = $^1/_2$ cup (125 milliliters) evaporated milk + $^1/_2$ cup (125 milliliters) water

  or 1 cup (250 milliliters) skim milk + 2 tablespoons (30 milliliters) melted butter

  or $^1/_4$ cup (50 milliliters) powdered milk + 1 cup (250 milliliters) water

  or 1 cup (250 milliliters) soy milk

For eggs:

- 2 egg yolks = 1 whole egg
- 4 extra-large eggs = 5 large eggs

For sweetening:

- 1 cup brown sugar = 1 cup (250 milliliters) granulated sugar + $1^1/_2$ tablespoons (22 milliliters) molasses

Miscellaneous substitutions:

- 1 tablespoon (15 milliliters) prepared mustard = 1 teaspoon (5 milliliters) dried mustard
- 1 cup (250 milliliters) broth or stock = 1 bouillon cube dissolved in 1 cup (250 milliliters) boiling water
- 1 square (1 ounce/28 grams) unsweetened chocolate = 3 tablespoons (45 milliliters) unsweetened cocoa + 1 tablespoon (15 milliliters) butter, margarine, vegetable shortening, or oil
- 1 ounce (28 grams) semisweet chocolate = 3 tablespoons (45 milliliters) unsweetened cocoa + 2 tablespoons (30 milliliters) butter, margarine, vegetable shortening, or oil + 3 tablespoons (45 milliliters) granulated sugar

Suppose that a recipe calls for 1 pound tomatoes, and you don't own a kitchen scale. (You should, you know.) Or maybe you can't remember how many tablespoons are in a cup. Table B-1 lists common equivalent measures. Table B-2 deals with food items, giving cup and weight measures for some often-used ingredients. All measurements are for level amounts. Note that some metric measurements are approximate.

Table B-1	Conversion Secrets	
This Measurement...	*... Equals This Measurement...*	*... Equals This Measurement*
Pinch or dash	less than $1/8$ teaspoon	0.5 mL
3 teaspoons	1 tablespoon	15 mL
2 tablespoons	1 fluid ounce	30 mL
4 tablespoons	$1/4$ cup	50 mL
5 tablespoons + 1 teaspoon	$1/3$ cup	75 mL
8 tablespoons	$1/2$ cup	100 mL
10 tablespoons + 2 teaspoons	$2/3$ cup	150 mL
12 tablespoons	$3/4$ cup	175 ml
16 tablespoons	1 cup	250 mL
1 cup	8 fluid ounces	250 mL
2 cups	1 pint or 16 fluid ounces	500 mL
2 pints	1 quart or 32 fluid ounces	1 L
4 quarts	1 gallon	4 L

Table B-2	Food Equivalents	
This Measurement...	*... Equals This Measurement...*	*... Equals This Measurement*
1 pound all-purpose flour	4 cups sifted	1 L sifted
3 medium apples or bananas	approximately 1 pound	500 g
2 slices bread	1 cup fresh bread crumbs	250 mL
1 pound brown sugar	$2 1/4$ cups packed	550 mL packed
8 tablespoons butter	1 stick	125 mL or $1/2$ cup
4 sticks butter	1 pound	454 g
6 ounces chocolate chips	1 cup	250 mL
1 pound confectioners sugar	4 $1/2$ cups sifted	1.125 L sifted

(continued)

Table B-2 *(continued)*

This Measurement...	*...Equals This Measurement...*	*...Equals This Measurement*
1 cup dried beans	2 cups cooked	500 mL
1 large garlic clove	approximately 1 teaspoon minced	5 mL minced
1 pound granulated sugar	2 cups	500 mL
$1/2$ pound hard cheese (such as Parmesan)	approximately 2 cups grated	500 mL grated
1 cup heavy whipping cream	2 cups whipped	500 mL whipped
1 medium lemon	3 tablespoons juice, 1 to 2 teaspoons grated peel	45 mL juice, 5 to 10 mL grated peel
4 ounces nuts	approximately $2/3$ cup chopped	150 mL chopped
1 large onion	approximately 1 cup chopped	250 mL chopped
1 pound pasta	4 cups raw, 8 cups cooked	1 L raw, 2 L cooked
3 medium potatoes	approximately 1 pound	500 g
1 cup raw rice	3 cups cooked	750 mL cooked
1 large tomato	approximately $3/4$ cup chopped	175 mL chopped
3 medium tomatoes	approximately 1 pound	500 g
1 28-ounce can whole tomatoes	3 $1/2$ cups	875 mL

Appendix B

Glossary of Spanish Terms

● ●

A

achiote (ah-chee-OH-teh): The seed of annatto tree commonly used for making achiote paste, a seasoning mixture from the Yucatán.

adobado (ah-doh-BAH-doh) or adobo (ah-DOH-boh): A sweet, tart Mexican barbecue sauce or seasoning paste.

agave (uh-GAH-vee): The succulent used for making tequila.

agua fresca (AH-gwah fres-kah): A non-alcoholic fruit juice or tea.

ajo, al mojo de ajo (AH-hoh, ahl-moh-HOH deh AH-hoh): Garlic; a sauce or marinade whose main ingredient is garlic.

ancho (AHN-choh): The dried form of the poblano chile.

añejo (ah-NYEH-hoh): An aged food stuff. Most typically associated with a type of tequila and a Mexican cheese.

arbol (AHR-bohl): A type of paper-thin dried red chile.

arroz con pollo (ah-RROS kohn POH-yoh): A dish of rice with chicken.

atole (ah-TOH-leh): A traditional drink made of corn meal.

B

banda (BAHN-dah): A Mexican band specializing in polka music.

blanco (BLAHN-koh): White; often refers to a clear and unaged type of tequila.

bollillo (boh-LEE-yoh): A plain, crisp white bread roll used for making tortas.

brazo de reina (BRAH-soh deh ray-NAH): A special, large tamale called "the queen's arm."

buñeulo (boo-nyoo-WEH-loh): Sweetened fried dough fritters served for dessert.

burrito (boo-RREE-toh): A snack food of beans, rice, and other fillings wrapped inside a flour tortilla and eaten out of hand.

burro (BUH-roh): A donkey.

C

cabrito (kah-BREE-toh): A young goat; also known in cooked form as *birria*.

cacao (kah-KAH-oh): Cocoa.

café del olla (kah-FEH del OH-yah): Mexican spiced coffee.

cajeta (kah-HEH-tah): Caramel sauce.

caldo (KAHL-doh): Broth.

caldo de pescado (KAHL-doh deh pehs-KAH-thoh): Fish broth.

caldo de pollo (KAHL-doh deh POH-yoh): Chicken broth.

canela (kah-NEH-lah): Cinnamon.

capirotada (kah-pee-ROH-tah-thah): Mexican bread pudding.

carne asada (KAHR-neh ah-SAH-thah): Roasted or grilled meat, usually skirt steak.

carnitas (kahr-NEE-tahs): A dish of pork chunks simmered in lard.

carnitas norteñas (kahr-NEE-tahs nohr-TEH-nyahs): Northern-style carnitas.

Cascabel (kahs-kah-BEL): A small, dark red, round smooth dried chile.

cerveza (sehr-BEH-sah): Beer.

ceviche (seh-VEE-cheh): A dish of small bits of fish and vegetables marinated in lime juice.

chayote (chah-YOH-the): A small, pale green, wrinkled squash common in Mexico.

chilaca chile (CHEE-lah-kah): A long, thin, dark brown fresh chile.

Chilaquiles (chee-lah-KEE-lehs): A dish made of day-old tortillas and salsa.

chile negro (CHEE-leh NEH-groh): A long, narrow, dark brown dried chile used for grinding into moles.

chiles rellenos (CHEE-lehs reh-YEH-nohs): A dish made of whole chiles that are stuffed and fried.

Chinaco Anejo (chee-NAH-koh ah-NYEH-hoh): A brand of aged tequila.

chipotle (chee-POT-tleh): A smoked and dried jalapeno chile.

chipotle in adobo (chee-POT-leh in ah-DOH-BOH): Canned chipotle chiles in a sweet and sour sauce.

chorizo (choh-REE-soh): Spicy sausage.

churros (CHEW-rrohs): A Mexican pastry of fried dough sprinkled with cinnamon and sugar, often sold on the street.

cochineal (KOH-cheh-neel): An insect used for red dye.

cochinita pibil (koh-chee-NEE-tah pee-BEEL): A dish of small pig cooked in a pit barbecue.

Comal (ko-MAHL): A cast-iron griddle used for making tortillas.

Comino (koh-MEE-noh): The spice cumin.

cotija (koh-TEE-jah): A type of Mexican cheese.

crema (KREH-mah): Mexican sour cream, similar to crème fraiche.

E

El Tresoro Añejo (el treh-SOH-roh ah-NYEH-hoh): A brand of aged tequila.

empanada (em-pah-NAH-thah): A filled pastry similar to a turnover.

Encantado (en-kahn-TAH-thoh): A premium brand of mezcal.

enchilada (en-chee-LAH-thah): A dish of tortillas coated with chili sauce, stuffed and rolled.

enfrijolada (en-free-hoh-LAH-thah): A dish of tortillas dipped in bean sauce.

enmolada (en-moh-LAH-thah): A dish of tortillas dipped in mole sauce.

epazote (eh-pah-SOH-teh): A wild herb used to flavor Mexican dishes.

escabeche (ehs-kah-BEH-cheh): A sweet and sour marinade.

F

fideo (fee-DEH-oh): Angel hair pasta.

fiesta (fee-ES-tah): A celebration.

flan (flahn): A traditional vanilla custard.

Fuerte (FWEAR-teh): A type of avocado.

G

gazpacho (gas-PAH-choh): A typical Spanish style cold tomato soup with vegetables.

guacamole (gwah-kah-MOH-leh): A mashed avocado dip.

Guanajuato (gwan-ah-hwah-toh): A state in central Mexico.

gusano (goo-SAH-noh): The caterpillar often found in a mezcal bottle.

H

habañero (ah-bah-NEH-roh): A type of fresh chile.

horchata (or-CHAH-tah): A drink made from ground rice.

huevos rancheros (WEH-vohs rahn-CHEH-rohs): A dish made of eggs, refried beans, tortillas, and salsa.

J

jalapeño (hah-lah-PEH-nyoh): A type of fresh red or green chile.

Jalisco (hah-LEE-skoh): The Mexican state along the Pacific coast west of Mexico City.

jamaica (hah-MY-kah): Tea brewed from dried hibiscus blossoms.

jícama (HEE-kah-mah): A tuber eaten like a fruit, with crisp white flesh and thick brown skin.

Joven Abocado (HOH-vehn ah-boh-CAH-doh): Gold tequila which is unaged, colored, and sweetened.

L

limón (lee-MOHN): Lemon.

liquados (lee-KWAH-dohs): A fruit shake made with milk or water.

M

magueros (mah-GWEH-rohs): The workers who gather maguey.

maguey (mah-GWEH): The succulent from which mezcal tequila is made, also known as agave.

maiz (mah-EES): Corn.

mañana (mah-NYAH-nah): Morning or tomorrow.

Manchego (mahn-CHEH-goh): A type of Mexican cheese.

manzanillas (mahn-sah-NEE-yahs): Small green Spanish olives.

margarita (mahr-gah-REE-tah): A cocktail consisting of tequila, orange liqueur, and lime or lemon juice.

mariachis (mahr-ee-AH-chees): Mexican band and music, typical of Guadalajara.

masa (MAH-sah): Corn dough.

masa harina (MAH-sah ah-REE-nah): Powdered, dried masa for making tortillas.

masa para tamales (MAH-sah PAH-rah tah-MAH-lehs): Dough made out of dried corn that has been cooked with limestone and water and then coarsely ground for tamales.

menudo (meh-NOO-thoh): A traditional stew of tripe, chiles, and hominy.

mesa (MEH-sah): Table.

metate (meh-TAH-teh): Flat stone used for grinding corn and chiles.

mezcal (mehs-KAHL): A type of tequila from Southern Mexico.

mixto (MEES-toh): A type of tequila made with 60 percent blue agave and 40 percent grain alcohol.

molcajete (mohl-kah-HEH-teh): Mortar of basalt used to grind spices and ingredients.

mole (MOH-leh): A traditional stew made of ground roasted chiles, seeds, and nuts.

mole colorado (MOH-leh koh-loh-RAH-thoh): A reddish-brown mole.

mole poblano (MOH-leh poh-BLAH-noh): A mole from the city of Puebla in central Mexico.

mole verde (MOH-leh BEHR-theh): A green, herb-based mole.

molinillo (moh-LEE-nee-yoh): A traditional wooden whisk for blending hot chocolate.

molino (moh-LEE-noh): Local tradesperson who grinds ingredients for seasonings, moles, and cacao.

mollettes (moh-LEH-tehs): A sandwich made of toasted bread with beans.

morita (moh-REE-tah): A small brown dried chile.

N

naranja agria (nah-RAGHN-hah AH-gree-ah): A bitter orange from Yucatán.

nopale (noh-PAHL): A cactus paddle.

nopalitos (noh-pahl-EE-tohs): Small, young cactus paddles.

P

palapas (pah-LAH-pahs): Beach shacks.

palenque (pah-LEHN-keh): Mezcal distilleries.

pan de yema (pahn deh YEH-mah): An egg-based bread traditionally served on the Day of the Dead and decorated with skull and crossbones.

panela (pah-NEH-lah): A type of fresh white Mexican cheese, similar to Mozzarella.

pasilla (pah-SEE-yah): The dried form of the chilaca chile.

Patrón Añejo (pah-TROHN ah-NYEH-hoh): A brand of aged tequila.

pepita (peh-PEE-tah): A pumpkin seed.

picadillo (pee-kah-DEE-yoh): Seasoned, ground, fried meat, often used for stuffing.

picholines (pee-choh-LEENS): Large, green French olives.

pico de gallo (PEE-koh deh GAH-yoh): A salsa made of chopped fresh tomato.

pina (PEE-nah): The heart of the agave, or maguey plant, used to make tequila.

piñata (peen YAH tah): A hanging hollow paper decoration filled with candy and gifts to be broken in a game by blindfolded participants.

pipiáns (pee-PYAHNS): A sauce of ground nuts or seeds and spices, similar to mole.

Plata (PLAH-tah): A type of tequila which is unaged and clear.

poblano (poh-BLAH-noh): A type of fresh green chile used for rajas and stuffing.

Porfidio Silver (pohr-FEE-dee-oh SIL-vehr): A brand of aged tequila.

posole (poh-SOH-leh): A traditional stew of meat and hominy served with several vegetable and herb garnishes.

Puebla (PWEH-blah): City in Central Mexico.

Q

quesadilla (keh-sah-DEE-yah): A flour tortilla with melted cheese filling.

queso fresco (KEH-soh FREHS-koh): A type of fresh white Mexican cheese.

queso fundido (KEH-soh fuhn-DEE-doh): A dish made of melted cheeses and chiles.

quinoa (Aztecan quinoa) (KEEN-wah): A high-protein grain from South America.

R

raja (RAH-hah): A roasted chile strip.

ranchero (rahn-CHEH-roh): Country-style.

Reposado (reh-poh-SAH-thoh): A type of tequila that is aged and light gold in color.

rompope (rohm-POH-peh): Traditional eggnog, usually served at Christmas time.

S

salsa cruda (SAHL-sah CREW-dah): A chopped fresh tomato salsa; also known as pico de gallo.

salsa fresca (SAHL-sah FREHS-kah): Fresh salsa.

salsa verde (SAHL-sah BEHR-theh): A green salsa usually made with tomatillos.

salud (sah-LEWD): A popular toast meaning "to your health."

sandia (sahn-DEE-ah): Watermelon.

sangria (sahn-GREE-ah): A drink made of wine, fruit juice, and marinated fruits.

sangrita (sahn-GREE-tah): A drink made of orange and lime juice, grenadine, and Tabasco.

serape (sah-RAH-peh): A colorful woolen shawl worn over the shoulders.

serrano (seh-RRAH-noh): A type of small, fresh green chile.

sopa (SOH-pah): Soup.

sopa de lima (SOH-pah deh LEE-mah): Lime soup.

sopa seca (SOH-pah SEH-kah): Dry soup served as a side dish.

T

taceria (tah-keh-REE-ah): A taco stand.

taco (TAH-koh): A soft, corn tortilla with savory filling and garnish eaten like a sandwich.

tacos al carbon (TAH-kohs ahl kahr-BOHN): Grilled meat tacos.

tamale (tah-MAH-leh): Corn husk stuffed with corn dough and savory fillings and steamed.

tequila (teh-KEE-lah): A Mexican liquor distilled from the heart of the agave or maguey plant.

texate (teh-HAH-teh): The fruit of the mamey tree used to make a slightly sweet, milky drink.

Tikin-Chik (TIK-in-chik): A Yucatecan dish of marinated and grilled fish.

tomatillo (toh-mah-TEE-yoh): A small, green, acidic Mexican fruit used for salsas and marinades.

torta (TOHR-tah): A sandwich.

tortilla (tohr-TEE-yah): A round thin cake of unleavened, ground, dried corn eaten as bread in Mexico.

tostada (tohs-TAH-thah): A salad served on a fried corn tortilla.

V

vitriolla (bee-tree-OH-yah): A street vendor of cold juices and teas.

Z

Zapotec (SAH-poh-tehk): Indian tribe of Oaxaca, Mexico.

zócalo (SOH-kah-loh): Mexican public square located in the center of town.

Index